NEW ESSAYS ON CANADIAN THEATRE
VOLUME THREE

LATINA/O CANADIAN THEATRE
AND PERFORMANCE

NEW ESSAYS ON CANADIAN THEATRE
VOLUME THREE

LATINA/O CANADIAN THEATRE AND PERFORMANCE

EDITED BY NATALIE ALVAREZ

PLAYWRIGHTS CANADA PRESS
TORONTO

PLAYWRIGHTS CANADA PRESS
202-269 Richmond St. W., Toronto, ON M5V 1X1
416.703.0013 • info@playwrightscanada.com • www.playwrightscanada.com

We acknowledge the financial support of the Canada Council for the Arts, the
Ontario Arts Council, the Ontario Media Development Corporation, and the
Government of Canada through the Canada Book Fund for our publishing activities.

Cover photo by Mercedes Fidanza, a video still from Colombian Québécois per-
formance artist Claudia Bernal's *Escritura X Escritura*, performance in situ at Ex
Padelai, Cultural Centre of Spain, in Buenos Aires, Argentina, in 2010.
Cover design by Leon Aureus
Book design by Blake Sproule

LIBRARY AND ARCHIVES CANADA CATALOGUING IN PUBLICATION

Latina/o Canadian theatre and performance / edited by Natalie Alvarez.

(New essays on Canadian theatre ; vol. 3)
Includes bibliographical references and index.
ISBN 978-1-77091-148-2

    1. Canadian drama--Latin American Canadian authors--History and
criticism. 2. Canadian drama--20th century--History and criticism.
3. Canadian drama--21st century--History and criticism. 4. Latin Americans
in literature. I. Alvarez, Natalie, 1974- II. Series: New essays on Canadian
theatre ; vol. 3

PS8089.5.L3L37 2013   C812'.5409868071   C2012-907949-9

First edition: May 2013
Printed and bound in Canada by Marquis Book Printing, Montreal

To my parents, who continue to withstand the winters in Saskatchewan by finding solace in their Spanish-speaking friends from across the Americas.

CONTENTS

GENERAL EDITOR'S PREFACE

RIC KNOWLES

New Essays in Canadian Theatre (NECT) is a book series designed to complement and replace the series Critical Perspectives on Canadian Theatre in English (CPCTE), which published its last three of twenty-one volumes in 2011. CPCTE was primarily a reprint series, with each volume designed to represent the critical history since the 1970s of a particular topic within the broader field of Canadian theatre studies. Most volumes, however, also included essays specially commissioned to fill gaps in the coverage of their respective topics and to bring the books up to the moment. These new essays, some of them scholarly prize winners, were often among the volumes' most powerful, approaching the field and the discipline from important new perspectives, regularly from those of minoritized and other under-represented communities.

NECT consists entirely of newly commissioned essays, and the volumes themselves are designed to fill what I perceive to be gaps in the critical record, often, once again, taking new approaches, often, again, from minoritized and under-represented perspectives, and always introducing topics that have never before received book-length coverage. NECT volume topics may range as broadly as did those of CPCTE, from the work of an individual playwright to that of a whole community, however defined, and they are designed at once to follow, lead, and instantiate new and emerging developments in the field. Volume editors and their contributors are scholars, artists, and artist-scholars who are doing some of the most exciting and innovative work in Canadian theatre and Canadian theatre studies.

Like those published in CPCTE but more systematically, NECT volumes complement the catalogues of Canada's major drama publishers: each volume serves as a companion piece either to an already existing anthology or to one published contemporaneously with it, often by the editors of the NECT volumes themselves. As a package, NECT and their companion volumes serve as ideal introductions to a field, or indeed as ready-made reading lists for Canadian theatre courses in these topic areas.

But generating new materials and entirely new fields of study takes time, and while CPCTE published at the heady pace of three volumes per year, the production of NECT is more leisurely with, initially at least, only one volume launched each spring, beginning in 2011. The first of these was *Asian Canadian Theatre*, edited by Nina Lee Aquino and myself and designed to ride the tide of a flurry of activity in the first decade of the twenty-first century among Asian Canadian theatre artists. It complements Nina Lee Aquino's two-volume anthology *Love + Relasianships*, published by Playwrights Canada Press in 2009. The second, third, and fourth volumes are concerned with new Canadian realisms (edited by Roberta Barker and Kim Solga), Latina/o Canadian Theatre (edited by Natalie Alvarez), and affect in Canadian performance (edited by Erin Hurley), and each of these are or will be accompanied by companion anthologies.

It has been exciting for me to see the development of Canadian theatre criticism since its inception as an academic discipline in the mid 1970s, when the first academic courses on the subject were offered, and the first journals were founded, together with the then Association for Canadian Theatre History (now the Canadian Association for Theatre Research)—the first and only scholarly association to specialize in Canadian theatre. It was also very satisfying to serve as founder and general editor for the CPCTE series that tracked that development and made some of its key writings widely available and key critical histories and genealogies visible. In embarking on this new series, I am equally excited by the opportunity to contribute to the further development of the field by opening up new areas of study, introducing fresh new voices, and making innovative new work readily available to scholars, teachers, students, and the interested general public.

ACKNOWLEDGEMENTS

I would like to thank Ric Knowles for his generosity, support, and mentorship and for recognizing the need for collections that acknowledge the work of Latina/o playwrights and theatre artists in Canada. Annie Gibson and Blake Sproule at Playwrights Canada Press have been positive, responsive, and patient interlocutors throughout this process and have been an utter pleasure to work with. I thank them for their keen editorial eye and professionalism. The work of Gabrielle Etcheverry, my editorial assistant, has been outstanding and has effectively made the completion of these books possible. I am grateful for her willingness to jump into the project *in medias res*. I am also indebted to Marilo Nuñez for her encouragement and advice. She has created a hub for Latina/o theatre artists across Canada and her passionate commitment to the goal of fostering a professional Latina/o theatre culture in Canada is an inspiration. I also extend thanks to my dear friend, who also happens to be the savviest of researchers, Natalie Harrower, for her unconditional and unwavering support, both personal and professional. Many thanks, as well, go to Laura Levin, Marlis Schweitzer, and Kim Solga for the occasional "research swap" and their invaluable insights on works in progress. These acknowledgments would not be complete without mentioning the boundless moral support of my parents, Eduardo and Rosario Alvarez, and my in-laws, Narinder and Swarsha Kaushik. Last but not least, I would like to thank my husband, Rajiv Kaushik, for taking time away from his own book in order to make the completion of these books possible in the wake of the birth of Violeta, who kept us both sleepless (with joy).

LATINA/O CANADIAN THEATRE AND PERFORMANCE: HEMISPHERIC PERSPECTIVES

NATALIE ALVAREZ

This collection of essays begins a conversation about Latina/o theatre and performance in Canada. It initiates a cross-border dialogue between Canadian and US Latina/o theatre and performance studies scholars in order to advance shared disciplinary discourses and cultural practices that imbricate our seemingly discreet nation-states and to think more inclusively about the hemisphere. As Rachel Adams argues, the hemisphere has proven to be a useful framework for those interested in a more expansive and inclusive optic that considers the plurality of the Americas that lie beyond US borders ("Northern Borderlands" 314). Yet despite this interest, Canada is rarely included in these studies of the hemisphere.[1] The most significant intervention of this collection is to extend the conversation in hemispheric studies north through an examination of *latinidad* in Canadian theatre and performance. But the collection is also an enjoinment to turn our attention away from what has historically been our eastward view across the Atlantic to the Mother

---

1   Winfried Siemerling and Sarah Phillips Casteel share this observation about Canada's limited inclusion in hemispheric studies. In the introduction to their edited collection *Canada and its Americas: Transnational Navigations*, which surveys a transamerican body of literature that has motivated a "hemispheric turn" in US studies and cultural criticism, they note that, "Whereas hemispheric American studies has by now become established in the United States academy as an approach and a field of study, much less discussed is Canada's place and participation within such projects and perspectives. Canadian culture and criticism are frequently marginalized in hemispheric comparative work, in borderlands criticism, and even in North American studies" (7–8).

Country and the colonial traditions of Europe, and look southwards toward the continental traditions of which we, as Americans to the north, are a part.[2]

Scholars on both sides of the border have expressed their bewilderment that there has not yet been a compendium devoted to the study of Latina/o theatre and performance in Canada. Searching for possible explanations as to why this field of study has not yet found its footing on Canadian soil, some point to the relatively "recent" phenomenon of Latin immigration to Canada. But as Juan Flores reminds us, the characterization of "Latin" Americans as recent immigrants is a fallacy, since "Latin" Americans, particularly the Indigenous populations of the Americas, existed on the continent long before borders were drawn and the hemisphere was cut along a north-south axis.[3] While Canadian theatre and performance studies have not yet paid tribute to existing scholarly investigations of emerging and established "Latina/o" artists in book-length form, Flores's remarks remind us that this discipline's critical antecedents lie in the volumes devoted to the active fields of First Nations theatre and performance in Canada.[4]

Despite the historical presence of "Latinas/os" in the Americas, the twentieth century witnessed marked demographic shifts due to political and economic unrest in Latin America, which effectively produced successive waves of neocolonial migrants and refugees seeking political asylum beginning

---

2   I'm indebted here to very productive conversations with Beatriz Pizano, artistic director of Aluna Theatre, in my capacities as a company board member and chair of the conference program committee for its 2014 Panamerican Routes/Rutas Panamericanas international festival. Brian Damude, fellow Aluna board member and professor of film studies and media production at Ryerson University, recently made these useful observations about Canada's historic preoccupations with Europe. For an overview of how our gaze toward Europe and England has shaped Canadian theatre practice and its politics in the context of an emerging Latina/o theatrical culture, see my article "Realisms of Redress."

3   On this point see Flores 615.

4   See, for example, the critical work of Canadian scholars Jill Carter, Heather Davis-Fisch, Ric Knowles, and Monique Mojica, particularly Knowles's and Mojica's co-edited anthologies of First Nations plays, *Staging Coyote's Dream*.

in the 1970s.[5] The waves of migration from Latin America to Canada produced by neo-liberal economic restructuring, globalization, and neo-colonial forces in the Americas are "shrinking historic divisions between Canada and the rest of the Americas," as Adams asserts in her introduction to *Fronteras Americanas* in the companion anthology to this collection ("Guillermo" 46). In 2005, for example, Mexico became the number one source country for refugee claims within Canada,[6] a statistic that is "indicative of new connections with Latin America that destabilize the United States from its position as the mediator of continental relations and the desired endpoint of all Latina/o migration" (Adams, "Guillermo" 46). In this collection of essays, readers are introduced to a Canadian theatrical culture that shoulders Latin America with its own set of relations, investments, collective memories, and cultural practices. It also widens the scope of our view to those left in the periphery and invisible in Canada's official policy of multiculturalism, focusing our attention on our nation's transnational borderlands and "worlding," as José David Saldívar might say, Canadian theatre and performance studies in turn (xiii).

Despite its place as one of the principal destinations for emigration from Latin America and its reputation as a peaceful harbour of multicultural values, Canada has recently revealed itself to be Janus-faced with respect to its relations with Latin America. In July of 2009, Citizenship, Immigration, and Multiculturalism Minister Jason Kenney, under Prime Minister Stephen Harper, announced a visa requirement for all Mexican nationals travelling into Canada. Positioned as an attempt to manage "significant delays and spiraling new costs" in its refugee program due to the increased volume of claimants, the timing of the new legislation was suspect ("News Release"). Kenney's

---

5   See my introduction to the companion anthology of plays, *Fronteras Vivientes*, for a more detailed overview of Latin American immigration in Canada.

6   For more details about Mexican immigration and Minister Jason Kenney's announcement see "News Release." It is important to note that while Mexico has exceeded other countries for refugee claims in Canada, a very small percentage of those claims are successful; both immigration and tourism from Mexico has decreased significantly since the imposition of the visa requirement for Mexican nationals in 2009.

announcement came on the heels of a series of drug-related murders that gripped Vancouver earlier that year. British Columbia law enforcement linked these murders to the Mexican government's crackdown on its cocaine market, in which BC marijuana circulates as barter, resulting in diminishing profits and escalating competition for market share among the province's gangs (Murphy). A media-fuelled hysteria left Canadians thinking that Mexico's drug war had infiltrated Canada's borders. This new immigration legislation aiming to tighten the grip on the flow of Mexican nationals into Canada now operates alongside Canada's Seasonal Agricultural Worker Program (SAWP), established in 1974[7] as a "labour mobility program" that maintains an "effective and regulated flow of migrant workers" between Canada and Mexico ("Seasonal Agricultural"). The program ensures a steady population of cheap labour that can be found in Canada's agricultural lands, most notably in the orchards and vineyards in southwestern Ontario, where a collision in February of 2012 that killed eleven migrant workers brought concerns over migrant workers' rights to national attention.

This schizoid relationship with Mexican nationals through legislation that enables and restricts the flow of its citizens operates within the larger framework of the Harper government's Americas Strategy, a program initiated in 2007—following the appointment of a secretary of state for Latin America in 2006—to increase relations with Latin America in three principal areas: economic security and opportunity, the advancement of democratic governance and human rights, and the establishment of Canada's engagement and influence in the hemisphere.[8] Judging by the Harper government's recent attempts at the 2012 Summit of the Americas to "reinvigorate" what is largely considered a "muddled" initiative, trade and economic development seem to be the strategy's principal motives (Canadian Press). A November 2012

---

7   A 1974 start date for SAWP is uncertain. A CBC news story on migrant workers' rights and SAWP, contrary to the Mexican Consulate's website, notes that this program was established in 1966. See Stastna.

8   For more on the Americas Strategy and its support from the Department of National Defense see "Canada-Latin America."

segment on CBC's *Lang & O'Leary Exchange* titled "Latin American Lover" reported on Canada's increasing economic interests in Latin America, which are currently governing its foreign policy for the continent. Stereotypes of the Latin American other in the Anglo imagination, it seems, inevitably frame and constitute in advance our nation's engagements with its southern partners, who are positioned either as members of drug cartels or, in the case of economic interests, more amicably as "Latin lovers." It is the circulation of images such as these that compel many of the artists examined in this collection to produce work that exposes and redresses the damaging stereotypes and estrangements that persist under the banner of a multicultural Canada.

Some of the artists in this collection may not even self-identify as "Latina/o"—a contested and densely polycultural category. Some might argue that Canada does not have a "Latina/o" theatrical and performance culture. But what if we adopt an entirely politically naive position for a moment and simply say that there is? The self-designation and appropriation of "Latina/o" might allow us to identify points of contact between and alliances among theatre and performance artists who are reshaping our national identity while establishing hemispheric networks beyond our national borders. Perhaps an act of self-naming is a critical way of cohering a body of work, which then enables us to take account of the vital role it has played, and continues to play, in the ongoing formation of our theatrical culture as well as our national identity. As Juan Flores says, "the search for a name, more than an act of classification, is actually a process of historical imagination and struggle over social meaning at diverse levels of interpretation" (617). This collection of essays is an invitation to begin this process of historical imagining and take stock of how the works examined in these pages have been changing the Canadian theatrical landscape.

In the anthology that accompanies this volume, before tracing the emergence of Latina/o theatre and performance in Canada, I ask what it means to invoke the term "Latina/o" within Canada's borders. I briefly survey the history of the referent "Latin" America as a colonial invention during shifting geopolitical forces in the nineteenth century. I then consider the critical appropriation of the moniker "Latina/o" during the civil rights movements in the US as a "positive designation of social space" amongst those of Mexican, Cuban, Puerto Rican, and Central and South American origin and descent living in the US in resistance to the imposed and homogenizing term "Hispanic" (Vélez-Ibáñez and Sampaio 2). This collection of essays draws on the spirit of that self-naming strategically as a means of building additional coalitions north and, in the spirit of Arjun Appadurai's "ethnoscape,"[9] deterritorializing the term in order to build cross-border alliances in the hemisphere. I adopt this terminology with caution, recognizing that such terms risk homogenizing the diversity of ethnicities they encompass, but do so as a means of acknowledging shared "colonial relations of hemispheric inequality," as Flores reminds us, that "underlie not only the historical logic of Latino migration but also the position and conditions of Latinos" (614). Taking up the term "Latina/o" in a Canadian context is a gesture of diasporic belonging, strengthening transnational connections in the hemisphere as Americans, belonging as we do to the Américas. As Guillermo Verdecchia avows in *Fronteras Americanas*, "Somos todos Americanos. We are all Americans" (2). In their multi-faceted invocations of what Latina/o theatre and performance means in Canada, these essays reveal that the demonym Latina/o is not fixed or static but, in transnational and transgeographic contexts, always contested, localized, and processual, and formed as a result of continued movements across and between borders.

While this publication marks the first collection of critical essays on Latina/o theatre and performance in Canada, it builds on the momentum of important antecedents, critical essays that have surfaced periodically since roughly the 1980s, that track the early figures and tendencies of this still emerging theatrical culture. The *Canadian Theatre Review* (*CTR*) has been a vital forum for analyses on and by important figures in Latina/o theatre and

---

9   Arjun Appadurai coined the term "ethnoscape" as one of the ways in which we might account for the "new global cultural economy" as a "complex, overlapping, disjunctive order" that can no longer be understood in terms of "existing centre-periphery" critical models (296). "Ethnoscape" refers to a landscape of global flows of people "who constitute the shifting world in which we live" and who "appear to affect the politics of and between nations to a hitherto unprecedented degree" (297).

performance. In the 1980s, *CTR* featured articles and performance texts on the groundbreaking work of the Chilean Québécois performance–theatre artist Alberto Kurapel, as well as his own critical reflections on works in development.[10] Kurapel's work has received critical attention both internationally and within Canada, most notably by Huguette Le Blanc[11] and by Mayte Gómez, who examined Kurapel's self-titled "Latin American Performance of Exile" for its capacity to immerse its audiences experientially in an exilic condition, turning them effectively into subjects of exile.[12] Hugh Hazelton, who offers the most sustained examination of his performance oeuvre for this collection, contributes to this recurring theme of exile in Kurapel's work by focusing on how his bilingual performance theatre conveys the plight of the liminal, hybrid subject negotiating multiple worlds.[13]

Latina/o Canadian theatre artists have also attracted the interest of US scholars seeking to look beyond US borders to investigate Latina/o cultural and performance politics in a broader hemispheric context. US Chicano scholar Michelle Habell-Pallán's review of Carmen Aguirre's *¿Qué Pasa Con La Raza, Eh?* (1999) for *Theatre Journal* opens by noting the novel idea of Latinas/os in Canada: "When we think about the culture of *Las Américas, con acento*, Canada rarely comes to mind. However, the recent moving premiere of *¿Que Pasa Con La Raza, Eh?* by the Latino Theatre Group (LTG) located Vancouver, British Columbia on both the cultural and geographical map of *Nuestra América*" (112). Habell-Pallán's invocation of Cuban journalist,

---

10　See, for example, Sher; Walker; Kurapel, "Montreal/Santiago"; as well as the publication of Kurapel's performance text *La bruta interférence* in CTR 79.

11　See Le Blanc.

12　See Gómez, "Infinite Signs." For additional Canadian work on Kurapel, see also the prologues to Kurapel's plays published by Montreal's Humanitas. The international scholarly attention Kurapel has received is too extensive to include here, but see, for example, Alfonso de Toro, "Figuras" and " 'Transversalidad;' " Faúndez Carreño, "La repetición"; Fernando de Toro, "Identidad"; and Moss.

13　Aside from Hazelton's essay featured here, see also his "Latin American" and "Quebec Hispánico."

essayist, and poet José Martí's continental optic of "*Nuestra América*" or "Our America" conveys a degree of intrigue, even mystification, as to how Latina/o artists have escaped critical attention despite historical and critical attempts to think more inclusively about *latinidad* in the hemisphere. Habell-Pallán continued to develop her principal study of LTG's *¿Qué Pasa Con La Raza, Eh?* in subsequent publications, which track, in part, the cross-border movements of Chicano popular culture in order to propose how shared cultural practices in the hemisphere might foster strategic alliances.[14]

Efforts to include Canada in US hemispheric studies have also centred on the work of Guillermo Verdecchia. For Rachel Adams, Verdecchia's *Fronteras Americanas* and his short fiction *Citizen Suarez* serve as a foil for more nuanced thinking about the distinctions between international borders, specifically the Mexico–US, US–Canada borders. Verdecchia's work also presents a "way out" of conversations about the hemisphere, which are "often framed in terms of a dichotomy between the United States (or the more amorphous North America) and Latin America" ("Northern Borderlands" 314). Canada introduces an "important third term," Adams contends, that interrupts this dichotomy within scholarship on the hemisphere (314).[15] One advantage of introducing a collection of essays on Latina/o Canadian theatre and performance is that it repositions Canada as not so much a "third" as a "first" term where it can occupy a critical centrality within hemispheric studies, amplifying studies on the ramifications of Canada's increasing proximity to Latin America.

Aside from his own pioneering work in Latina/o theatre in Canada, Verdecchia continues to make significant contributions to its development as a critical field of study, publishing in national and international journals

---

14   Habell-Pallán's subsequent works on LTG's production of *¿Qué Pasa Con La Raza, Eh?* can be found in her essays "Epilogue" and " 'Don't Call Us Hispanic.' "

15   See also Adams's introduction to *Fronteras Americanas*, "Guillermo Verdecchia's Northern Borderlands," in this volume's companion anthology of plays, *Fronteras Vivientes*, as well as her book *Continental Divides*. For additional international scholarship on Verdecchia see, for example, Zorc-Maver and Maver and Fellner.

and essay collections on the role of memory, exile, and Canada's hemispheric relations in the work of Latina Canadian playwrights.[16] Of course, the critical writings about Verdecchia by Canadian scholars such as Mayte Gómez, Anne Nothof, Ann Wilson, and Pablo Ramirez are plentiful and deepen our understanding of its resonances within Canada, particularly in how Verdecchia's work exposes the limits of multicultural discourse and the complex valences of Canada's borderlands as a domain that encompasses the lived, political reality of the border as well as its conceptual and theoretical possibilities.[17]

Elsewhere in this series, I have attempted to trace the development of Latina/o theatre and politics in the important artistic, advocacy, and developmental work of Toronto's Alameda Theatre, a company that, due to unfortunate circumstances, is conspicuously absent among the studies featured in this collection. In that essay, I focus on the theoretical and political quagmire companies like Alameda face in attempting to redress the systemic marginalization of Latina/o theatre artists by casting almost exclusively and, at times, militantly from among the Latina/o diaspora.[18] Other scholars, such as Jeannine Pitas here and elsewhere, have focused their attention on companies that attempt to counter such marginalization by forming grassroots, community-driven companies.[19] Lina de Guevara, the former artistic director of Victoria's PUENTE Theatre—examined in this volume by Tamara Underiner—has written her own self-reflexive essays on how theatre provides

---

16   For some of Verdecchia's critical writings see "Tango's," "*Leo*," "Mapping," "We Win," and "Contending."

17   See Gómez, "Healing"; Nothof; Wilson; and an earlier, albeit distinct, iteration of Pablo Ramirez's essay presented for this collection, "Collective Memory and the Borderlands in Guillermo Verdecchia's *Fronteras Americanas*."

18   See "Realisms of Redress" and my forthcoming essay, which engages in a comparative study of Canadian and US Latina playwrights, "Transcultural Dramaturgies."

19   Aside from Pitas's essay featured here, see her article "Performing Communities."

an avenue for immigrant actors and non-actors to find not only their place in Canada but also to participate in its civic life.[20]

As this brief and by no means complete critical history reveals, the terrain is rich for the establishment of Latina/o Canadian theatre and performance studies as a field of study and inquiry. This volume consolidates the work of these independent investigations by presenting a collection of new essays that fortify the view of theatre and performance in the Americas from a Canadian vantage point. These new essays on Latina/o theatre and performance make efforts to consider Latina/o Canadian particularity while acknowledging the cross-border travels of cultural and critical traditions, as well as the trans-national impacts of neocolonization, that require a framing of Canadian *latinidad* in a more expansive hemispheric topography.

The collection begins with Alicia Arrizón, who uses migration and "intersectional humour" as a framework for her examination of Nicaraguan Canadian stand-up comic Martha Chaves. Chaves's humour highlights the multiplicity of identities that intersect in shaping who she is as a lesbian, middle-class Nicaraguan, immigrant, and comedian in order to undermine how these identity markers function as "categories of domination." Arrizón cleverly extends a metaphor Chaves invokes, aligning Chaves's comic persona with a "bull-fighter" in order to demonstrate how she uses humour as an "emancipatory strategy of liberation"; Chaves dismantles patriarchal rhetoric and systems of domination with her stand-up, which opens up spaces for self-representation in turn. Her sardonic humour, Arrizón shows us, also targets the intense homophobia that runs through Latin American communities, as well as how the male-dominated arena of stand-up comedy, which largely holds that women "aren't funny," intersects with patriarchal attitudes toward femininity. Chaves's loud, bold, and feminist comedic edge inspires Arrizón to reflect on one of the lessons on gender-appropriate behaviour for *señoritas* that she was taught as a child: "*calladita te ves más bonita*" (when

---

20   See Lina de Guevara's personal website for full-text articles she has published on her writing, directing, and production work for Latinas/os and other immigrants in Victoria, BC, such as "Civic Participation Through Theatre."

you are quiet you look prettier). Arrizón's analysis reveals how the unique performer-spectator relationship Chaves fosters through her "intersectional humour" effectively turns the performance space into a "contact zone" in which ideas about identity and difference are co-generated and negotiated in the exchange.

How the performance space might become a critical "contact zone" of intercultural negotiation and exchange is further advanced in Ric Knowles and Jessica Riley's careful and detailed analysis of Aluna Theatre's *Nohayquiensepa (No One Knows): A Requiem for the Forcibly Displaced.* Based on the stories that have emerged from Colombia's Magdalena River region, where Canadian mining companies have decimated local populations and resources, the performance "created environments, for artists and audiences," Knowles and Riley argue, "in which differences could come together on equal terms and new, self-reflexive and non-appropriative ways of seeing and relating to difference could be proposed and explored." This attention to the creation of an environment was present in the early stages of the devising process, in which scenographer and Aluna artistic producer Trevor Schwellnus made the rehearsal space "part of the improvisation, by proposing (and adapting) environments in real time." In their analysis of this environment, Knowles and Riley reveal how the intermedial serves to mediate the intercultural. More specifically, they demonstrate how difference and understanding might be achieved without resorting to forms of appropriative empathy, which colonizes the experiences of the other. Knowles and Riley make urgent and critical contributions to current discussions about empathy and performance by tracing the development of the question that served as the genesis for *Nohayquiensepa*—namely, "How do we deal with the death of a stranger?"— and raise provocative questions of their own about the limits of empathy as a means of fostering understanding across difference.

Other essays in the collection reveal how Latina/o theatre companies attempt to bridge understanding across difference by moving beyond narrowly conceived identarian terms and building pan-ethnic and trans-indigenous alliances. In the first scholarly essay on PUENTE Theatre, Canada's longest-running Latina/o theatre company, Tamara Underiner invokes the metaphor of a woven fabric—an image that arises in one of their productions—to frame her examination of their work's "warp and weft," like "the threads that go in perpendicular directions in a woven cloth." The metaphor serves to capture the complex and intersecting commitments of the company to foster "pan-immigrant solidarity" while maintaining "cultural specificity" and "calls for inclusion and targeted critique"; these "relationships and tensions," Underiner contends, "form much of the texture of PUENTE's work." This ethics of interdependence is reflected in Underiner's own methodological approach: her analysis is intimately, and very poignantly, tied to her own positioning and lived experience, which serves to demonstrate how the researcher becomes ethically responsible and bound to her research subject. Her analysis also demonstrates what can be gained from a hemispheric analysis that bridges the concerns of immigrant theatre in her locality in Arizona to those in Victoria, BC.

Underiner's analysis of PUENTE's community-engaged theatre is followed by Jeannine M. Pitas's study of its Toronto allies. Like PUENTE, Toronto-based community-theatre companies such as Double Double Performing Arts, the Apus Coop, and Grupo Teatro Libre are seeking to build a pan-ethnic *latinidad* in a Canadian context; company members come together in the interest of forming a "pan–Latin American Canadianness that transcends the borders of any individual nationality and seeks to assert a self-determined, self-aware, visible presence within Canada's cultural landscape." Pitas very usefully situates the efforts of these emergent companies within the context of a consciousness shift she is witnessing broadly in the Americas that is turning toward Pan-American alliances and solidarity, such as the Bolivarian Alliance for the Peoples of Our America (ALBA) and the Community of Latin American and Caribbean States (CELAC) as well as international artistic and cultural festivals founded throughout the Americas. Turning to Walter Mignolo, Pitas frames these alliances within larger efforts to build a "culturally specific, self-determined form of modernity" that informs the praxis of these companies. These alliances, Pitas argues, are often formed on the basis of their "common yet unquestionably diverse Spanish language," in which some companies, such as Grupo Teatro Libre, perform almost exclusively. As company member Jorge Henríquez avers, "Our language empowers us . . . This is part of our ideological message" (Henríquez).

In the bilingual experimental performance theatre of Chilean Québécois poet, essayist, musician, and theatre artist Alberto Kurapel, language also functions ideologically, registering not merely Kurapel's unapologetic disinterest in attracting wider, mainstream audiences but, more significantly, the conditions of exile. In his comprehensive and illuminating analysis of Kurapel's particular form of "teatro-performance" or "post-teatro," Hugh Hazelton reveals how Kurapel's Spanish-French performances create a "hybrid language" that "deftly subverts the intention of having a transparently bilingual text accessible to speakers of either language." Kurapel's characters "speak in two tongues in their new environment, giving rise to a process of repetition, linguistic self-consciousness, and even a slightly schizoid reality" that conveys the exilic condition of existing between multiple worlds. As Hazelton relays, Kurapel's "post-teatro" practice germinated in his native Chile, where he found Aristotelian conventions to be stifling artistic development, but came to fruition in Montreal, stimulated by its multidisciplinary arts scene among Chilean refugees. While also drawing on European and American avant-garde traditions, Kurapel's commitment to anti-realist experimentation was also, according to Hazelton, "distinctly Latin American, infused with Indigenous traditions, historical and cultural references, denunciations of oppression, poverty, and marginalization, calls to action, collective focus among the cast, and shamanistic rituals."

In his examination of Carmen Aguirre's *¿Qué Pasa Con La Raza, Eh?*, Ramón Rivera-Servera targets the commonplace critical continuity between anti-realist aesthetics and political intervention in order to advance the potentialities of what he calls a "critical dance realism." Examining the critical literature on Aguirre's play, Rivera-Servera highlights how "the codes and conventions of realism" are often "ideologically set up against the marginal imaginaries of *latinidad*" in both performance practice and scholarship. His analysis of Aguirre's 1999 ensemble piece reveals what can often be overlooked in the almost default deference to experimentation as the only viable mode of political intervention. While he is careful to acknowledge how realism has operated in service of a rhetoric of authority and authenticity in the tradition of "Spanish Fantasy Heritage" that consolidated ideas about "ethno-racial otherness," Rivera-Servera identifies how moments of aesthetic realism in Aguirre's play, conveyed through mimetic movement and dance, circumvent conventional representational economies in favour of Latina/o embodiment. Where the play's use of hip-hop dance, in its "eye-popping slickness," risks naturalizing and re-entrenching Latina/o stereotypes, the play's use of the Chilean *cueca sola* and a tender slow dance allows for affective exchanges, which make possible the emergence of a "pan-ethnic *latinidad*."

While embodiment makes possible a pan-ethnic *latinidad* in Rivera-Servera's essay, we witness the complex ways in which the biopolitical intersects with the geopolitical in Martha Nandorfy's reading of Verdecchia's *The Terrible But Incomplete Journals of John D*. Nandorfy takes up Portuguese sociologist Boaventura de Sousa Santos's notion of "abyssal thinking" as a form of Eurocentric epistemology that operates biopolitically, evident in the lines John D draws, which circumscribe his "first world" from the "third world" he encounters in his journey from Canada to Mexico. Through a close analysis of the title character's transnational journey, both literal and figurative, Nandorfy analyzes how John D's initial attempts "at self-deception, strategically separating political critique from personal contemplation" evolve into a political praxis in which the abyssal lines—"separating self from others" and the personal from the political—are dissolved. Nandorfy's insightful analysis of *The Terrible But Incomplete Journals*, which has received very limited scholarly attention, makes a vital contribution to the study of Verdecchia's oeuvre.

The idea—and promise—of a lived praxis in *The Terrible But Incomplete Journals* also emerges in Guillermo Verdecchia's own study of the revolutionary politics that run through the work of Carmen Aguirre. Using Paul Ricoeur's idea of *anamnēsis*, which conveys a mode of "active recollection" that requires "effort" as opposed to a more passive mode of recollection in which memories recur unexpectedly and spontaneously, Verdecchia demonstrates how the characters in Aguirre's plays actively sustain the "memory of a revolutionary ethics." They engage with this mode of active recollection not only in order to continue—and resuscitate—what was ultimately a failed political project but also to make sense of and draw meaning from their current circumstances as political exiles. A revolutionary paradigm operates as both a "framework" and a "touchstone," one that "subsumes and transforms immediate, personal conditions and situations into an aspect of a larger historical dynamic." This ability to draw on a revolutionary paradigm is, Verdecchia argues, "key to the survival and well-being of Aguirre's characters." Verdecchia's essay very importantly discloses the ways in which this commitment to a Latin American revolutionary politics is a current that extends beyond Aguirre's work into the emerging corpus of Latina/o Canadian theatre.

In the essay that follows, the process of *anamnēsis* and active recollection that served as a framework for Verdecchia's analysis finds resonances in his own groundbreaking play, *Fronteras Americanas*, as examined by Pablo Ramirez. Ramirez's engaging analysis takes a fresh look at a play that has received substantial critical attention by scholars in Canada and the US by considering how Verdecchia as Verdecchia actively tries to "heal his 'border wound' " by searching for a way to instantiate his own memories within a Canadian multicultural script and national collective memory that do not yet have a place for those who fall outside its official cultures of English and French. But rather than integrating his own memories into existing historical narratives that have shaped Canada's national identity, Verdecchia turns the performance space into a "locus of enunciation," envisioned here as a "no-place," an *atopic* "borderlands collective memory" where individual counter-memories are made possible. In Ramirez's study, the tradition of a "non-territorial" borderlands space in US Chicana/o discourse becomes newly configured in a Canadian context.

The creation of a discursive space for the formation of a sense of identity as well as a sense of home extends into the essay that closes this collection, Jimena Ortuzar's compelling examination of the Art Gallery of York University's (AGYU) *Imaginary Homelands* project. Artists from Colombia migrated to Canada for a three-year residency in order to explore issues of displacement "from the perspective of being *in* and being *from* two places simultaneously." The installations capture the movements of the artists between Bogotá and Toronto and the critical vantage point of the exilic position, which reveals how a sense of place and national borders are contingent upon the body that encounters them. The project's emphasis on ideas of home that are constituted and performed through bodily movements and migrations across transnational borders serves as a reminder of the broader hemispheric connections linking Latinas/os and all Canadians to a larger network of relations within the Americas.

The vantage points offered in the *Imaginary Homelands* project compel us to consider how ideas of *latinidad* in Canada cannot be confined to our national borders exclusively. An understanding of Canadian *latinidad* requires tracing the constellation of hemispheric movements each individual carries with her, allowing those traces to lead to a sense of Canadian Latina/o particularity. The essays featured here, in the singular plays and performances, the performance practices, as well as the specific devising and rehearsal processes they examine, underscore the heterogeneous instantiations of Latina/o Canadianness. Yet together, these essays also reveal how this irreducible specificity of Latina/o identity often serves as the starting point for artistic processes and works that allow for the articulation and formation of pan-ethnic Latina/o Canadian and Indigenous subjectivities, alliances, and ethos that supersede ideas of nation and national difference.[21] This ideological commitment to the formation of a polycultural Latina/o and Indigenous solidarity carries strains of Martí's "*Nuestra América*," which sought to unite the Americas, north and south, while embracing "the hemisphere's heterogeneous people and multiple geographical borders" (Arrizón 21). The essays collected here enlist Canada in that project of *Nuestra América*, reminding us that, to echo Verdecchia's words in the form a refrain, "Somos todo Americanos. We are all Americans."

---

21   Such alliances are demonstratively at work in the forthcoming collaboration of Aluna Theatre and Native Earth Performing Arts for the 2014 Panamerican Routes/Rutas Panamericanas Festival.

MARTHA CHAVES'S "STAYING ALIVE" NARRATIVE: COMEDY, MIGRATION, AND FEMINISM

ALICIA ARRIZÓN

In 1978 we are at the height of the repression by the dictatorship. There's a military curfew. The Sandinistas are coming down from the mountains to the city. The revolution is on.

The theme of my high school prom is "Staying Alive" and in my High School Yearbook, I was voted, "most likely to talk under torture."

Most people my age are interested in toppling the dictatorship. The nuns of our school embrace the "Theology of Liberation" and they are teaching us to . . . not to be indifferent to the suffering. My favorite nun tells me, "The problem is that the children in this school need to grow a pair—of eyes. You must learn to see the people so you can help them." And I started seeing, all right, seeing a lot. I see children begging at the traffic lights, I see slums where those children live when we go from our middle class home to our private school. I see children sniffing glue to stop the hunger. I see the children that most North Americans only see in UNICEF commercials.

> The theme of my high school prom is "Staying Alive" and in my
> High School Yearbook, I was voted, "most likely to talk under tor-
> ture." (Chaves, *Fragile*)[1]

The above fragment is part of *Fragile*, a one-woman show in progress by
Martha Chaves, considered one of Canada's most prolific and entertaining
comedians.[2] Chaves's narrative marks the beginning of the Sandinista National
Liberation Front–led Nicaraguan Revolution (Revolución Nicaragüense or
Revolución Popular Sandinista) in 1978, which ousted the dictator Anastasio
Somoza Debayle. In addition to the presentation of this historical event, the
performing subject evokes her sheltered middle-class experience and situates herself as an eyewitness to the revolution. While the nuns taught her
"not to be indifferent to the suffering" of the less fortunate, Chaves acknowledges her relatively privileged existence as a student in a private Catholic
school, where one can joke—albeit with some hint of conscious or subconscious anxiety—about torture. The abrupt shifts in her narrative—from the

---

1   Tracey Erin Smith, an award-winning solo performer based in Toronto, is the founder
and teacher of the SoulOTheatre class developed at Ryerson University's ACT II Studio
where Chaves developed *Fragile: A Play in Progress*. The class is designed to help and in-
spire professionals and non-professionals to create, write, direct, and perform in their own
one-person show "by transforming raw material from their lives into creative personal
story telling performances. Smith's process turns personal experience into compelling and
entertaining theatre, with no prior acting experience necessary" (Smith). Consult www.
soulo.ca for more information about the program and Smith.

2   Currently based in Toronto, Ontario, Chaves performs regularly at Yuk Yuk's, a
Canadian comedy club chain, and at the Montreal Comedy Nest. Chaves has won a Soul'd
Award and has been nominated for six Canadian Comedy Awards in the category of Best
Female Stand-up. She has performed in Central America, Germany, for the UN peace-
keeping troops in the Middle East, and has appeared in numerous festivals around North
America and in countless humanitarian fundraising events. As an invited speaker at Lasalle
Secondary School in Greater Sudbury, she told students to never back down from bullies
when it comes to hatred toward their sexuality. Accordingly, she left students with the
following message, "Keep staying alive. And keep kicking the ass-----!" (Carmichael). For
more biographical information regarding Chaves, see "Roster Acts."

dramatic representations of a repressive regime to her high-school yearbook designation as "most likely to talk under torture"; from the images of children surviving the slums of Nicaragua to her prom theme of "Staying Alive"—reflect Chaves's dramatic-sardonic humour, anchored in a consciousness-raising form of self-representation.

I aim to situate Chaves as a Latina comedian confronting her multiple subject positions as an immigrant living in Canada. Paying attention to her use of cultural signifiers to produce laughter, I intend to analyze the modality of her style, which I will refer to as "intersectional humour." In what context does Chaves contribute to expanding the definition of stand-up comedy while negotiating cultural difference, her exile, and feminism? How is the comical awareness of the subject positions—claims of identity, identification, and disidentification—produced in Chaves's comedy? Considering that humour and satire depend on transgressive acts and behaviours against the status quo, in the second part of the essay I will respond to these inquires by placing Chaves in a broader context. If women have traditionally been discouraged from embracing comedy because it is too "unfeminine," how does Chaves's comedy function as psychological survival skill and an emancipatory strategy of liberation?

"STAYING ALIVE": THE SEARCH FOR LATINA/O CANADIAN IDENTITY

According to Chaves, she was drawn to stand-up comedy and playwriting because of her passion for acting but her opportunities as an actress in Canada were limited "due to [her] ethnicity"(Chaves, Telephone 22 Oct.). This socio-economic polarization along racial/ethnic lines is ironically represented in a public service announcement (PSA) released nationally on Canadian television in 2009, wherein she plays an immigrant with a Master's in Business Administration (M.B.A.) forced to work as an office cleaning lady in Canada. The PSA begins with Chaves sitting in an office with two Caucasian male executives. The men appear to be listening to her intently as she provides them with business advice on ways to improve their bottom line. At the end of the consultation, Chaves stands up from her chair, picks up her cleaning spray and rag, and pushes her janitorial cart away. The men have a surprised look on their faces, showing in their reaction that they cannot reconcile the fact that this woman, who just gave them sound financial advice, is a cleaning lady. The PSA ends with the following caption: "If Canada is a land of opportunity, why is an MBA cleaning offices?" (Chaves, "Martha Chaves"). To be more specific, I would say, "If Canada is a land of opportunity, why is a Latina M.B.A. cleaning offices?" Often praised as a success story of multiculturalism and diversity, Canada's immigration system attracts highly skilled workers to better compete in the global economy. However, the caption and the overall content of the PSA announcement evinces Canada's self-awareness about the economic marginalization correlating with racial/ethnic/immigrant status within its borderlands. This issue is an ongoing subject in Chaves's comedy.[3]

In one of my interviews with Chaves, she explained her choice of profession as a stand-up comedian: "I think I was born to be a comedian. In stand-up, I write, I direct, I act." She laughs before continuing, "That way, I don't have to be cleaning houses or offices, selling drugs or selling a younger Latina into prostitution every time I am on-screen" (Chaves, Telephone 5 Nov.). As an actress, Chaves sees herself typecast in the stereotypical "Latina" roles of cleaning lady, madam, or drug dealer. She finds greater freedom to self-represent as a stand-up comedian while also having the opportunity to raise consciousness regarding the limitations imposed by the mainstream media on her and other women of colour. As a result, comedy becomes a tool of liberation and empowerment for Chaves while also becoming a process of self-typecasting. In his study *Stand-up Comedy in Theory, or, Abjection in America*, John Limon considers abjection as a self-typecasting mode in

---

3   See also Chaves, "Canada Immigration." At the end of this YouTube video, viewer discussion is included. In response to Chaves's role as an M.B.A., an angry viewer writes: "If this bitch is so smart then why doesn't she start her own business? I am sick of hearing how hard immigrants have it in this country. It is hard for everyone. Immigrants figure that if they are not the president of a company in 6 months; it is because of racism."

stand-up comedy. He borrows the term abjection from Julia Kristeva, arguing that stand-up comedy is an art form best exemplified by its fascination
with the abject. The theory of abjection embodies figures that are in a state
of transition or transformation, a state of in-betweeness or liminality. For
Kristeva, the link between psychoanalysis and the subconscious produces
"abjectifying" subjects and practices. Either in the form of scatological references in some cases or in relation to what makes "us" laugh (at times, an
uncomfortable laughter), all of a comedian's life, Limon asserts, is abject. He
says, "When you feel abject, you feel as if there were something miring your
life, some skin that cannot be sloughed, some role (because 'abject' always,
in a way, describes how you *act*) that has become your only character" (4).
The many applications that abjection can have to stand-up comedy and its
often crude content certainly applies to Chaves's comedic work. For example,
references to the word "ass" (or *culo* in Spanish) are common in her comedic
monologues. In one of her shows I recently attended, references to her ass as
having Alzheimer's were hilariously articulated in the context of discussing
her weight and body size.[4] *Coño*, a word that has different meaning across
the Spanish-speaking countries, is also a signifier in her repertoire. She has
also jokingly called the audience "drunken asses" for peeing in their pants
while laughing at her jokes.[5]

   After all, laughter, she suggests, is the best remedy to survive: "I know this
show will kick ass with the power of a bionic mule that just snorted lava off a
Nicaraguan volcano. I will work it baby! Laughter is the best . . . exorcist! To

---

4   I attended two of Chaves's shows that took place at the Yuk Yuk's in Ottawa on January
25 and 26, 2013. During the same weekend, I interviewed her during her participation as
a living "book" at a Human Library event that took place in the Ottawa Public Library's
North Gloucester branch.

5   *Coño* is a common expression used in Spain and several Latin American countries. It
originated in the Dominican Republic. Its meaning differs according to use, but in Spain
and several Latin American countries it is also used in its literal form as slang for the female genitalia, the vulva. It is important to point out that those references to the audience
as "drunken asses" were made in regards to some audience members who have the potential to behave disrespectfully during her shows.

perform an exorcism you do it in LATIN! For Latinos to endure all we have
endured we had to have laughter" (Chaves, "Sunday Feature: First-Person").
For Chaves, endurance and survival are signifiers marking the trajectory of
her comedy. She makes sense of her life by creating humour that not only subverts stereotypical images but also tells her individual story within a collective
sense of self, which binds together the Latina/o community. In the following
passage, she uses "staying alive" as a sardonic metaphor of self-subjectification:

> Staying alive, besides being the title of that Bee-Gees tune and the
> John Travolta movie, has been one of the main motifs of my existence.
> Not only because I'm from Nicaragua, a war-torn country plagued
> with poverty and social injustice. Not only because I was born in
> the midst of a fundamentalist Christian family, in a macho-oriented
> society and I am a lesbian. Not only because I am an uprooted im-
> migrant who was sent away to Canada by her parents, all alone, at
> the ripe age of 17. But staying alive has been my quest also because
> I am a stand-up comedian dammit! To stay alive is the name of the
> game in stand-up comedy as much as it is in bullfighting. (Chaves,
> "Sunday Feature: Dying is Easy")

In the Foucauldian sense, "the mode self-subjectification" or self-imagin-
ing acts through which Chaves confronts her existence, function as strategies
of representation. Her position is clear as she resists the constraints exercised
on her subjectivity or individuality. The context of the revolution is undeni-
ably a dramatic event in her life experience, justifying her survival story and
the reflective comedy it produces. While speaking as a survivor, she identifies
as a Nicaraguan immigrant living in Canada. The "imagining" of Nicaragua,
the place of origin, appears continually in Chaves's comedy.[6] Suggested in
the discursive configurations of a "war-torn country" are the allusions to

---

6   I use the notion of "imagining" here in reference to Benedict Anderson's book *Imagined
Communities: Reflections on the Origin and Spread of Nationalism*, which first appeared in
1983. For further discussion of *Staying Alive* by Martha Chaves, see Chaves, "De Colores."

the revolution, which was the main reason her parents "shipped her off" to Canada at the age of seventeen. The revolution is the cause and effect of her exile. Her parents sent her away to Montreal in 1978, the year the civil war in Nicaragua began, and she subsequently became a Canadian citizen. As a result of this upheaval, her parents and siblings also left for Guatemala a year later. According to Chaves, her parents sent her abroad with the excuse that they wanted her to learn a second language but "it was really because they feared that I would join the revolution" (Chaves, Telephone 22 Oct.). She successfully escaped the Nicaraguan Revolution, but in her Canadian exile she joined the "vaginista" revolution, as she suggested in a raunchy show at the Goodhandy's bar in the gay village in Toronto. In her interactions with the audience, she announced that she was a "vaginista" and that she was part of "the frente vaginista de la liberación nacional." While showing the audience the word "vaginista" written on her T-shirt, she asked how many people in the audience had a vagina and "how many people came to this world through the vagina" (Chaves, "Leather Bar").[7] The audience responded with laughter and applause when hearing the word "vagina," but, most significantly, Chaves's brilliant articulations make reference to the Frente Sandinista de la Liberación Nacional (the Sandinista National Liberation Front), the group that defeated the Somoza dictatorship and governed Nicaragua from 1979 to 1990.

It is clear that Chaves's exile to Canada is fundamental to her personal/professional being. However, her journey as an immigrant is not the story of an undocumented "border-crosser"; it "is based on an immigrant experience that not too many people talk about because usually people talk about immigrants who left and have to go with coyotes in tunnels with rats biting them or came through Niagara Falls in a bubble and stuff like that" ("De Colores").[8]

---

7   The word "vaginista" can be translated as a vagina activist, or, in certain contexts, as a lover of vaginas.

8   Originally *Staying Alive* was used as a working title of a semi-autobiographical piece by Chaves. Although she now uses *Fragile* as a working title for her one-woman show, she continues to use "staying alive" as a metaphor describing her life. Part of her material from *Staying Alive* was conceived at Alameda Theatre Company's 2010 De Colores Festival

Instead, her middle-class parents sent her to Canada to further her studies (and escape the revolution). The pain of her exile and the consequent loss of identity that Chaves describes, however, are similar to every immigrant's journey: "The suffering of not having a home has been always in my heart, of not having roots, of having lost my roots because my parents left to Guatemala while I was already here and never went back [to Nicaragua]" ("De Colores"). While she has lived in Canada the majority of her life, feelings of displacement are symbolically and comically performed in the trajectory of her work. As introduced in her biographical sketch, this feeling of being uprooted and having an uncertain identity are characteristics of a true Canadian: "She has lived in Canada most of her life, feeling uprooted, cold and confused about her identity, which, incidentally, is what makes her a true Canadian, eh?" ("Roster Acts").[9]

Chaves's use of the metaphor "staying alive" reflects her experience not only as a Latina immigrant but also as a lesbian and as a comedian. Most importantly, "staying alive" symbolizes her enduring the exile from Nicaragua. Her use of biting humour and the embodied knowledge and diverse contexts implicit in the signifier "staying alive" point to the rhetoric of marginality in

---

of New Works. The De Colores Festival focuses on providing developmental support for works in progress written by Latina/o Canadian artists.

9   Whether she feels like a true Canadian or not, her migration/exile to Canada was a necessity for her safety. As a result of the revolution, Nicaraguans preferred to migrate to neighbouring countries in Central America, as in the case of Chaves's parents, but those Nicaraguans who chose to go to North America were more attracted to the United States than to Canada. There were almost no Nicaraguans in Canada until the mid-1980s; however, their numbers gradually increased after 1983. It has been reported in the *Encyclopedia of Immigration* that in 1991 and 1992 alone more than 3,500 Nicaraguans were admitted into Canada. It was established that "[m]ost Nicaraguans were young and poorly educated and had often lived for some time in Honduras, Costa Rica, or the United States. In 2001, of 9,380 Nicaraguan immigrants living in Canada, only 170 came before 1981. About 88 percent (8,255) arrived between 1981 and 1995, most as refugees" ("Nicaraguan Immigration"). Numerical estimation of the Nicaraguan community in Canada has been difficult to conceive in absolute terms but both official and community sources have indicated that there are between 10,000 and 20,000 Nicaraguans in Canada today (Kowalchuk 1011).

the patriarchal cultural trajectory embedded in stand-up comedy and the social limitations confronted by female comedians. The marginal sites in Chaves's discourse not only indicate a positionality that is best understood in terms of the limitations of a subject's access to power but also represent a model of resistance to cultural/male hegemony (the "macho-oriented society") and Christian fundamentalism. In a feminist study that situates the woman comic culturally, Philip Auslander notes that "the processes by which cultural expression is disseminated in a patriarchal culture all create obstacles for the comic woman and the woman comic" (316). For Chaves, staying alive is a valuable metaphor responding to the many obstacles she has confronted since her exile: feeling compelled to perform her Nicaraguan self in a foreign country, marking her lesbian subjectivity, and fighting for recognition as a female, Latina immigrant comedian.

MULTIPLE SUBJECT POSITIONS AND INTERSECTIONAL HUMOUR

Chaves's multiple subject positions or the implications of being an immigrant/Latina/lesbian/comedian configure within the sites of intersectionality. While she understands the power of parody and humour to subvert established norms and transgress social taboos, Chaves's sardonic discourse illustrates what I conceptualize here as "intersectional humour." When Chaves emphasizes the paradoxes of her experience as a Latina immigrant (middle-class Nicaraguan) in Canada who happens to be a lesbian and a comedian, the sites of intersectionality pinpoint multiple dimensions and modalities of social relationships and subject formations. While intersectionality can be defined as a theory to analyze how social and cultural categories intertwine, it has been fundamental in feminist studies, implying more than the study of difference and diversity.[10] Chaves's multiple identities, marked in performances

10   Intersectionality attempts to capture the relationships between socio-cultural categories and identities, focusing on diverse and marginalized positions. Gender, sexuality,

analyzed here, capture the complexity of her intersectional subjectivity: the multiple specificities delineate difference (and her uniqueness) as a source of empowerment. If race, gender, sexuality, nationality, and other identity categories are most often treated in mainstream liberal discourse as categories of domination, Chaves's insistence on highlighting her multiple subject positions in her work intrinsically empowers her and her audience while challenging those who marginalize "the other." As Homi K. Bhabha has noted in a different context, the power of representation "as a theoretical and cultural intervention in our contemporary moment represents the urgent need to contest singularities of difference and to articulate diverse 'subjects' of differentiation" (74).

Chaves explores questions of identity and subject formation from different vantage points while performing the experience of living in two or more cultures, languages, and realities simultaneously. As pointed out in her biographical sketch, "Chaves is fluent in four languages (five when intoxicated or praying) and one of the few comics in the world who has the rare gift of doing comedy in a second language . . . and a third . . . and a fourth" ("Roster Acts"). Whether she is speaking of her experience as an immigrant, talking about the Canadian Latina/o community, or critiquing the Nicaraguan or Canadian governments, the essence of her humour comes from the necessity to integrate her Nicaraguan/Latina/o narrative with her Canadianness. She is a border subject who encourages her audience to think about the possibilities of understanding the Latina/o diaspora within the Canadian context. While she sees Canada as her new home, she often questions its identity. In *Queerly Canadian: An Introductory Reader in Sexuality Studies*, Scott Rayter begins the introduction by quoting some of the remarks made by Chaves at the tenth annual comedy night, Accent on Toronto: "I love this country. When Jack Layton died, the funeral for the leader of Her Majesty's Loyal Opposition was presided over a gay minister married to a man. And the right-wing prime

---

ethnicity, race, class, and nationality are categories that help to explain the complexity of intersectionality while pointing toward identities in continual processes.

minister had to pay for it!" (xv).[11] Rayter uses the irony embedded in Chaves's remarks to address the complexities of Canadian identity. He says that she is not the first to point out

> what many in a long line of cultural critics, historians, and, yes, comedians have noted: there appears to be something contradictory or paradoxical about this country, a quality often remarked upon whenever someone attempts to define Canadian identity. And yet, as others have suggested, we seem to take great pleasure in pointing this out, just as Chaves does above. (Rayter xv)

The use of Chaves's irony to introduce *Queerly Canadian* is intriguing to me. While the purpose of the book is to examine sexuality and its role in the building of Canadian identity, Chaves's inclusion is extraordinarily suggestive and significant. Her sardonic humour situates her in a continual search for a "new" identity, one that incorporates the specificities of Canada along with her multi-layered experience. This identity differentiates her not only within mainstream culture but also within the marked heterogeneity that defines the Latina/o diaspora in Canada. In one of her routine jokes, the Latina/o diaspora is suggested while making fun of mainstream Canadians for failing to differentiate between Nicaraguans and other Latinas/os. She introduces herself: "My name is Martha Chaves from Nicaragua. But at the end of the night people always think that I am Maria from Mexico, which is in the Dominican Republic" ("Martha from Mexico" and "Leather Bar"). Beyond the production of humour, Chaves urges her audience to continually recognize her ethnic background and differentiate it from that of other Latinas/os. This was also made evident when she described a day in her life as a comedian:

> Forget "Spanglish" l'espectáculo will have to be in Spanfranglish, franchement. Now, there's a myth that Latinos learn French easily

---

11 Layton was a Canadian social democratic politician and Leader of the Official Opposition. He was leader of the New Democratic Party from 2003 to 2011.

because French and Spanish are very similar but that is pure un-
adulterated "Le toro caca" [sic] Not even Spanish and Spanish are
very similar. For example, Costa-Rican Spanish is not even close to
Guatemalan Spanish—not to mention how differently those two
nations kick a soccer ball! Holy Saint Frijoles! The audience is going to be a casa divided! There will be Rightists and there will be
people who love Fidel. There will be Leftists and there will be people who wear Ché Guevara t-shirts thinking the face belongs to the
singer from Rage Against the Machine. There will be homos in the
closet and there will be queers in the cupboards. Latin people are
very diverse and are in constant dispute with each other but—in
my experience—they are united in one common thought, "Fear the
homo". And as you know, fear is a killer; but not on a comedy stage.
("Sunday Feature: First-Person")

Chaves's representation of Latina/o heterogeneity is both funny and on
point. She describes a community that is impossible to categorize in absolute terms. On one hand you have the Costa Ricans and on the other the
Guatemalans, each group speaking their own "Spanish." When imagining a
"Latina/o audience," she suggests that this will be a divided house because
Latinas/os are "in constant dispute," only uniting (in her view) when it comes
to homophobia, or "fear of the homo." As harsh as this may sound in the
light of day, Chaves is using self-deprecating humour to insert her critical
commentary regarding homophobia in the Latina/o community. The jokes
about differentiating Latinas/os remain as the primary "punchline" and the
subtle reference to homophobia becomes secondary, suggesting that she is
more invested in addressing the complex characteristics of the Latina/o community. Although Chaves's subtle references to homophobia are intersected
in the background of her joke, its inclusion is strategically configured. As a
social commentary, the use of this humorous "double entendre" technique
aims to sensitize and raise awareness while laughing about the complexities
and prejudices embedded in Chaves's community. References to a diverse
Latina/o population are significantly marked in the trajectory of Chaves's

comedy work. She represents a newly emerging community that has gradually expanded over the past thirty years. In *Continental Divides*, Rachel Adams examines the Latina/o diaspora, suggesting that the understanding of Latin Americans in Canada as a "new" North American constituency is fundamentally paramount to the integration of Canada in hemispheric relations. Her study demonstrates that these relations involve the need to "decentralize" US hegemony and to understand the cultures of North America in a new era of "continentalism." In particular, the cultures she includes in her study cross the borders of Canada, the United States, and Mexico. By highlighting the differences between the three countries, and the embedded cultural diversity within each other, she proposes a model envisioning the Americas of José Martí, *Nuestra América* (Our America). While his vision unified Latin Americans south and north, it resisted the imperial designs of the United States. Adams's attempts to move beyond the US nation and its cultural hegemony imagines the notion of the borderlands as a "borderless" divide, "since the entire continent has become a contact zone where Anglo and Latin American meet up, clash, and interpenetrate" (227). Chaves's comic configurations of *latinidad* imagine this "borderless" divide while emphasizing the possibilities of cultural heterogeneity and difference within difference.

"STAYING ALIVE" WITH THE POWER OF FEMINIST LAUGHTER

When I go out to do my job—whistling a joyful song and mentally dressed in full matador regalia including my red cape—I am often thinking how lucky I am. Honest. I may be on my way to a gig in a little town located in the cozy confines of the devil's rectum—northern Alberta—to play for an audience that is not remotely used to seeing a woman on stage—let alone a woman whose mother tongue is not English, let alone a woman who uses that tongue to (ideally) sexually satisfy other women and has no qualms about saying it in public in her broken English and still . . . I know it won't be as hard as being

> Josey Aimes, the character of Charlize Theron in "North Country."
> (Chaves, "Sunday Feature: Dying is Easy")

In Chaves's consciousness, a comedian must be psychologically prepared like a matador (including the "red cape") in order to survive. As demonstrated in her overall narrative, the intersectional forces she must confront to stay alive are not only associated with her ethnic background or her sexuality but with the challenges she confronts as a stand-up comedian. This matador/stand-up comedian analogy is fundamentally a feminist imaginative technique counteracting the belief that women are not funny. This belief has persisted as a negative stereotype in Western cultures and has been perpetuated by some male comedians like John Belushi and Jerry Lewis. Jane Curtin attested to this when she appeared on *The Oprah Winfrey Show* as part of a panel on women in comedy, sitting alongside Tina Fey and Chevy Chase, among others. Curtin said that the women writers on *Saturday Night Live* were often unable to contribute their work due to sabotage by the show's male comedians, especially breakout star John Belushi. She spoke about being in constant battle to be recognized by Belushi, who believed women were just fundamentally not funny. Curtin said, "So you'd go to a table read, and if a woman writer had written a piece for John, he would not read it in his full voice. He felt as though it was his duty to sabotage pieces written by women" ("Tina Fey").

Likewise, Jerry Lewis commented that he did not like any female comedians during a question and answer session with Martin Short: "A woman doing comedy doesn't offend me but sets me back a bit. I, as a viewer, have trouble with it. I think of her as a producing machine that brings babies in the world." "How about Lucille Ball?" Short asked him. "You must have loved her," he said to Lewis, who replied, "No" ("Jerry Lewis"). According to Lewis's logic, women are incapable of making people laugh because he can only imagine them as mothers. Lewis's statement was later supported and expounded upon by Christopher Hitchens in a 2007 issue of *Vanity Fair*, in which he used a "scientific study" to explain women's appreciation for—and lack of—a good sense of humour. He pointed out that his " . . . argument doesn't say that there are no decent women comedians. There are more terrible female comedians than there are terrible male comedians, but there are some impressive ladies out there. Most of them, though, when you come to review the situation, are hefty or dykey or Jewish, or some combo of the three." In short, Hitchens is implicitly suggesting that the only good female comedians are those he considers unattractive or unfeminine. The following year, in 2008, a response to Hitchens's piece was printed in *Vanity Fair*. Written by Alessandra Stanley, "Who Says Women Aren't Funny?" featured funny women and television stars, emphasizing the fact that female comedians are considerably more visible on television than before. According to Stanley, the history of women's humour, "or supposed lack thereof, is a joyless and increasingly moot subject, but it boils down to the point Virginia Woolf argued in her essay about Shakespeare's sister in *A Room of One's Own* and it's analogous to the case Larry Summers made so clumsily with regard to women in the sciences that cost him his job as president of Harvard: namely, that society has different expectations for women." Increasingly, female comics are emerging and finding their own voice in this male-dominated field—as "bull-fighters," to use Chaves's analogy, employing humour as a psychological survival tool. For feminists, laughter serves many functions essential to their survival and emancipatory tactics; it has evolved as a protective shield against male hegemony. The subversion of sexism and patriarchy not only legitimizes women's concerns, deflating anti-women positions, but serves as both an attack weapon and a call for feminist solidarity. Through the matador analogy and metaphor, Chaves's feminist imaginative technique responds to the effects of patriarchy. The analogy serves its purpose: it communicates an awareness of resistance and always the desire to win the "fight." Humour is the weapon she must use to stay alive. Implicit in her defensiveness is the need to assert her position as comic woman, because as Joan Rivers once said, "Men find funny women threatening. They ask me, 'Are you going to be funny in bed?' " (qtd. in Stanley). The most basic level of comedy, the telling of a joke, has been considered aggressive and "unfeminine" behaviour. I remember being told many times while growing up that decent *señoritas* will never laugh out loud. I heard my aunt saying, "*Calladita te ves más bonita*" (when you are quiet you look prettier). Producing noise and being loud have been practices associated with the "unfeminine." Being as subversive as Chaves's "unfemininity" is always a powerful act. When Chaves self-describes as "a woman who uses that tongue to (ideally) sexually satisfy other women," her insubordinate "tongue" dismantles the "normality" of femininity. For the Latina feminist, the subversion of "normative" femininity is coupled with the dismantling of the virgin/whore dichotomy embedded in the gender relations in Latina/o cultures. This dichotomy implies that women must assume subservient roles, either as Madonnas/virgins to be protected, or as whores to be desired and punished by men.

The gendered system embedded in the virgin/whore dichotomy affects not only Latinas, but also women collectively. First presented by Sigmund Freud in 1915, this dichotomy places the polarization of women into two categories: good girls versus bad girls. The good girls become wives and mothers and bad girls become the object of male sexuality and desire. The view of women as either virgins/Madonnas or whores has proven to limit women's sexual expression in patriarchal cultures. Patriarchy, Norma Alarcón contends, is the basis for the servile role of women in heterosexual relationships. She also argues that "when the wife or would-be-wife, the mother or would-be-mother questions out loud and in print the complex 'servitude/devotion/ love,' she will be quickly seen as false to her 'obligation' and duty, hence a traitor" (186). Although this dichotomy is foundational in the development of a Latina feminist's thought, the need to subvert its negative effects is imperative and constituted new gendered expression and sexualized female subjectivities in the late twentieth century. Since the late 1970s, Chicana and Latina feminists have developed a type of intellectual mobility in order to reconceptualize gender relations and gendered bodies outside the boundaries of binary knowledge systems embedded in heteronormative patriarchies. In their studies, heteronormativity and homophobia have been contested for stigmatizing alternative concepts of both sexuality and gender, and for making certain types of self-expression more difficult. By considering the social structures that construct gendered/sexualized identities (such as gay and lesbian) and the sexual politics that separate men and women, the emergence of self-identified "queerness" has transformed common understandings of new

Latina/o gendered bodies and spaces. In Chaves's configuration of lesbian desire, when she uses "her tongue"—not only to produce laughter but to satisfy women sexually—the subversion of the feminine body appears in multiple layers of meaning. Defiantly, lesbian desire binds the politics of identity with those of visibility.

Women as producers of laughter have a long history; however, they have been marginalized and demonized.[12] In her introduction to *Women's Comedic Art as Social Revolution*, Domnica Radulescu suggests that female comedians or mimic actresses were as important as men throughout some of the early Christian era, "before the fathers of the church started in due manner to link them to Satan and consider them 'children of Satan' " (6). It is not by accident that the words hell, evil, or devil, are familiar configurations in Chaves's discursive humour, if not in the comedy of many comic women. Chaves describes sardonic laughter as the "byproduct of evil":

> People think that humour comes from a rosy place but hell they are wrong! Laughter is a byproduct of evil! You can bet that in Paradise they didn't laugh. What were they going to laugh at? Everything was perfect until the Fall of Man you know, when a monkey threw a banana peel on the scale of evolution and Adam slipped making Eve laugh uncontrollably when she saw his goofy privates for the first time! Coño! ("Sunday Feature: First-Person")

The feminist technique inherent in Chaves's matador-analogous and symbolic humour is also evident in her commentary regarding the origins of laughter. Since humour and laughter are considered evil forces when produced by women, they must have subversive ends. They disrupt the social order. In her discussion of laughter, Chaves uses another analogy, but this time she

---

12   Comic women have existed since ancient times, having had a particularly strong presence in the *commedia dell'arte*, where female roles were generally played by women as early as the 1560s.

uses the Christian origins of "mankind" to relate laughter to Eve, the first woman in paradise:

> Of course there's the risk that I may be humiliated and that I may even be putting my physical integrity in serious danger but the other side of that coin is that there's a bigger chance that I may be able to slaughter that "bull" and that those people who may have never thought they would give the time of the day to someone as "different" as me, may partake in the greatest equalizer: the sacrament of laughter which says their minds are opened even if just a little bit! I don't mean to sound like the pompous ass that uses "sacrament" and "laughter" in the same sentence nor do I mean to imply that in the great scheme of things our contribution to society is as grandiose as we, comedians, may be inclined to believe it is . . . but there's indeed an undeniable healing power in the elixir of laughter and that healing may not be as potent for the audience as it is for ourselves. ("Sunday Feature: Dying is Easy")

CONCLUSION

While some performers have used comedy to make fun of themselves and other women, others use it to deal with the ironies of daily life. Some comic women openly address the intersectionality of gender, race, sexuality, and disability, among many social categories. I place Chaves's intersectional humour in this context, which reinforces the re-enactment of individual and collective identity. While she conceives her comedy as a means of enacting the world(s) of difference, or the enactment of "someone as 'different' as [her]," she sees comedy and the laughter it produces as feminist vehicles for transformation. Chaves belongs to a generation of comic women who have pushed the boundaries of stand-up comedy while negotiating cultural difference: the comical awareness of the subject positions inhabited in acts of self-representation—claims to identity, identification, and disidentification.[13] From the work of Chaves to the contributions of Sara Contreras, Monique Marvez, and Sandra Valls, to mention a few, Latina comedians are raising their diverse voices across all mainstream media spaces from east to west of the US–Canada border. While Sandra Valls jokes about growing up Mexican and lesbian in Texas, Sara Contreras self-represents as a Puerto Rican single mother, living in an upper-class Jewish neighbourhood in New Jersey. Monique Marvez, a Cuban from Miami, has been featured at the Just for Laughs Festival in Montreal and hosts her own radio show in San Diego.[14]

Chaves's distinctiveness represents forms of resistance disguised in the power of laughing, the power of telling her own story, because, as she points out, "[T]here's indeed an undeniable healing power in the elixir of laughter and that healing may not be as potent for the audience as it is for ourselves" ("Sunday Feature: Dying is Easy"). She enacts the reality of her multiple selves, the middle-class Nicaraguan immigrant, the comic woman, and her lesbian subjectivity while acknowledging the many borders that criss-cross her identity and give it a distinctive shape. The markings of a split subject demand a space for representation across diverse social categories.

---

13   Consult my books *Latina Performance* and *Latinas on Stage* for an analysis of the works of Latina comic performers in the US.

14   Marilyn Martinez, who died on 3 November 2007, can be placed as part of this generation. She used to say that she was a triple minority because she was fat, she was a woman, and she was Hispanic. She was based in Los Angeles and was a regular at the Hollywood Comedy Store. Before she died, she was featured along with Sara Contreras, Monique Marvez, and Sandra Valls in the DVD *The Original Latin Divas of Comedy*.

ALUNA THEATRE'S *NOHAYQUIENSEPA*: THE INTERMEDIAL INTERCULTURAL AND THE LIMITS OF EMPATHY[1]

JESSICA RILEY AND RIC KNOWLES[2]

We attended *Nohayquiensepa (No One Knows)*, the signature production of Aluna Theatre, as part of Aluna's Panamerican Routes/Rutas Panamericanas[3] festival, which took over Toronto's Theatre Passe Muraille for three weeks in May 2012.[4] The crowd in the lobby and spilling out onto Ryerson Avenue was charged with energy. English and Spanish mixed in lively conversations about the festival's workshops, classes, and showcases and about the two shows most had already seen: *Urban Odyssey*, an interdisciplinary dance puppet theatre piece by Federico Restrepo and Loco7 of Bogotá and New York, and *Parting*

---

1   The phrase "the limits of empathy," though not new, recently entered popular discourse through a September 2011 article with that title in the *New York Times* by David Brooks. "The problem comes," Brooks writes, "when we try to turn feeling into action."

2   We would like to thank Natalie Alvarez for her extremely helpful comments and suggestions. Research for this essay was supported in part by the Social Sciences and Humanities Research Council of Canada.

3   Aluna used the spelling "Panamerican" to reflect the Spanish "panamericana." We have retained their usage when referring to the festival, but elsewhere have used the more standard "Pan-American."

4   Some of the festival's workshops also took place at Buddies in Bad Times, Nightwood/ Tapestry Studios in the Distillary District, and Aluna's own studio space.

Memories, a performance piece by the luminous Violeta Luna of Mexico City and San Francisco. Yet to come on the main stage was *Blue Box* by Carmen Aguirre, of Valdivia, Chile, and Vancouver.

Nohayquiensepa was in good company. All of these shows had been invited by Aluna's founders Beatriz Pizano and Trevor Schwellnus with the explicit purpose of "going beyond divisions and making connections," to achieve a festival that was "Interdisciplinary. From Across the Americas" (Aluna, *Panamerican*). Their own interdisciplinary video-dance theatre performance was listed as having arrived by way of a Pan-American route that passed through Medellín, Montevideo, Mexico City, Caracas, Bogotá, Edmonton, Ottawa, and Toronto, all cities directly involved in its development. In addition to complex pre-recorded and (mostly) live video projection, live drawing on screen, original sound and music, and striking choreography, the show used spoken text in both English and Spanish. In doing so, *Nohayquiensepa* made significant interventions into the fraught and often appropriative practice of intercultural performance[5] through the mediation of the intermedial and the interdisciplinary. The show created environments, for artists and audiences, in which differences could come together on equal terms and new, self-reflexive and non-appropriative ways of seeing and relating to difference could be proposed and explored. But the process toward understanding was not an easy one.

When the audience entered the main space at Theatre Passe Muraille on that evening in May of 2012, they saw a large screen downstage on which a live hand was drawing shapes, squares, crosses, words, and phrases that at first seemed random. When the house lights dimmed to black, the screen went blue and the shapes of two female dancers in outstretched skirts appeared in silhouette behind the screen (Fig. 1)—moving through water, perhaps?—but soon emerged to the front and engaged in ritual movements based on the Colombian *cumbia* (a dance form tracing back to Yoruban traditions in

---

5   For a discussion of the problems of interculturalism in performance that *Nohayquiensepa* mediates, see Knowles, *Theatre*.

Fig. 1. Victoria Mata and Lilia Leon dance in silhouette behind the blue screen at the opening of *Nohayquiensepa*. Photo by Katherine Fleitas.

West Africa),[6] making offerings in the direction of the audience and lighting candles at the sides of the forestage that would remain lit throughout the show. This ritualistic sequence was followed by the projection of an animated map of the Magdalena River region of coastal Colombia, fragments of a corporate report from a Canadian mining company, and the again shadowy, silhouetted figure of a man who seemed to be presenting it. This show was full of shadows. This in turn was followed by projected charts, with the occasional intervention of the live onscreen hand highlighting phrases such as "missing persons" and "AFRO COMMUNITY FACES EVICTION BY ANGLO GOLD ASHANTI IN COLOMBIA." The sequence dissolved into a "soup," as the creators put it (Pizano and Schwellnus),[7] of seemingly naked bodies on the stage floor, their images shot from above and projected onto the again blue screen, while their limbs also reached up to form disconnected

---

6   For a version of the *cumbia* closest to what was used in the production, see Xiomara.

7   All subsequent quotations from Pizano and Schwellnus are from their interview with Riley and Knowles unless otherwise indicated.

onscreen silhouettes. This complex image was accompanied by reverberating, watery music that was oddly serene. We were fifteen minutes into the show before a word was spoken, and even when words were introduced they were fragmentary, and they characteristically moved freely between the show's dominant spoken languages.

What were we to make of this? To answer this question, we need to consider briefly the company's history and process before moving to a closer analysis of the creation of *Nohayquiensepa* and its reception within the context of the Panamerican Routes festival.[8]

Aluna Theatre was founded in 2001 by Pizano as Artistic Director and Schwellnus as Artistic Producer out of a felt need to create roles for Latino, particularly Latina, actors—chiefly Pizano herself—and to develop a process—one which they would ultimately describe as "design dramaturgy"—to accommodate Schwellnus's ambitions and interests as a scenographer. The company's mandate, however, has evolved over the years. Its cultural specificity as Latin American has given way to a more interculturally Pan-American vision, while at the same time Aluna's work has become increasingly intermedial and interdisciplinary. It is the purpose of this essay to explore the relationships between the intercultural and intermedial in the work of Aluna, specifically in their signature piece, *Nohayquiensepa (No One Knows): A Requiem for the Forcibly Displaced*. In particular, we are interested in the ways in which the show used the intermedial and interdisciplinary to produce an affective longing that is different from and more productive than the kind of "crude empathy" that Jill Bennett finds critiqued by Brecht: "feeling for another based

---

8   Our analysis is based on two performances of the play at this festival and a video of a festival performance provided to us by Trevor Schwellnus, and all quotations from the performance are from that video. But we have also consulted a video of the 26 March 2011 performance in Toronto (see Schwellnus, "Nohayquiensepa"), and Ric Knowles attended earlier workshop presentations of the show there. We are grateful to Pizano and Schwellnus for making material available to us, for answering our questions, for providing illustrations, and for engaging in a lively discussion of their work with us on 29 August 2012.

on the assimilation of the other's experience to the self" (Bennett 10).[9] Indeed, *Nohayquiensepa* may serve as an example of a different kind of work—and a different kind of empathy—not unlike the kinds that Bennett says "refuse to yield to sympathetic identification" but allow the viewer to "*feel into* another": "it stages a perceptual experience that threatens to take us outside of ourselves"—to unsettle us (34, emphasis in original).[10]

According to their published mandate, "Aluna Theatre is a not-for-profit charitable company that creates, develops, produces and presents artistically innovative and culturally diverse performance work with a focus on Latin Canadian and women artists." More specifically,

> The artistic mission of Aluna Theatre is to embrace the myriad of voices, cultures, and stories of our population, which are transforming the landscape of Canadian theatre. In our plays, works in translation, and international co-creations, people are complex individuals who exist beyond the restrictions of cultural labels. We encourage new hybrids of theatre evolved from a rich collaboration of experiences, performance traditions and media by engaging both emerging and established theatre professionals. Our work reaches out to diverse audiences in Canada and abroad. We build liaisons that promote art as a way to empower, and a way to share with each other and the world the idea of living in harmony. (Aluna, "Artistic")

---

9   Brecht never uses the word "assimilate," and the passage in "A Short Organum" that Bennett cites is talking about an actor's empathetic identification with her or his character, which he calls "the crudest form of empathy": "what should I be like if this or that were to happen to me?" (Brecht 195). But Bennett's phrase accurately represents the force of Brecht's argument.

10   It is striking, given *Nohayquiensepa*'s focus on Colombia as seen from Canada, that Bennett twice invokes "the plight of Colombians" when discussing the need "to *understand* their situation insofar as this entails an acknowledgement of an alterity, irreducible to our own experience," and "the failure of the First World to think outside of itself—to understand its differences from other places" (19, 21). One of Bennett's case studies, moreover, is the work of Colombian artist Delores Salcedo (50–54, 60–69).

The focus on the (implicitly multicultural) Canadian experience, on international outreach, on collaboration, on language, and on hybridities of various kinds is a result of the company's evolution, its experiences working with theatre artists in Colombia and elsewhere since 2008, and its increasing politicization in the realms of human rights and social justice.[11] It is also the result of an increasing awareness of the problematics of the term "Latin America," particularly as it relates to the Indigenous peoples of the Americas. Returning from working in the Amazon region in Brazil in 2012, Pizano describes an encounter with a man who told her, "We're not Latin American. We're Indigenous." This acute awareness of Indigeneity across the Americas is reflected in the company's name ("Aluna is a Kogi word that refers to an inner world of spirit and memory through which the world around and outside of us is kept in balance" (Aluna, "About")),[12] and in a current Aluna dance/theatre production, *Ixok'*, by Edgar Flores and Carmen Samayoa, which concerns Indigenous women and the struggle of the Mayans in the face of the 1978–84 genocide in Guatemala. It is also reflected in an increasingly engaged interest in what Pizano calls "this [multicultural] experiment that is Canada."

The integration of the intermedial and intercultural has been incipient, however, in all of Aluna's work, and is reflected not only in Pizano's interests, but in those of Schwellnus, who now holds a fellowship with the Chalmers Foundation to explore the integration of artistic disciplines and intercultural practices. Indeed, they describe the company's earliest work, *Meeting Place*, created by Schwellnus and directed by Pizano at Toronto's SummerWorks Festival in 2003, as "a post-dramatic montage," and Pizano's trilogy of plays

---

11   The company "History" provided on its website now includes, in addition to an emphasis on its goals of redressing the mis- and under-representation of diversity and on its efforts "to form a new and distinct theatrical language of presentation," an indication that "[f]or over a decade, Aluna Theatre has been attempting to shift the scales of imbalance by bringing social justice, equality, and human rights to the forefront of all productions" (Aluna, "History").

12   The Kogi are Indigenous to Colombia, the unconquered descendants of the Tairona civilization, living primarily in the higher regions of the Sierra Nevada (see Mejia).

about women and war, *For Sale* (Theatre Centre, Fall 2003), *Madre* (Theatre Passe Muraille Backspace, 2008), and *La Comunión* (Buddies in Bad Times, 2010), have increasingly been developed scenographically in the studio, incorporating live video into the process, not simply into the production, in order that the actors could work with the projections actively (see Fig. 2). "We didn't want wallpaper," Schwellnus says, indicating an impulse to move beyond video and other intermedial dimensions as purely aesthetic effects toward their incorporation as inherent, integral dramaturgical elements informing how and what the performance evolves to communicate. At the same time, *La Comunión*, the third play in the trilogy, introduced the mixing of languages that has also become important to the company's work, and did so through a characteristic emphasis on the intrinsic communicative potential of design elements. Rather than the traditional use of surtitles, Aluna's

Fig. 2. Live video was incorporated into the process of creation for *Nohayquiensepa*, not simply the production. Above is a rehearsal photo in which Carlos González-Vio (as Claudio) is seen working on the show's "running" sequence while facing the on-screen image so that he could work with the shadow image as the choreography evolved. Photo by Trevor Schwellnus.

strategy, since *La Comunión*, has been to incorporate such textual translations into the "literary architecture" of the design as an essential move toward the hemispheric perspective cultivated by their multilingualism. As Schwellnus puts it, "Visual poetry is a way to transcend language."

But a major turning point in the company's process came in 2008 when they worked in Bogotá with a diverse team of ten Canadian and fourteen Colombian artists on *the defenestration project*, a cross-cultural collective creation in collaboration with Bogotá's Corporación Colombiana de Teatro, Toronto's Theatre Revolve (theatre for young women), and Toronto's Tridha Arts Association (for the creation of international co-productions, especially between Canada and Latin America). The director of the project was Patricia Ariza, the award-winning artistic director of La Corporación.[13] The process, first developed in the 1960s by Teatro La Candelaria to help find a unique Colombian voice (and a kind of Jungian collective unconscious, according to Pizano and Schwellnus), was adapted by Aluna for the creation of *Nohayquiensepa*. The process involves a tripartite focus on the ensemble, the space of creation, and the audience. It consists of unmotivated improvisation (improvisers are not told what to improvise *about*) in front of members of the ensemble who stand in for future audiences, non-interpretative reflection (observers simply describe what they see as "a chain of actions"), and reflective analysis.

---

13   The program for Aluna's 2012 Panamerican Routes Festival, where both *Nohayquiensepa* and *Ixok'* were performed and where Ariza offered a workshop on collective creation, describes her as "one of the most important women in Latin American Theatre": "She is Artistic Director of La Corporación Colombiana de Teatro, a beacon of hope and awareness in engaged theatre in a context of civil war. In 2007 she was given the Prince Claus Award (Denmark) for her efforts in counteracting injustice, restoring social memory, for her energetic commitment to the reduction of conflict and for her outstanding work over the decades to empower the disadvantaged, enabling them to transform their lives through cultural activities" (Aluna, *Panamerican*). For more information on Ariza and the company, see La Corporación's website. See also Cawly for information on Teatro La Candeleria, the country's first independent experimental theatre, with which La Corporación is associated.

Nohayquiensepa is a result of Aluna's adaptation of this process to its own cultural and creative contexts. This involved finding ways to work with—and against—artists coming out of conventional North American conceptions of theatre, modifying the year-long Colombian process to suit Canadian the-atre-making timetables and introducing some of the characteristics of Aluna's style and working methods into the process of collective creation. For example, for Schwellnus, who directed and designed *Nohayquiensepa* as "lead artist," "[V]ideo projection works best when the performer works with it from the beginning, making it part of her space." Consequently, he says, "My twist on [La Corporación's] formula is to make the room in which we work part of the improvisation, by proposing (and adapting) environments in real time. The improvs, based on some source material and ideas, are analyzed, and then we do another round. Everyone in the room creates, but the director definitely assembles and tweaks the work as the process matures and the improvs slow-ly transform into a series of related sequences" (Schwellnus, "Interview").

Thus the emphases on ensemble, space, and audience learned from La Corporación were adapted through Aluna's characteristic "design dramaturgy." Aluna constitutes its Toronto studio as a "meeting place," to invoke at once the title of their first production and the supposed Huron name for the city in which they are located. "Toronto" is popularly believed to derive from the Huron word for "meeting place,"[14] a derivation that invokes the city's history, even before contact, as a place in which different cultures and (First) Nations came together—a point of intercultural mingling that also evokes a Pan-American history predating the borders of nation-states and such concepts as "Canada" and "Latin America." The studio, then, serves consciously as the *locus* for the intersection of the (multi)cultural, transnational, and (multi) medial, an intersection that provides the Aluna process with much of its gen-erative force. The emphasis on audience in the creation process, moreover, extends beyond improvisation exercises that involved participants responding

---

14   The etymological claim is disputed (see, for example, Merritt), but it has the force of popular tradition behind it, and the historical role of Toronto as actual meeting place is not in question.

to the work as spectators. At later stages, in its multiple Pan-American iterations, *Nohayquiensepa* continued to evolve in response to spectatorial
feedback, most notably in their critical discovery—on performing an early
version of the piece in Bogotá to an invited "first audience" of the families of
people being killed in Colombia—that the play was about Canadian mining
practices. Thus, the ensemble creation of the show, in its particular spaces of
creation, is integrally related to the eventual involvement and engagement
of the spectator.

The ensemble, too, was essential to the role played by interdisciplinarity in the development of *Nohayquiensepa*. Reflecting on this, Pizano and
Schwellnus speak of the "freedom" from traditional North American—for
them, specifically Torontonian—dramaturgies that intermediality and interdisciplinarity, as well as collaborative development practices, has allowed
them. Pizano and Schwellnus talk about the excitement of working with choreographer Olga Barrios and other dancers, citing the dancers' freedom from
the post-Stanislavskian assumptions about motivation that can sometimes
constrain actors. Modelling a different approach to development, "the dancers just *launch*" into the process, as Schwellnus puts it, giving the rest of the
ensemble "something right off the bat to react to" and helping members un-
used to the "risky [Colombian-influenced creation] process" to overcome
their conventional inhibitions. As Pizano puts it, "We had to shut up as actors.
Because they [the dancers] don't ask—they start going, and going, and going,
and they start *finding*." Resisting impulses toward conventional Western acting
and dramaturgy, performers from both disciplines engaged in cross-cultural,
cross-genre "jamming with composer Thomas Ryder Payne in the rehearsal
hall." Likewise, intermedial "jamming," with live drawing by Lorena Torres
Loaiza, with cameras, projections, abstract shadows, and Mylar, and with
co-director Heather Bratten as observer/describer, produced a process that
resisted traceable, causational, appropriative narratives. "We didn't want to
re-enact anything," says Schwellnus, describing a process not of "explaining
but explor[ing]," a process which avoided approaches to acting that require
the performer to absorb rather than present the "character" she is playing.
"Throughout the creation process we always tried to reflect from our own

perspective. We were not trying to embody somebody else unless a very particular moment demanded it." What Schwellnus is describing echoes in theatrical terms Dominick LaCapra's "empathic unsettlement," a kind of critical, self-reflexive empathy, "a virtual, not vicarious experience . . . in which emotional response comes with respect for the other and the realization that the experience of the other is not one's own" (40). "Empathic unsettlement," according to LaCapra, "poses a barrier to closure in discourse" (41).

The process cut across cultural backgrounds and influences as well as across creative disciplines, with company members from throughout the Americas and Europe. Different parts of the show were inspired by the *cumbia* dance form, by Indigenous songs, and by pre-Columbian art. The influence of Western dramaturgy entered the mix during the stages of reflection and analysis, as Schwellnus and the company assembled the pieces out of the creative, "interwoven" dramaturgical material to constitute, through alternative ways of working, what is essentially an alternative performance form that is not based on (re-en)acting, in the traditional sense of creating "characters," but on the prompting and reacting that characterize Aluna's creation process *and* the reception of their work by audiences.

Nohayquiensepa, which is based on stories from the Magdalena River in Colombia and the devastating effects of Canadian mining operations there, is loosely focused on the largely subconscious final moments of a hunted man and the local people who react to his death. It has been variously described over the several manifestations in the course of its development as a *cri de coeur* for victims of violence, a requiem, and "an investigation on what it means to be on the fringes of violence—to confront its effects not in our personal lives, but where public meets private":

> [I]t is about the death of strangers, and what people do to cope with the realities of violence when we have our own seemingly disconnected lives to live. What kind of answers could we propose in the face of human rights violations against people we don't know? Nothing truly honest (no hay quien sepa—there is no one who knows)—and

yet we feel the pull of that need to try to answer the why and how of resolving someone else's pain. (Aluna, *Nohayquiensepa* Program)

It is also about using the techniques of collective and collaborative creation across disciplinary, artistic, and cultural difference to find "new ways of creating hybrid performances" (Aluna, *Nohayquiensepa* Program).

The show uses the intermedial to mediate key issues in intercultural performance on several fronts, all of which are related to the initial and overarching issue of empathy and its limits across difference as raised by the project's inciting impulse to explore our "capacity for empathy"[15] through the question, "How do we deal with the death of a stranger?" Debates about empathy have been renewed in theatre and performance studies in the past decade in part because of cognitive studies discourses around the discovery by Vittorio Gallese in 1996 of "mirror neurons" in macaque monkeys (see Gallese et al.; Gallese). Theatre, performance, and dance studies scholars such as Bruce McConachie, Rhonda Blair, and Susan Leigh Foster have been quick to explore the implications of these theories for theatre and performance. Foster's work, *Choreographing Empathy: Kinesthesia in Performance*, is particularly pertinent to our discussion here because of her attention to social and cultural determinants that frame empathetic responses. Perhaps less well known to the field is the work of trauma scholars such as Sara Ahmed, Jill Bennett, and Dominick LaCapra, who are useful in addressing our own concern with empathy's tendency to "eat" its other, appropriating and ultimately negating the other's experience by making it one's own. LaCapra warns against "unchecked identification, vicarious experience, and surrogate victimhood" (40), while Sara Ahmed characterizes empathy as "a 'wish feeling,' in which subjects 'feel' something other than what another feels in the very moment

---

15   This description of the inciting impulse behind *Nohayquiensepa* was offered by Schwellnus during the Panamerican Routes/Rutas Panamericanas Festival conference session "Theatre and the Law II: The New Gold Rush and Corporate Responsibility" on Friday, May 25, 2012.

of imagining they could feel what another feels" (*Cultural Politics* 30). "Even when we feel we have the same feeling," she argues, "we don't necessarily have the same relationship to the feeling" (*Cultural Politics* 10). Bryoni Trezise parses Ahmed's argument as "intimating that at the heart of empathy there exists an important, but often overlooked, discordance between an intention to enact it and the actuality of performing it." "Perhaps," she suggests, "empathy might always already be diverting itself from its own central cause" (216). Finally, both Ahmed and Susan Leigh Foster relate empathy to the cultural production of "the stranger" in ways that illuminate *Nohayquiensepa*'s central question concerning how we relate to the death of a stranger, both historically and in the contemporary context of globalization and multiculturalism. Ahmed argues that "emotions may involve 'being moved' for some precisely by fixing others as 'having' certain characteristics. The circulation of objects of emotion involves the transformation of others into objects of feeling," and thereby "objectifies" them (*Cultural Politics* 11). In her earlier book, *Strange Encounters*, Ahmed speaks of this reifying and objectifying "fixing" of others as an act of (creative? rhetorical?) figuration that "*invents the figure of the stranger with a life of its own insofar as it cuts 'the stranger' off from the histories of its determination*" (5, emphasis in original): "[I]t is the very gesture of getting closer to 'strangers' that allows the [reifying] figure to take its shape" (4). And as Foster points out, empathy has as part of its history and genealogy a definitional field that involves recognition, and therefore the very constitution of the (*un*recognizable) other *as* other, in the service of justifying the colonial project (see Foster 142–47).

Jill Bennett nevertheless holds out hope for LaCapra's "empathic unsettlement," finding in the contemporary visual and performance art world's response to trauma "the possibility—for both artist and viewer—of 'being spectator of one's own feelings' "[16] (23) in a way that allows for the kind

---

16   Bennett is quoting from Swiss psychologist Édouard Claparède's 1911 work, "La Question de la 'mémoire' affective," where he argues, "It is impossible to feel emotion as past . . . One cannot be a spectator of one's own feelings" (qtd. in Bennett 22). Trezise sees in Bennett's position a conflict, not only with Claparède, but also with Ahmed, for whom

of self-reflexive, non-appropriative empathy that we are exploring here in the creation and reception ("for both artist and viewer") of *Nohayquiensepa*. Indeed, we suggest that *Nohayquiensepa*, in foregrounding the limits to proximity between strangers (on stage and in its performer-spectator dynamic), works against the impulse to elide the distance that Ahmed sees as part of the reification of the stranger through what she calls "stranger fetishism" (*Strange Encounters* 5).

Initially for the Aluna company, the question "How do we deal with the death of a stranger?" was prompted by the story of Colombians in Puerto Berrio who were dealing with the deaths of other Colombians, strangers from upriver rendered all the more strange and unknowable by the fragmentation of their remains. Retrieving these unidentifiable body parts from the Magdalena, the people there adopted the remains, giving names to the strangers, and creating a mausoleum in which to bury them. Entering into this project, Schwellnus and Pizano themselves became part of the question, extending it into the realms of the intercultural and intermedial by the nature of their involvement and working process. The story first came to the attention of Pizano and Schwellnus mediated and mediatized; that is, it came by way of a televised news story, which led to Internet research. Thus artists in Canada, now, were "dealing with the deaths of strangers"—and with how strangers deal with the deaths of strangers—across media and culture, and their next step was to use intermediality and interdisciplinarity to work through this extended strangeness and directly explore our "capacity for empathy." This exploration intriguingly brought together the traditionally "kinaesthetic" kinds of connections that Susan Leigh Foster explores in the history of dance and the "phenomenological aural experience" that Marcus Cheng Chye Tan finds in what he calls "acoustic interculturalism" (36) ("sound/music," he argues, can "create new culture-scapes" (43)) with a degree of detachment that is produced through a frustrated need to perform semiological decoding—to *comprehend*—that is highlighted throughout the production in ways that we

---

"empathy only ever operates in the future, as a wish, as deceptively multiple or even *dissimulating*" (Trezise 216, emphasis in original).

explore below. The pure affective power of Barrios's choreography and of Ryder Payne's soundscape can, in fact, be understood to *produce* the longing for meaning and understanding that the performance itself productively frustrates. Ultimately, then, the problem of dealing with the deaths of strangers extends one step further, to *Nohayquiensepa*'s audiences, who can be understood directly to engage the initial impulse of the project, to test, mediate, and experience the power and limits of empathy in ways that reflect the paths traced by the artists' own intercultural and intermedial process of discovery as they worked through an evolving sense of the politically, psychologically, and affectively charged initial question. The production might be understood to produce what Bennett calls "affective responses [that] can be thought provoking as well as emotive [and] can produce a form of empathy that is more complex and considered than a purely emotional or sentimental reaction" (24). She draws on Gilles Deleuze's notion of the "encountered sign" that, "far from foreclosing on thought, . . . agitates, compelling and fuelling inquiry rather than simply placating the subject" (36), becoming "the means by which thought proceeds and ultimately moves toward deeper truth" (37). And that truth, arrived at "when one allows the violence of an affective experience to truly inform thinking" can, for Bennett, "inform understandings both about the nature of relationships to others and about the *political* nature of violence and pain" (56, emphasis added). For as Ahmed argues,

> The call of such pain, as a pain that cannot be shared through empathy, is a call not just for an attentive hearing, but for a different kind of inhabitance. It is a call for action, and a demand for collective politics, as a politics based not on the possibility that we might be reconciled, but on learning to live with the impossibility of reconciliation, or learning that we live with and beside each other, and yet we are not as one. (*Cultural Politics* 390)

The "strength of the Arts," Schwellnus writes, is "the sensitivity to hear the softer voices that don't cut through the daily noise of our overmediated lives" ("Why"). Given that Schwellnus's own art is intermedial theatrical design, this assertion expresses the paradox of media as both the barrier to and the agent of intercultural exchange that operates in the development and reception of *Nohayquiensepa*. Intermedial effects that are integral to the creation and presentation of the work frequently express, simultaneously, both the impulse toward and the self-reflexive limitations of empathy. This paradox is closely related to the intermedial paradox discussed by Bruce Barton in his essay "Paradox as Process: Intermedial Anxiety and the Betrayals of Intimacy." Barton productively examines the ways in which intermediality, by heightening the anxiety and vulnerability of both performers and spectators, can simultaneously heighten the possibilities of intimacy. He talks about the tensions between "vicarious identification" and "an intimacy informed by investments in lucidity, consistency, and comprehension," and he usefully (for our purposes) cites "Yvonne Spielmann's assertion that the primary mode of intermedia performance is 'self-reflection' " (581). We are attempting here to extend his insights on intimacy into the different but related realm of empathy. In *Nohayquiensepa*, however, the issue is less about the anxiety that intermediality might produce in spectators than about the capacity for intermediality to mediate between the production of direct kinaesthetic or phenomenological response, as suggested above in the work of Barrios and Ryder Payne, and the self-reflection produced by fragmentation and the frustrated longing for semiological "lucidity, consistency, and comprehension." The large screen, for example, which dominates the setting (particularly in the first half of the show when it is located far downstage in the position of a proscenium curtain), at one level represents the tantalizing possibility of easy access to another's experience implicit in our regular engagements with televised news, or with naturalistic dramas or films. The screen in *Nohayquiensepa*, however, intrudes on the space in ways that also serve to remind us that this perception of access is illusory, that there is inscrutable life behind, before, and at the peripheries of its projected representations. And throughout the production it is used at once to produce and complicate our empathetic relationship to the action. Like the show in which it features, the screen is full of shadows.

When Pizano as actor finally, at first timidly, speaks over fifteen minutes into *Nohayquiensepa*, she offers a narrative, and with it the tantalizing possibility of some access to meaning, a definitive elaboration on the series of images, on screen and on stage, that have been presented thus far. Speaking in front of a screen onto which is projected a disembodied hand, Pizano (or the "character" she presents) names and begins to narrate the life of the Magdalena victim she has adopted. As she describes his life with increasing confidence, the disembodied hand on screen gains a body: a live camera pans up the arm until the torso and head of "Claudio" (Carlos González-Vio) come into view behind her (Fig. 3). What is at issue here are the limits of Pizano's access to the unknowable victim: he both is and isn't reachable through Pizano's creative attempt to know him—in Ahmed's terms, to "figure" him—and this self-reflexive articulation of the limits of empathy—and the possibilities of creativity—in communication between strangers is made explicit by the operations of the intercultural and intermedial in this scene. They communicate, she in English, he in Spanish, from stage to screen, seeming to re-enact conversations drawn from his life. They speak lines in unison. He comments on—even contradicts—the details of her narrative. For spectators such as us, fluent in only one of the two languages, there are limits to understanding the nature of this interaction. Indeed, there are other, non-linguistic limits as well, which, taken together, serve to disrupt the spectator's certainty about what she is seeing: if Pizano, or the character she is presenting, has conjured this "Claudio" from an unknown fragment or body part, if she has given him life through imagining his life story, then who is this man that we see on screen? Is he the embodiment of her fabrication, a fragment turned into a man? Or is he the man, the victim, who became Pizano's fragment?

At one level, Pizano virtually breathes (onscreen) life into the body fragment that she has discovered. At the same time, however, we are made self-reflexive by the seemingly provisional ontological status of the "characters," including the "hunted man" that the show is purportedly about. As we "*see ourselves feeling*," in Bennett's phrase (47, emphasis in original)—as we "catch [ourselves] in the act" (123)—we are made aware of the limits of empathy across difference through the mediating and mediatized disruption of an impulse toward intercultural engagement that is potentially appropriative and distorting. We experience a type of empathy that "comes into play

Fig. 3. The live camera panned up from the image of a hand
to reveal the torso and head of Carlos González-Vio (Claudio)
as Beatriz Pizano named and described the imagined character's life with increasing confidence. Photo by Katherine Fleitas.

when . . . we inhabit the space—the difference—between ourselves and others" (Bennett 123), and our certainties about shared understanding, in this
instance, are experientially unsettled. As LaCapra argues, such unsettlement
"places in jeopardy harmonizing or spiritually uplifting accounts of extreme
events from which we attempt to derive reassurance or a benefit (for example unearned confidence about the ability of the human spirit to endure any
adversity with dignity and nobility)" (41–42).

And then Pizano exits and "Claudio" comes to life. González-Vio enters the auditorium through the audience-centre aisle, climbing onto the
stage and beginning violently to interact with his silhouettes/doubles on the

screen. To the ragged, unsettling sound of machinery he runs, literally shadowed by a multi-figured, multi-limbed image behind him, seeming to run from the screen toward the (embrace of the?) audience, but trapped in motion, making no progress. The surprise of first seeing an embodied rather than onscreen Claudio is not, however, accompanied by a greater sense of empathetic identification. Perhaps because of our familiarity with filmic naturalism, on screen the figure seemed somehow more engaging, more "real," than this nevertheless desperate figure enmeshed in his own shadows in an increasingly claustrophobic *mise en scène*. Claustrophobic, that is, until, in an extraordinary moment, the screen that has kept the stage so foreshortened to this point lifts in what Pizano and Schwellnus call "the opening-up moment," when the stage is taken over by dancers as the screen adjusts and settles itself farther upstage.

Thus, the freedom from conventional dramaturgical constraints that is cited by Pizano and Schwellnus as the product of their interdisciplinary and intermedial collaborative-development processes also operates in the possibilities for reception that emerge in performance. As indicated in our description of the play's first "dramatic" moments, through Pizano's narration and animation of the life of "Claudio," *Nohayquiensepa* invokes and disrupts assumptions that commonly inform conventional theatrical reception, at least in Canada. Audience members seeking to know "What does it mean?" both get their answer and don't. Indeed, as Pizano aptly notes, spectators asking "What does it mean?" register not only the disruption of their inherited assumptions, but also, significantly, their engagement: "That [is] the thing they are so interested in." This fixation conveys the theatrical power of the unexplained, replacing "What does it mean?" with "What are we to *make* of this?," the need for comprehension (and therefore control) with the impulse, like the artists and their original subjects, to imagine, or create.[17] Drawn in by the

---

17   Jill Bennett also proposes a shift away from "What does it mean?" as the question to ask of an artwork, but rather than "What are we to make of this?" she proposes "How does it work?—how does it put insides and outsides into contact in order to establish a basis for empathy" (45).

disruption of convention and denied the conventional routes to meaning associated with control and comprehension (with complete and discrete, definitive and unquestioned understanding), an alternative, non-appropriative communication model—a model, even, for a different form of empathy—becomes possible for the spectator, one which includes the reflexive recognition of its own limits and incompleteness.

The most ostensibly "dramatic" scene in the piece occurs at the midpoint of its hour-long duration, and might serve as a further example. Here the more traditional "character" of a journalist is introduced (though one with neither backstory nor through line). The audience's expectation of a conventional "scene" is initially evoked with the sound of a ring tone and an opening line spoken realistically into a cellphone—"Hello, yeah, I'll be right there." There is even a revealing expository detail: "I woke up this morning in a hotel. . . . I thought I'd learn some Spanish before I got here, but you know how that goes. Best intentions. . . . " However, the staging of the scene and the incorporation of projections disrupt these expectations of realism. The reporter's interview subjects are bodies writhing on the floor, projected on screen in a wash of blue light that evokes the Magdalena and its victims of violence, and his extending microphone becomes a fishing line, dredging the river for its secrets. Most of these secrets are delivered in Spanish, which the journalist struggles to translate and relays to us in fragments: "something about a door . . . flowers, water, and salt," "something about a mountain . . . ," "something about no water in the tank." Eventually one of the women "climbs" him, literally enmeshing him in a struggle that he initially ignores. When he finally drops his microphone to the floor, another woman crawls to it, crying out in Spanish, and eventually crying *tout court*, as the journalist moves his body, apparently experiencing pain akin to that which is registered in the woman's voice. His writhing seems to respond to something that is not there; the unseen assailant who prompts the woman's cries seems also to prompt the journalist's contortions. Or do the cries themselves bring on the journalist's pain? Is his pain analogous to hers, brought on by the same assailant, or is it an echo, a personal expression at a remove, an onstage depiction of Ahmed's "wish feeling" empathetic experience that creates distinct, subject-specific emotion in the place of any direct appropriation of feeling or experience? This uncertainty is amplified by our own empathetic impulses, prompted simultaneously by the aural encounter with the woman's suffering and the onstage image of the writhing man. As in Ahmed's definition of empathy, we are powerfully affected by this feeling, prompted to "imagin[e] we [can] feel what another feels," but the very fragmentation of this feeling, the onstage illustration of the dislocation of empathetic "wish feeling," fractures and makes plain the limits to this impulse toward a unifying—and universal—experience of suffering. Meanwhile, the upstage screen shows images of the squares that we had seen in the pre-show, which we come to understand to be the individual graves of a large mausoleum. As the journalist points to or touches these cells, the projected hand of the live drawer blacks them out while the previously writhing and whispering bodies on the stage floor assume fetal positions, deadly still, and are projected onto the screen from overhead cameras. The scene dissolves into a video of walking feet that fill the screen as a voice-over sings lines from Emilíana Torrini's haunting "Beggar's Prayer," highlighting the refrain, "Mama said eventually this hurting will end."[18]

The sequence seems to cry out for an empathetic response as we see the journalist move from his initial casual composure to kinaesthetically embodying and enacting a version of his subject's struggles, as we ourselves witness and experience viscerally something that resembles-at-a-distance the wrenching pain of the depicted victims, and as we finally hear the moving lyrics of the song. But neither the journalist nor the dancers are figures who invite identification, and finally the video that accompanies the song, featuring the apparently indifferent feet of passersby, serves as a distancing, and puzzling, distraction from conventional pity or fear. The audience in Canada understands that something terrible has happened, and through other clues in the production knows that this ecological and human disaster is an outcome of the practices of Canadian mining companies and the policies of Canadian governments. But we are not allowed to own the grief that we see depicted, to feel the pleasures of purgative identification, or to let ourselves emotionally

---

18   For the complete lyrics of the song, see Torrini.

off the hook for what we are coming to understand. Perhaps what we experience is less the vicarious and dubious pleasures of empathetic involvement and more the longing to respond actively and adequately to something that we cannot fully comprehend.

The audience's experience of this central sequence, moreover, once again replicates that of the theatre company, as the journalist's questions and research into the ultimately unknowable may be seen to represent those of the company itself, while the audience's piecing it all together—"something about body parts and a river," perhaps, "something about ecological disaster," "something about mining"—replicates both.[19] Here and throughout the show the audience, like the creators, are "working within environments," reacting to prompts rather than witnessing re-enactments that are always and inevitably inadequate. In these ways the show models and prompts an affective, differently empathetic way of connecting across difference that is at once powerful, provocative, and deeply moving.

Against the backdrop of the apparently indifferent passing feet, the transition from this sequence to the next occurs through the limited and ultimately unsettling onstage depiction of the spectator's impulse to reach out across difference and offer assistance. Pizano crosses the stage and reaches out to aid a dancer, lifting her from the ground, but this ostensibly simple act of assistance is implicitly complicated by the operations of costumes and props. Pizano, dressed in what registers as the first recognizable "costume" in the performance, wears a corporate ensemble, glasses and a jacket. Is this, then, to be understood as an empty gesture? Far from a fulfillment of our fantasy for an easy connection across difference, Pizano's costume reminds us of

---

19   As scholars and theatre historians we have experienced a further replication of this process in piecing together fragments and traces of a show that, as we have worked on it, only exists in our memories and reconstructions, and in archival videos of its different iterations. In piecing together our account of the show's first "dramatic" scene, discussed above, we built a complex argument concerning a particular unsettling split-screen effect, only later realizing that the documents we were working with were rehearsal videos made for the purposes of introducing a new actor into the cast. The split-screen effect we had so carefully analyzed had never existed in any performance before an audience.

the contentious issue of "corporate social responsibility" (CSR) that is to be the subject of a public debate as part of the festival, immediately following *Nohayquiensepa* on one of the days we were in attendance. Though the dancer accepts Pizano's assistance in rising from the stage floor, she notably rejects Pizano's proffered microphone, refusing to be "given" a voice.

Moments later, this refusal is repeated by the audience. Extending the microphone in our direction, Pizano invites spectators—specifically the Torontonian audience of which we were a part—to fill the gap left by the dancer's refusal, to say what needs to be said in response to the suffering we've witnessed. Finding the audience silent, however, the corporate figure herself attempts to speak, but she too finds herself lost, stuck at the expression of self, literally as (grammatical) subject, uttering "I . . . ," and struggling to move beyond it. At the same time, the screen functions intermedially to extend the implications of this limited "I." As the show has evolved the hand of the live drawer has come to feel like an extension of the audience, and here, as it visibly transcribes and then falters in its self-expression, spectators are once again invited to reflect on the limits of empathetic engagement. Across languages, too, we see this expressed, as González-Vio comes forward to utter, and falter at, his own "Yo . . . ," duly recorded by the hand on screen. The hand that writes, finally, completes in Spanish the sentence that neither Pizano nor González-Vio were able to finish "live," and in so doing expresses the limits to knowledge across difference, to certainty in the face of violence, to the capacity for words to atone for the devastating practices of Canadian mining companies in Colombia, adding on screen, "No se" ("I don't know"). As the show's title tells us, no one does.

Not knowing—the limits to knowledge and therefore to empathy—is then illustrated experientially by what the creators call the "eulogy scene." The performers line up, initially one behind the other and later in a row across the base of the screen, and deliver eulogies in overlapping languages and voices. Arising directly out of one of the improvisation exercises used to create the piece, in which the performers were asked to offer eulogies to strangers, the scene is staged in order to recapture what emerged in the development process as an "exercise in listening." The scene remains unscripted, so the actors, improvising every night, are forced not only to create but to listen to one another in performance. "The listening is key," Schwellnus says, "giving your thing, but also letting someone else talk. It was like creating a choir." Experiencing these multiple, bilingual, and overlapping speeches from the position of a spectator, however, the effect of this listening exercise is to disrupt the conventional expectation that what we hear, in the theatre, defines and delineates our ability to make meaning, that everything we receive as spectators is everything there is to know. Here, instead, the experience highlights the limits to our knowledge, to our ability to make meaning. We can't hear everything, no matter how hard we try; we are necessarily limited in our access to the experiences of others. Thus we experience the impulse to understand, straining as we do to distinguish particular voices, to make whole the fragments of speech we are able to discern, while simultaneously confronting experientially the limits to that understanding.

Moreover, those fragments that we do piece together serve to make plain the very real limits to meaningful cross-cultural communication surrounding the mining practices of Canadian companies in Colombia. The English fragments discernible in this eulogy scene range from bureaucratic ("I would have preferred more time to prepare something more suitable on this terrible day. I want you to know that the company is . . . regretful," "inappropriate for me at this time to comment as the investigation is going on; however, we believe in the community. We believe in the project") to ridiculous (a "closet vegetarian" impulsively confesses, "When there is a chicken I eat chicken"), and they compete against Spanish voices for provisional dominance as the microphone passes from hand to hand in mid-sentence, even mid-phrase. At one point, one of the figures is asked about life in Canada. "It's a good life," she responds, to which the questioner replies, "Señora, we also want a good life."

Here, as in many other scenes in *Nohayquiensepa*, the onstage action is accompanied by the onscreen hand of Lorena Torres Loaiza, engaged in live drawing in dialogic, intermedial response to the action (the hand rarely prompts or precipitates what happens on stage). Loaiza's live drawing, in an instance of process as performance, recreates the responsive, collaborative, intermedial dynamics of the collective creation of *Nohayquiensepa*. The artist's hand, in the development process and in the live performance, helps to create the space in which the performers, and later the audience, come together. Perhaps most importantly, however, the hand also has the potential to literalize reception, at certain points in the show functioning as a live, responsive prosthetic for the audience, within which the artist herself is physically situated (the technical requirements of the show necessitate her positioning in the tech booth) and out of which the hand is literally projected. In the eulogy scene, as elsewhere, Loaiza's projected hand serves as a potential conduit for spectators' own responses both to that which is represented and to the experiential discoveries fostered by the performance. As the eulogists speak, the hand makes marks over their bodies in groups of five slashes on a projected transparency, keeping a kind of tally that, multiplying to cover the entire surface of the constantly shifting transparency, becomes a kind of prison for the eulogists (Figs. 4 and 5). Perhaps enacting a sort of justice on the part of the audience, this tally-keeping also simultaneously reads as futile, experienced as it is alongside the impossible aural track-keeping of the listening exercise itself.

The hand often does things in response to the action that *we* want to do. But the impulse toward identification (those hands are "my" hands, with all the attendant intercultural implications concerning the appropriations effected by traditional empathetic cross-cultural response), as with other similar impulses, is evoked only to be disrupted. The intermediality of the hands' projection on screen, for example, serves as a constant reminder that those hands are manifestly *not* "mine." A culminating instance of the productive affect of this dynamic comes in the final moments of the show. The hands—fully established, by now, as both "my hands" and not—engage in their penultimate task: the piecing together of fragments of a torn-up letter that has spilled out of an envelope addressed to the "Minister of Foreign Affairs and International Trade Canada." As the hands assemble the fragments, the audience may recognize words and phrases that had seemed random in the live drawing during the pre-show. Fully assembled, the letter reads:

Figs. 4 and 5. The hand of artist Lorena Torres Loaiza, projected live, keeps a count as Carlos González-Vio, Mayahuel Tecozautla, Christopher Stanton, and Beatriz Pizano deliver their overlapping eulogies to strangers, in Spanish and English. The tally escalates as they speak. Photo by Katherine Fleitas.

Let me be clear, saying these things to you today puts my life in danger. Already, four Embeca leaders have been killed by paramilitary forces for challenging the negative impact of the Urra mega project . . . Anyone who dares to speak out about Urra is accused of being involved with the guerillas and with that pretext, both our communities and leadership have been deemed a military target.

It is signed "Kimy Pernia Domico."

For those in the know, the letter has documentary force. The words are taken from a deposition made by Kimy Pernía Domicó,[20] a leader of the embattled Embera Katío Indigenous people, to a Canadian parliamentary commission in 1999. Domicó had come to Canada to draw attention to the hunger, disease, and rainforest habitat destruction on the upper Sinú River in northern Colombia, brought about by a hydroelectric megaproject funded in part by Export Development Canada. On 2 June 2001 he was abducted by three gunmen believed to belong to army-backed paramilitary groups and has not been seen since. In January 2007, paramilitary leader Salvatore Mancuso confessed to participating in Domicó's murder.

Literalizing as it does the repeatedly evoked and limited impulses to make meaningful wholes out of fragmentary parts, which also recalls the project's impetus, this onscreen assembly of the letter is the culmination of our identificatory impulse toward the hand throughout the production. In this moment, our longing to make sense of what we have been presented with, even to assign or assume responsibility, is to some extent fulfilled. A whole and comprehensible document emerges, and it demands our attention. The question of what to do with this letter—posed by the fact that it is directed to a minister of the Canadian government—is raised by way of our evolving sense of the onscreen hands as audience prosthetic.

---

20   The accents seem inadvertently to have been dropped from Domicó's name. For more information on Domicó see, among many online sources, Council of Canadians "Update." For information on the Embera Katío's struggle see, also among many online sources, World Rainforest Movement, "Colombia."

This culminating moment of identification and complicity precedes the hands' final intervention. While the letter is assembled and as the show draws to a close, the two *cumbia*-inspired dancers, with the same outstretched white skirts that they wore at the opening, reappear, by now identified with the peoples of the Magdalena region, after which the hand, protective now, arches on the screen above them, fulfilling the audience's urge to offer shelter (Fig. 6). The sheltering of the dancers, then, expresses our longing through a prosthetic gesture that is not appropriative, but that symbolizes and provokes social engagement and responsibility. A numbered list of names appears on the screen, the disappeared, to which is added, as number 667, "Kimy Pernia Domico, Disappeared, June 2001." And as the rest of the cast and the audience watch, the women . . . dance.

This dance—a celebration, a wake?—and the shelter of a hand that represents at once an audience's need and inability to protect, its longing and incapacity for empathetic identification, juxtaposed so closely with the letter and the long and growing list of the disappeared, is productively unsettling rather than purgative, enabling and provoking rather than forestalling or replacing thought and action. We feel ourselves feeling. In the words of Susan Leigh Foster in another context, the dancers "foreground the partiality and incompleteness of empathy even as they invite viewers to dance along with them" (218).

Fig. 6. Lorena Torres Loaiza's projected hand functions as an audience prosthetic to shelter *cumbia*-inspired dancers Victoria Mata and Lilia Leon, as Beatriz Pizano and Carlos González-Vio watch. Screen capture from a video by Trevor Schwellnus.

"LIVING BETWEEN TWO OR MORE CULTURES": ON THE POLITICAL INTERVENTIONS OF PUENTE'S COMMUNITY-ENGAGED THEATRE

TAMARA UNDERINER[1]

LINA AND *PINA* AND PUENTE AND ME

One evening a little over a year ago, Lina de Guevara, freshly retired after twenty-three years as founder and artistic director of Victoria's PUENTE Theatre, was watching Wim Wenders's film *Pina*. Throughout this documentary tribute to the legendary dance-theatre choreographer Pina Bausch, Guevara found herself increasingly struck by a feeling of familiarity with Bausch's aesthetic, a connection that she felt very viscerally but couldn't quite place. A Chilean emigrant to Victoria, Guevara had never seen a Bausch performance live. What was it about the film that made her feel so strongly, as she watched it, that she was "coming home"? Later, reading an interview with Wenders, it clicked: Lina and Pina shared an artistic ancestor, another legendary German choreographer, Bausch's mentor Kurt Jooss. In 1940 (coincidentally, the year of Bausch's birth) Jooss's company, in exile from Nazi Germany, toured to

1   I would like to acknowledge the excellent research assistance provided me for this essay by Dr. Néstor Bravo-Goldsmith (ASU/Universidad de Chile) and Martha Herrera-Lasso (University of British Columbia). I would also like to thank PUENTE artistic directors Lina de Guevara and Mercedes Bátiz-Benét for the time they granted me in interviews and email exchanges.

Guevara's hometown of Santiago. The repertoire included his groundbreaking *The Green Table* from 1932, which had established Jooss as an innovator of expressionist dance-theatre. The impact of this tour was so great in Chile that, when it ended, three company members were invited to return to establish the School of Dance at the University of Chile, which would train dancers for the Chilean National Ballet, formed four years later. Their Chilean proteges in turn became the movement teachers associated with another new enterprise in Chile, Pedro de la Barra's Teatro Experimental, which came to be housed at the university. In 1949, the School of Theatre was established; it was there that, in the mid-1960s, a young Lina de Guevara came to study movement with three of Jooss's artistic descendants from the Chilean National Ballet, the dancer/choreographers Patricio Bunster, Malucha Solari, and Alfonso Unanue (L. Guevara, Skype interview).[2]

Situating PUENTE's political interventions within this genealogy of artistic influence is my attempt to make an intervention of my own—against the temptation to reduce what follows into an overly simplified view of the kind of theatre Guevara, her successor Mercedes Bátiz-Benét, and PUENTE Theatre have done over nearly a quarter of a century. I am aware that this gesture is not without its own ideological freight, given its apparent appeal to a European pedigree, and ask that you stay with me: this is just where the story begins, and is not its only or principal point. As I hope to show in this review of some of PUENTE's signal accomplishments in creating a space for Latina/o Canadian staged subjectivity, not all roads in political or community-engaged theatre lead back to Brecht and Boal, although PUENTE has certainly travelled them at length; at the same time I want to point out that not all important theatre companies in Canada trace their own artistic genealogy back to Stanislavsky (although that was a principal component of Guevara's theatre training in Chile as well).[3] As Guevara put it to me, "I feel a political

---

2   For the Chilean training context, see also Bloch, Cifuentes, Fischer, Markard, Sepúlveda, Solari, and Villegas.

3   Laurin Mann estimates that 90% of Toronto-based theatre teachers trace their training back to Stanislavsky's ideas.

objective is always present in PUENTE's productions, but I have tried, to the best of my ability, to never compromise the artistic quality of the work for political expediency. In a way, to have high artistic quality in work done by minority artists is a political goal" (Message).

Situated on an island, in a relatively small city not known as one of Canada's theatre capitals, PUENTE—with its mandate to "use theatrical experience as a bridge between cultures" ("Mandate"),[4] its commitment to working with immigrant artists and audiences, its penchant for collective community- and research-based theatre—might seem easy to dismiss as being too local, too particular, too non-professional, and, perhaps, at once too foreign and too familiar. Too foreign given Canada's pervasively Caucasian theatre culture and PUENTE's focus on the stories of immigrants from all over the world (as well as works in translation that often receive their Canadian premieres through PUENTE's Worldplay play readings series and Workplay staging initiative); too familiar given Canada's own mandate to self-identify as a multicultural country and therefore to fund efforts that "bridge cultures." Nevertheless, there is still that gap, identified by PUENTE performer and scholar Nikki Shaffeeullah, between "big-M Multiculturalism" in policy and law and the realities of a society that does not see itself in pluralistic terms at all. As she observed in a recent issue of *alt.theatre*, "Culturally diverse theatre makers often [fall] 'between the cracks of government agencies,' unable to fund their projects or be recognized as professionals," and she laments the fact that what she calls "The Conversation" about cultural diversity in Canadian theatre seems always "stuck in first gear" (12–13).

I myself am new to this conversation. I had not heard of PUENTE before Natalie Alvarez asked me to contribute to this collection, but I live and work in Arizona and have some experience thinking about and through theatre that dramatizes immigrant experiences. Like Victoria, Phoenix is far from being a theatre capital, but where I live there are many artists committed to exploring the immigrant experience (in circumstances, I venture to say, that have been more overtly hostile, but perhaps easier to get a handle on as a

---

4   Just in case, "puente" means "bridge" in Spanish.

result). My own position is nevertheless both literally and figuratively rather far away. I've not had the pleasure of seeing a single PUENTE production, except as excerpted on its website and on YouTube; I have been able to review only two manuscripts from the more than twenty original pieces PUENTE has developed or presented. I confess it feels very strange to be writing from such an experientially ungrounded position about a practice that is so very embodied. Although this is a dilemma for any theatre historian, I feel it particularly keenly in this case of work that is happening even as I write and which I have yet to see live.

Still, I share something of the sense of excitement, familiarity, and home-coming that Lina experienced while watching *Pina*. Even from this highly optic rather than haptic perspective, reading in and around the PUENTE online archive, I feel a kind of professional kinship with this work, which cannot help but colour my comments about it. The negotiations PUENTE has to make within its specific contexts of readability are richly illustrative of the binds facing many artists who do their work in the maddening gap between the rhetoric and the reality of proffered multiculturalism,[5] whether in Canada or in the United States. Possibly the most characteristic tension facing the work of artists who care about immigrants is between bridging cultures on the one hand (both immigrant/non-immigrant and inter-immigrant), and honouring cultural specificities on the other—and in finding the proper process, theme, and form for such work to take. "Living between two or more cultures" is thus the central problematic both thematically and aesthetically,

---

5   There are, of course, many legitimate criticisms of the word "multiculturalism," especially in the United States, where it has come to be almost synonymous with "tokenism"; in Canada, Mayte Gómez refers to it as "an ideology which has instituted acculturation behind a liberal discourse of integration" ("Healing"). For more on the Canadian critique, especially with regard to theatre, see Ric Knowles's introductions to the special issue on interculturalism for *Theatre Research in Canada/Recherches théâtrales au Canada* ("Performing") and to his co-edited collection with Ingrid Mündel, *"Ethnic," Multicultural and Intercultural Theatre*. I hope my general point is clear: that I am referring to rhetoric, official or otherwise, that ostends a utopian inclusivity to all comers, regardless of cultural or national origin.

and it extends increasingly from the stage to the world offstage in the "multicultural" societies in, for, and through which these artists do their work.

Given this important mandate and work—even allowing for PUENTE's resolutely community-oriented focus—I am a bit surprised at how little attention this company has received in Canadian theatre criticism and scholarship. It is thus a real privilege for me to join this "conversation" about an important contributor to the history of Latina/o Canadian theatre. Understanding my role to look, as Sonja Kuftinec calls for in her work on community-based performance, "beyond the particularity of the event to connect it to larger paradigms and practices" (16), I urge you to peruse the substantial amount of visual, textual, and video material you will find both on the PUENTE website and on Lina de Guevara's personal site[6] for a sense of PUENTE's theatrical texture, while I attempt to both trace its underlying warp and weft and situate it within the paradigms and practices of community-engaged theatre in the Americas.

PUENTE'S ROOTS

When Lina de Guevara embarked on the project that helped to establish PUENTE in 1988, she wasn't so much out to save the world as she was to save herself as an artist. Self-exiled from Chile since 1976, when the military regime closed the School of Theatre she directed at the Universidad Austral de Chile in the city of Valdivia, she spent twelve years looking for opportunities to use her professional acting and directing experience in Victoria. Perhaps her experience in Valdivia, a provincial city some six hundred miles from Santiago in the south of Chile, helped her to put things in perspective: in terms of a theatre scene, Valdivia is to Santiago as Victoria is to Toronto. As Juan Villegas has observed, theatre tended to flow from Santiago to the provinces and not vice versa, a unidirectionality that tracks with Canadian practice as well. In Chile, she had studied not only with the movement teachers

---

6   Many of Guevara's published reflections can be accessed on her website.

identified above, but also with Agustín Siré, founder of the School of Theatre at the University of Chile, who had himself studied at the Royal Academy of Dramatic Arts (RADA) and the Old Vic and had introduced Stanislavsky-based, US American–style theatre training to the school. She also worked with director Pedro Orthous, who had been trained at the National Academy of Dramatic Arts in France (with Louis Jouvet and Gaston Baty) and who upon his return to Chile worked with neuropsychologist Susana Bloch and Guy Santibañez, who laid the groundwork for what would become Bloch's Alba Emoting System (Bloch).[7]

From these theatre teachers she developed her abilities in the cognitive, emotive, and physical realms of performance and directing; from Bunster, the idea that theatre and dance could be harnessed toward awareness—and transformation—of social realities, especially among subaltern groups; from Solari, the notion that cultural expression could be uniquely Chilean; from Unanue, significant skills in the craft of *commedia dell'arte*. She also studied with Víctor Jara, who was a theatre director before he became a political activist and who had begun to develop a methodology for collective devisement of new work. Once in Canada, she continued her training via Theatre of the Oppressed workshops with Augusto Boal in New York and Canada; with Richard Fowler of the Canada Project (Eugenio Barba's assistant at the Odin Teatret); and with Judith Koltai, who had developed the integrative movement discipline of Embodied Practice®; among others. All of these experiences inform her evolving practice, a practice she now trains others in, called Transformational Theatre, which is as integrative of the personal and political as it is of the body, mind, and spirit.[8]

---

7   Biographical information related to Guevara's training comes from my interviews with her and from her personal website; the information on her teachers comes from the sources identified in note 2. Regarding the Alba method, this technique is described by its practitioners as "a safe, purely physical alternative to emotion memory and other psychological techniques for releasing, maintaining, and controlling emotional states on stage" (Alba).

8   In addition to Guevara's site, see also Koltai's website.

Over the course of some thirty-three years in Canada, Guevara has crafted a place for herself and her artistic vision. But at first it was difficult, having
enjoyed and then abandoned a full career in the theatre in Chile. Furthermore,
training for opportunities that didn't materialize in Victoria proved to be only
part of the difficulty. Another significant layer of discontent was more quotidian:
"I was no longer living among people with whom I shared a past, a culture, a
language and a history," she writes. Instead, conversations with her new neigh-
bours made her realize how much real cultural exchange was still necessary:

> Most Canadians knew that Chile had undergone a bloody military
> coup, and suffered under a cruel dictator, General Pinochet. Few
> knew that Chile had two Nobel Prize winning poets, that we had
> great architects, that the University of Chile was an internationally
> respected institution, and that our Social Security System had, at
> one time, been exemplary. It would be as if Canada was known in
> the world only by the clear cutting of its forests and the abusive res-
> idential schools. ("Telling Stories")

PUENTE emerged in part to address this cultural disconnect.

PUENTE'S ROUTES

For the most part, people don't emigrate in significant numbers from stable
countries. As Guevara began to meet other exiles from other Latin American
countries fleeing other oppressive regimes, civil wars, and social injustices,
she became increasingly interested in their ordeals not only of escape and
exile, but also of adjustment and alignment to their new Canadian realities.
This led to the founding of PUENTE theatre in 1988 and its first project, *I
Wasn't Born Here*.[9] This project brought together five other women from Latin

---

9   Scenes from this play, as well as interviews with Guevara, the performers, and audience were collected in the 1988 documentary *Creating Bridges*, which can be viewed in

America (none of whom had theatre experience in their home countries) to develop a collective piece about immigrant women's experiences. Under the auspices of a federal job-training grant, Guevara was able to employ these women full-time for six months, during which time they shared stories and received training in voice, acting, movement, and theatrical devisement (although that term was not yet available to describe this process). They also conducted their own interviews with some fifty other women immigrants to gather source material, a research-based process PUENTE has refined over the years for all of its collective creations. In this process, the commonalities and specificities noted in these interviews become the basis for improvisations and movement sequences that in turn lead to scenes. Throughout the process, during which "a hundred possibilities are tried and only a few are kept," the final play slowly takes shape (L. Guevara, "PUENTE Theatre"). The results often feature an eclectic mixture of performance styles and forms, such as blending the serious with the comical and farcical, incorporating music and dance, borrowing from other forms like TV soap operas to emphasize a point through exaggeration, utilizing other theatrical conventions like masks and puppetry, and finding innovative uses for found objects, etc. Reflecting on the process that led to that first production of *I Wasn't Born Here*, Guevera writes:

> During that first project we developed methodologies for our research, training and rehearsing. For people who were not actors and, in some cases, spoke very little English, it was a huge challenge to write, act in and produce a play, but our limitations became spurs. We found creative ways of overcoming those challenges: we used written signs when our English wasn't good enough; we found expressive images that didn't require words; we had scenes simultaneously in English and in Spanish; and found surprising ways to use props. As the director, I started to welcome the difficulties and obstacles. They seemed to provide a frame of reference, a springboard for our work. ("Civic Participation")

three parts on YouTube (Joy and Hood).

Thus, in *I Wasn't Born Here*, the room full of folding chairs in the rehearsal hall became the source of the play's scenic repertoire. Not only did they stand in for whatever the actors needed them for—from bus seats to factory machines to a large banquet table and more—they also provided movement and ensemble training to make the transitions between scenes go smoothly. "That's when they became actors," Guevara told me in an interview.

The response to the play, from immigrant and non-immigrant audiences alike, was enthusiastic. In interviews with some audience members included in the 1988 documentary *Creating Bridges*, one can detect a hint of surprise at the professionalism of the results. This is a reaction that chafes at Guevara's sensibilities and reveals something about the horizon of expectation such work operates within in Canada and, as scholars of community-based theatre have long pointed out, elsewhere as well: community-based artists often find themselves working against a pervasive and "underlying aversion to art that claims to 'do' something, that does not subordinate function to craft . . . That

Fig. 1. The factory scene from the 1988 production of *I Wasn't Born Here*, featuring, from left, Emperatriz Toledo, Magdalena Diaz, Ana Strauss, and Yolanda Huerta. Photo by Robin J. Hood.

their work intends to affect and transform is taken by its detractors as evidence that it is not art" (Lacy, qtd. in Kuftinec 15).

Guevara's response was to make more of such art. The success of the play about immigrant women's experiences led, two years later, to a similar process for telling the stories of immigrant men, in 1990's *Crossing Borders*.[10] Like the women in *I Wasn't Born Here*, the four men in *Crossing Borders* worked together for six months to develop this play; this time, because the men were all musicians, music became a key component of the play's entertainment and, I would argue, its historiographical values. It tells the story of Chepe, a young Central American who is literally roped into military duty against his will in his home country and who eventually escapes to Canada. (Many scenes/years later, the same rope reappears to symbolize the way Latin American immigrants are "drafted" into the worst jobs in Canadian society.) He eventually "makes it" as a car salesman, but only at the cost of his music. In *Crossing Borders*, music is much more than a plot point or theatrical accoutrement: it is part of the dramaturgical infrastructure, employed to suggest a historical sweep beyond the lifespan of one immigrant.

Crossing Borders opens with Andean music played on pre-Columbian instruments (drums, pan flutes, bird whistles, rainmakers). Soon, a baby boy is born; the men sing a song in Spanish to celebrate, which is immediately sung again in an Indigenous language. As the boy grows and begins to play childhood games, one of the men performs the traditional lullaby "Duerme Negrito," from the region of the Venezuela/Colombia border (a song popularized by many Latin American artists, from the Argentinean performer Atahualpa Yupanqui in the 1960s forward). Sung by a caregiver because the child's mother is out working in the coffee plantations, the song coaxes children to sleep by warning about what the "white devils"—the overseers—will do to them if they don't. Chepe makes his own musical debut in the play, whistling one of El Salvador's most beloved songs by Pancho Lara, "Las Cortaderas" (Women Coffee Cutters), accompanying himself on the guitar.

---

10   To view a two-part documentary about this play, *Changing Rhythms*, see Joy and Hood.

In the first few moments of the play, then, several hundred years of history is staged via the musical selections, ending with the semi-feudal nature of much Latin American society during the nineteenth and twentieth centuries, and also offering the possibility of Indigenous continuity and return. Throughout the play, music is used to provide targeted commentary on the unfolding action.

Once Chepe is forcibly "drafted" by the military, all music stops and stays silent throughout the military training (in which Chepe receives American shoes as a symbol of US involvement). It only returns again with "Oh, Susanna," playing over "Border Radio" at the Mexico/Arizona border as Chepe is trying to head north after escaping his superiors and dead comrades in Central America. The song provides a surreal accompaniment to the racist, if inept, attempts of the guards to capture him, as they'll get bonus points for his being an "OTM—Other Than Mexican." "Yankee Doodle" accompanies an allegorical scene soon afterwards, in which Uncle Sam has his shoes shined by Chepe, after making him kneel so he can use his back as a stepping stool in a classic Brechtian *gestus*. (Adding insult to injury, Uncle Sam not only doesn't pay Chepe for his service, but steals his bandana in the bargain.) Musical blues accompany Chepe's (unsuccessful) attempt to negotiate with the Devil for a way to make a living.

Nostalgia enters with another El Salvadoran favourite, "El Carbonero" (the Coalman), which Chepe plays to comfort himself and which endears him to the owner of a flophouse, who counsels him to go to Canada. "This Land Is Your Land" provides an ironic accompaniment to a pointed scene set in a Canadian immigration office, in which a wealthy foreign developer of dubious ethics receives an instant visa, while a medical doctor's prestigious Spanish and Latin American university credentials are questioned and deemed suspect, and a professional musician proves "not to be the type of immigrant we're looking for" (13). Chepe himself, having been refused entry as a refugee because, "According to the U.S. State Department [his] country is a fine democracy" (14), decides to sneak in anyway. The song "Start All Over" accompanies six years' worth of trying until at last, just before the intermission, the song "Canada" signals his successful, if illegal, entry.

Figs. 2 and 3. Uncle Sam in league with the Devil in the shoeshine scene from *Crossing Borders*. Masks by Maureen Mackintosh. Edgar Acevedo as Uncle Sam, Manuel Alberto as the Devil, and Oscar Cruz in foreground. Photo by Robin J. Hood.

The second half of the play features songs of nostalgia ("Canción Mixteca" from Oaxaca, the standard-bearer for Mexican longing), new-found patriotism ("Beautiful Nation"), and assimilation (the original "Linear Thinking, Your Mind is Shrinking," which pokes fun at the tacit violence of enforced monolinguality, especially when the language is English). In this act the play incorporates a soap-opera format that both acknowledges and gently mocks the melodrama of the immigrant dilemma; despite its exaggerations, the "real" characters in the play feel it tells a truth: that "to be an immigrant is the worse [sic] thing in the world" (26). The men decide to form a band to play Latin American music, but Chepe opts instead for a more lucrative way of earning a living, singing his farewell to music with the mournful "La era está pariendo un corazón" (The Era Is Giving Birth [To a Heart That's Dying of Sadness]). In the end, all the fully acculturated Chepe (now called "Joe") is left playing is his stereo—until a visit from an old El Salvadoran friend sparks a *Christmas Carol*-esque nightmare that returns him to his calling, and the song celebrating the birth of a baby boy heard in the first scene is reprised here. The play ends with the newly formed band playing a meringue, to which the audience is invited to join in the dance. Thus, in *Crossing Borders*, music is a key leit-motif for organizing the worldview of this play—a generous one that, despite its happy ending, doesn't sacrifice targeted critique to get there. Visually too, the masks and puppets, inspired by research on mask and puppet traditions in Latin America, coupled with the hybridity of other theatrical forms, offer an aesthetically rich and multi-layered theatrical experience.

Noticing that the women's stories in *I Wasn't Born Here* focused particularly on their roles as family members, while the men involved with and interviewed for *Crossing Borders* tended carefully to avoid discussing home life at all, Guevara decided to explore that tension more closely in *Canadian Tango* (1991),[11] which Guevara developed further from the research already begun. Staged in Vancouver (this time with professional actors), it explored the effects of immigration on couples' relationships once in Canada, using ballroom dancing as a metaphor for marriage and for the negotiations one makes with two different national cultures. A scene called "Waltz of Two Loves" features a woman trying to choose between two different "dance partners," i.e., her home country and Canada: "It's like having two lovers! You feel so guilty. You want to love one and forget the other, but it's impossible!" (L. Guevara, "Civic Participation").

While researching *Canadian Tango*, Guevara could not ignore the many stories of family violence she was hearing in the interviews, which led the company to experiment with Forum theatre in the play *FamilyA* (1993). From there, PUENTE went on to use Theatre of the Oppressed (TO) techniques in workshops and formal productions to explore issues of racism, workplace discrimination, human rights abuses, sexual harassment, and other forms of oppression, eventually also adopting Playback Theatre techniques to further audience involvement. Such involvement, in one way or another, had been there from the start in PUENTE's work. For example, the audience for *I Wasn't Born Here* was invited to partake in a communal meal prepared by the

---

11   PUENTE would also stage Carmen Aguirre's play of the same name in 2009, which dealt with intercultural marriages between established and new Canadians.

Fig. 4. In a nightmare, Chepe sees his name on a gravestone in the final scene of *Crossing Borders.* From left to right, Enrique Rivas, Oscar Cruz (without mask), Manuel Alberto (below), and Edgar Acevedo. Mask and puppets by Maureen Mackintosh. Photo by Robin J. Hood.

performers; those for *Crossing Borders* were invited to dance salsa and *cumbia* with the cast members. Another hallmark of a PUENTE production is the "TIMELINE," in which all participants in a given workshop or production are asked to line up according to where they come from and how long they've been in Canada—"all the way to First Nations participants, whose forebears have been here since immemorial" (L. Guevara, "Welcoming Speech")— wherein one can see both the roots and routes that make up Canada's evolving story.

Until 1995, PUENTE had focused on Latin American contributions to this story. After this date, the group opened to include explorations of oth- er immigrant-group experiences in their specificity and in what they share with other new Canadians. For example, *Sisters/Strangers* (1996) developed along the model of the "community play" concept introduced in England by

Ann Jellicoe and Jon Oram.[12] This was a year-long collaboration between
six professional actresses and a large chorus of immigrant women from all
over the world, now scattered throughout British Columbia, who nevertheless constituted what Guevara calls a "community of situation" ("Welcoming
Speech"). Throughout the year they participated in various workshops in
Victoria and Vancouver, incorporating music, movement, storytelling, and
image theatre. Each city to which it toured contributed its own community
chorus, sometimes with only three hours of rehearsal time available. As its
title suggests, the play explored the commonalities and differences among
this diverse group of immigrant women. Other plays from this period (all
developed collectively, research-based, and workshopped through TO techniques, though not all according to the community play concept) include
Of Roots and Racism (1995); *Act Now Against Racism* (1997); *Story Mosaic*
(1998); and *Storytelling Our Lives* (different versions in 1998, 2003, and 2006);
and *Journey to Mapu* (developed between 2005 and 2010 in a collaboration
between Chilean and Canadian First Nations artists and published in this
volume's companion anthology of plays).

During her tenure, which lasted until June of 2011, Guevara also inaugu-
rated two other important initiatives, WorldPlay and WorkPlay. The former
is a series of staged readings of works in translation, the latter a series of
readings of works in progress by and for emerging playwrights. Both address
her early desire to redress misperceptions of Latin America's contributions
to a world history of art and ideas. Eventually the series were expanded to
include some fifty works from all over the world. WorldPlay readings from
Latin America (most of which were Canadian premieres) include *The Woman
Who Fell from the Sky* (Victor Hugo Rascón Banda, Mexico), *Letters from
Tomás* (Malucha Pinto, Chile), *Evita and Victoria* (Monica Ottino, Argentina),
Happy New Century Dr. Freud (Sabina Berman, Mexico), and *The Pilgrimage
of the Nuns of Concepción* (Jaime Silva, Chile), while WorkPlay has nurtured

---

12   For a longer description of this play and the process of its development, see Guevara's
essay, "Sisters/Strangers," in *Canadian Theatre Review* 90. This issue of *CTR* is devoted to
the concept of the community play.

to completion the work of several Latina/o Canadian playwrights. PUENTE has also served as a presenting organization for immigrant and First Nation performing artists and dance ensembles.

In 2011, Mexican multidisciplinary and multimedia writer and director Mercedes Bátiz-Benét assumed the artistic directorship after having worked as a writer, facilitator, and deviser with PUENTE for almost a decade. Her 2010 *With Open Arms*, directed by Barbara Poggemiller, continued PUENTE's tradition of pan-immigrant storysharing, this time enhanced by giant puppets designed by immigrants in PUENTE workshops, subsequently scaled up by puppet master Tim Gosley. The play includes the following exchange between a Mexican immigrant and a Canadian border agent. Performed in story-theatre style, it is expressive of more than a particular story, standing also as a symbol of PUENTE's own aesthetic and worldview:

ACTOR: And I told him, "I'm a writer." He said nothing at all, for a surprisingly long time. I wondered what was happening. I waited, with that strange facial expression peculiar to the presence of border guards. You never know if they'll suspect you for smiling too much, or for not smiling enough. For giving too much information, or for not giving enough. For saying you're a *writer*, or that you're from Mexico. I try to look . . . pleasant. And unconcerned. Which probably means that I look nervous. Which I'm sure is setting off alarms, in his easily alarmable Border Guard mind. I also resent his power. Which makes my face slightly red, and my eyes slightly hard. I'm ready for a fight! Even though I haven't done anything wrong, and he doesn't have a reason in the world to detain me. Then I realized: The man was crying.

BORDER GUARD: "I always wanted to be an artist."

ACTOR: He said.

BORDER GUARD: "Do you think I wanted to be a *border guard*? I've ruined my life."

ACTOR: "Why don't you quit, and become an artist?" I asked him.

BORDER GUARD: "You're right. That's what I've got to do. Thank you. [Clears throat, more strongly:] Thank you."

ACTOR: He wiped his cheek and he stamped my passport.

BORDER GUARD: "Welcome to Canada." (ICA Victoria)

Even without the giant puppets in the background, the theatricality of this scene forfends the possibility of over-absorption into the immigrant narrative, preserving the crucial distance necessary for not reducing its subjects to heroes or victims. The actor/narrator, portraying someone from Mexico, speaks with a distinctly Anglo African accent; hers is a vocal performance of pan-immigrant solidarity, even as it preserves the differences between them as registered in accented English. (Both Guevara and Bátiz-Benét lament the fact that most Canadian theatre is closed to immigrant actors who speak English with a non-Canadian accent.) The Border Guard announces another Canadian subjectivity, and although his epiphany may seem too quick and too pat, it must be remembered that this isn't realism, it's a call to art—more pointedly, a call to art rather than to arms, given that the immigrant has prepared herself for a fight. And his final words announce that utopian performative every immigrant wants to hear—"Welcome to Canada"—but here they are stripped of their bureaucratic rubber-stampedness and endowed instead with a sense of true indebtedness for what the immigrant has already contributed to Canadian society.

THEMES AND FORMS AS PUENTE CONTINUES

Altogether, the work of PUENTE offers a panoramic view of the multiplicity of immigrant experiences in Canada and a chance for immigrants to see those realities reflected and affirmed in the public space that is theatre. Most of this work developed "from the stage to the page" rather than vice versa, and the resulting playscripts have yet to be collected, corrected, and archived, but Guevara notes the following themes that provide the emotional background to PUENTE's oeuvre:

> Many men have arrived here alone, as refugees, escaping wars in which they had been forced to take part, either as rebels or as soldiers. Women more commonly arrived as part of a family group, with husbands and children. As a general rule, the men were out in the workforce while women remained isolated at home. But there were also many examples of role reversals: women as wage earners, men doing housework, and children taking on the roles of parenthood, speaking for their parents and becoming their link to the new environment. Nostalgia was an emotion shared by all, and it could become paralysing and overwhelming. The relationships with the family back in the homeland were very complex. Guilt is another feeling that many immigrants share. Losing one's profession, changes in status, feeling misunderstood, diminished and discriminated against are some of the negative emotions we all experience. A sense of power in overcoming difficulties, the excitement of living in adventure, the broadening of horizons and the freedom provided by breaking loose from strict traditions are some of the positive aspects of being an immigrant we have experienced. ("Staging")

In a recent interview,[13] Bátiz-Benét echoed this last point about freedom from strict tradition. She came to Canada in 1997 to escape Mexico's escalating urban violence and to pursue an education at the University of Victoria in philosophy, dramatic and creative writing, and film. She stayed because of how freeing it was to be considered "before anything else, a citizen, free to speak her mind," whereas in Mexico she was always first and foremost "a woman, whose opinion didn't matter." A confirmed "Mexicanadian," she welcomes the

---

13   All quotes in this section come from a Skype interview on 2 Jan. 2013.

slower pace of artistic development that allowed for long periods of rehearsal and devisement, the workshop experiences that elicited the "stories and misconceptions we all had about each other. We all have preconceived ideas until we're in a room together." As a result, she is committed to continue the work that Guevara started and to expand from that base into new directions. Toward that end, she has adopted a three-pronged approach that builds on PUENTE's prior model of collective devisement, artistic incubation, and theatre training: first, to expand the regular season to a consistent three offerings per year; second, to expand the audience through more touring productions and participation in family- and community-oriented arts festivals; and third, to expand the artistry through collaboration with artists in other media and community groups in the creation of street, outdoor, and site-specific theatre and installations, which will incorporate more of the spectacular work manifested in recent pieces using giant puppets, masks, and virtuosic physical performance.

The 2013 season's offerings feature three plays co-written by Bátiz-Benét, each an intervention in its own way. The first, *gruff*, is an adaptation, with children's author and puppeteer Judd Palmer, of the fable *The Three Billy Goats Gruff*, here reconceived as an immigration story featuring a rich goat, a poor goat, and a troll who is actually a goat masquerading as a border guard. In *gruff*, Bátiz-Benét wanted to explore the notion that:

> Nobody really chooses where they're born. Some people can be born in a very poor country like Mexico or El Salvador or many other countries, and it's not anyone's fault. And somebody can be born in a wonderful country like the States or Canada, and they just appear there. But in the end, we're all—goats. And that's what I wanted to start sharing with very young audiences: If we're all goats in the end, then we should help each other out. Especially if there's plentiful land here, why can't we share it with others? Which is very much the Canadian ideal.

Calling Canada's "big-M Multiculturalism" to account materially for its rhetoric continues one aspect of PUENTE's vision. Expanding on PUENTE's mission to include perspectives from immigrants from everywhere in the world follows another: Bátiz-Benét is also collaborating on a one-man show by Iranian Canadian Izad Etemadi called *Borderland*, about the challenges of being a theatre artist in his home country and the new opportunities Canada offers him. Finally, she is working on another adaptation, this time of the Greek myth of Orpheus. In *El Jinete* (the Horseman), which Bátiz-Benét describes as a "mariachi opera," a mariachi must travel in time and space to rescue his wife who has been abducted and taken to the United States.

SOME CLOSING THOUGHTS, FOR NOW

Near the start of this essay, I wrote that I hoped to trace PUENTE's "underlying warp and weft"—the threads that go in perpendicular directions in a woven cloth. I suggested that one way these threads cross is between pan-immigrant solidarity and cultural specificity, another is between calls for inclusion and targeted critique; these relationships and tensions form much of the texture of PUENTE's work. Such a textile metaphor was deliberately invoked in the PUENTE play *Journey to Mapu* (2005–2010)—collected in the companion anthology to this volume—to discuss yet another aspect of these relationships, specifically the connections between Canadian First Nations peoples and Latin American immigrants (many of whom could have traced their roots back to Indigenous forebears, had the prevailing ideologies in their homelands made this something to be proud of rather than ashamed about). *Journey to Mapu* was developed over the course of five years through interviews and workshops between PUENTE's Latina/o Canadian participants and members of Canadian and Latin American Indigenous communities, including Mapuche (Chilean Indigenous) poet Elicura Chihuailaf; it was presented as a staged reading under the direction of Floyd Favel in 2010.

In the Indigenous Chilean language of Mapuzugun, "Mapu" means "Mother Earth," and the journey in this tale is one that deftly weaves contemporary political issues related to land management in both Canada and Chile with the personal story of a young Chilean emigrant to Vancouver,

who comes to learn about his own Mapuche roots. It is organized structurally as a memory play that reveals the life story of Lautaro, a Chilean
Canadian activist who named himself after a famous Mapuche warrior; his
family emigrated from Chile under duress during the military dictatorship.
The "journey to Mapu" of Tato (the young Lautaro) is told through scenes
of childhood reminiscence—particularly of the stories of his grandmothers
and aunts in rural Chile—juxtaposed with scenes of Canadian generosity
and racism as Tato and his family adjust to life in Vancouver. Throughout,
these scenes are woven together by Mapuzugun poetry, music, storytelling,
and ceremonial dances, which are also linked visually to Canadian First
Nation practices in the figure of Lorena, a young Kwakwaka'wakw woman
sewing her own ceremonial button blanket. Tato has been conditioned by
his (in many other ways superior) Chilean education to identify with the
Spanish colonists, some of whom were capable of extreme acts of brutality
against the Mapuche. As a result, when Canadian youth call him "Indian,"
he works hard to distance himself from the designation. With the help of
Lorena, however, he comes to learn that in Chile, as in Canada, aboriginal
culture is alive and well, and the stories he loves and remembers so fond-
ly from his childhood spring from that deep source. As a result, the adult
Lautaro is working to build bridges between the two Indigenous cultures,
particularly regarding their relations to Mapu—understood not only spiritually, but also as a political and economic matter of land rights and resource
management.

Thus, the play's "present" references a real-life hunger strike by the
Mapuche, staged in 2010, as a protest against their pervasive and persistent
disenfranchisement from the Chilean political process:

> At present the Mapuche question the almost constant exclusion of
> their people from the decision-making process, decisions that affect
> their lives directly. They denounce the illegality of the Chilean le-
> gality. They say: "Are we not all different threads of the same cloth?
> They are woven together to make the cloth strong. Together we can
> come to an agreement while we sing, tell stories, have conversations,

discussions, and negotiations. Together we will seek advice, we will offer prayers!"

The Mapuche demand to be included, demand to be heard! (399)

Reading this passage in the context of all the other PUENTE materials, I see in it not only the intent to align Mapuche and Canadian First Nation predicaments vis-à-vis national political participation, but also the more general plight—and promise—of the kind of minoritized theatre PUENTE represents. *Journey to Mapu*'s linking of singing and stories to the serious work of discussion and negotiation, its call to inclusivity and collaboration, is everywhere evident in PUENTE's process and, often, its artistic product as well. I can't help but be infatuated by the metaphor of the woven cloth, and I want to live in the stronger world it promises. But then I recall my long-ago days as a seamstress and my more recent experiences observing Mayan women weaving cloth in Mexico, which remind me that there are a few pre-requisites for guaranteeing a good, strong result: one needs more than just a number and variety of threads; the threads themselves need to be strong, in both directions. The loom—the underlying structure that brings them together—has to be well-constructed. And the weaver has to stay focused; otherwise the pattern wanders.

Through collective development, thematic exploration, and multi-formal experimentation, PUENTE has proven itself to be a careful weaver of work that imagines a larger possibility: a strong Canadian cloth woven out of many cultural particularities. Its utopic vision may not bear a direct relationship to immediate social change. But for its participants, audiences, and spect-actors, it helps to condition understanding among immigrants and non-immigrants about their relationships and responsibilities to each other. PUENTE's story is important to tell, for one, to help fill a gap in the historical record about the emergence of "Latina/o Canadian Theatre" and community- or research-based theatre in Canada. Its story is important also because this kind of theatre ex-ists, in part, to address why that gap is there in the first place and to propose alternate models for understanding historical subjectivity itself. PUENTE presents the possibility of a subjectivity that can no longer be nationally or linguistically bounded—one that instead comprises people who weren't born here, who cross borders, who dance with each other to changing rhythms, who recognize each other across Indigenous centuries, who experiment with canonical forms, and who use theatre to conjure a world of ever more opening arms, where everyone might live between two or more cultures.

HOUSES OF CORN AND FULL INCLUSION: ON LATINA/O COMMUNITY-BASED THEATRE IN TORONTO

JEANNINE M. PITAS

It's a Wednesday night, the final rehearsal of Double Double Performing Arts's production of *M.O.A.R.* The play tells the story of Monseñor Óscar Arnulfo Romero, the archbishop of El Salvador whose tireless commitment to the poor and oppressed led to his assassination in 1980. Now, seven actors and their director stand in a circle, their eyes closed. "We know that we have developed our capacity as actors to the point where we can tell this story," states Colombian Canadian actor Enrique Castro, who plays the title character. Meanwhile, Rodolfo Molina, who spent the first half of his life as a *campesino* in El Salvador and had the chance to meet Romero in person, focuses on the work's spiritual dimension. "We seek to present this play in a way that is faithful to the memory of Óscar Romero, and we trust that he is with us, aware of our efforts here," he says. "May we seek to follow his example in the way we lead our lives." After completing their final vocal exercises, the actors leave the circle and take their places.

While Oscar Laurencio Ortiz Quiroz, *M.O.A.R.*'s director, has much experience in professional theatre, none of the actors are professionals, and most of them never thought that they would end up on stage. "I never would have imagined myself as an actor twenty years ago," states Enrique Castro. Born in Colombia, he came to Canada at the age of twenty-two and started a printing business that he owned for twenty-five years. Eventually, he began writing poetry and wanted to read it publicly; however, the thought of performing in front of an audience intimidated him. "An acquaintance invited me to come to a theatre workshop, and I said, 'I can't even read a poem in public—how am I going to do theatre?' " But, he attended a workshop offered by the (now defunct) Teatro Crisálida. In the past five years he has performed with four theatre companies in Toronto and is a now well-known figure in the Latin American community. For Castro, the experience of doing community-based theatre has been truly transformative:

> To me, Latin American immigrants to North America get immersed in a sea of misinformation. All too often they fall into the trap of consumerism; they focus on buying cars and condos. But once that happens, they don't have a chance to breathe; they have to work for years and years to pay off all those debts. I myself led that life for the whole duration of my business career. People forget their roots, their values. Theatre is a way to wake people up and tell them what's going on. I've met people who claim to have been politically active in their home countries, but there's nothing revolutionary about them now. To me, a social conscience can't be buried away like old clothes.

NewTeatro. Teatro Crisálida. Double Double Performing Arts. The Apus Coop. Teatro Libre. These are just some of the Latin American theatre groups that have sprung up in Toronto over the past ten years. Although different in their structures and foci, they share important features. According to Julie Salverson, community-based theatre "throws professional artists together with people who have stories to tell and something to say, and who, just this once (unlike professionals or dedicated amateurs) choose performance as the best way to say it" (viii). This is truly the case with all of these groups, which provide a space where seasoned theatre professionals—often the groups' founders—work side by side with non-professional actors of different ages, cultural backgrounds, and levels of experience. All of these groups operate on shoestring budgets, relying on the voluntary support of the artists and using community-based media to reach their audiences. They all embrace an ethos of inclusion; rather than holding auditions, their directors open their doors to any actor willing to demonstrate the discipline and commitment that theatre requires. Most of them seek to present works with a socio-political message—to provoke serious thought and debate as well as delight among their audiences. And all of them are engaged in the process of forming a new cultural identity in the Canadian context: a pan–Latin American Canadianness that transcends the borders of any individual nationality and seeks to assert a self-determined, self-aware, visible presence within Canada's cultural landscape.

Benedict Anderson has famously argued that the nation is an artificial social construct created in the mind of its individual members; more recently, scholars of diaspora and transnationalism such as Robin Cohen reveal that diasporic communities—groups of people who have moved from an original homeland to two or more host nations—are also formed through the creation of a social self-image. In this essay I will discuss three Toronto-based theatre groups—Double Double Performing Arts, the Apus Coop, and Grupo Teatro Libre—whose visions transcend the ideas of nation and even diaspora. Instead, these groups are involved in the formation of a cultural consciousness envisioned around a common language, parallel histories of political repression and social revolution, and a shared desire to maintain and develop their cultural identity within the host country of Canada. For me, this phenomenon within Latin Canadian cultures bears more than a slight resemblance to the pan–Latin American consciousness that is currently occurring throughout the western hemisphere. Recently formed political and economic alliances like the Bolivarian Alliance for the Peoples of our America (ALBA) and the Community of Latin American and Caribbean States (CELAC), along with international artistic and cultural festivals throughout the Americas suggest that the kind of political and cultural links that are forming in the Latin American diasporas might be modified versions of those that are being formed within and among the home countries. While these alliances in the home countries bring diverse peoples together on the conceptual and political level, such alliances in the diaspora unite them at the level of everyday, lived experience. In general, within the Canadian context we can observe a growing tendency toward greater communication and sharing among different Latin American cultures, leading to the enrichment of each group.

In his essay "Modernity and Difference," Canadian philosopher Charles Taylor suggests that all human beings exist within the framework of a "social imaginary," which he describes as the way large groups of ordinary people envision their social surroundings, less by conscious rational thought than by more tacit processes such as customs, legends, and images (370). Along with nation and diaspora, one such social imaginary is that of modernity—a movement from what Taylor deems "traditional societies" to ones organized around globalization, urbanization, technology, capitalism, and secularization. But, it is important to understand that this "modernity" is not a single, homogenous path that all cultures are following. Instead, it is a network of related but distinct paths in which cultures draw on their own traditions to consciously create a new social imaginary that enables them to modernize on their own terms (368). Theoreticians of Latin American culture such as Walter Mignolo have argued that a concept such as modernity is highly problematic for the peoples of Latin America as it goes hand in hand with the discourses of colonialism and power. For Mignolo, even a concept like *latinidad* is a product of a colonialist mentality in which outsiders seek to categorize and reify those people over whom they seek control (*Idea* 144). However, he demonstrates the ways in which people throughout the Americas are rejecting such imposed identities and seeking to create new social imaginaries that "allow each [diverse history] its own dignity without reduction, and maintain the autonomy of local, non-dependent histories . . . We open [these histories] to the different identities, possibilities and contradictions both inside and outside them" (144).

It is this kind of opening, I argue, that is occurring with the recent advent of groups like Double Double Performing Arts, the Apus Coop, and Grupo Teatro Libre. However, one concern that Salverson addresses about community theatre is its tendency to reinforce dominant narratives of modernity—particularly that of Canadian multiculturalism (viii). These groups, in their respective ways, reveal a reflective stance toward such Canadian narratives, often keeping them at arm's length. Comparing and contrasting these three independent theatre companies, I argue that while they draw on the cultural resources of their countries of origin—such as the Mexican Day of the Dead celebration and iconic historical figures like Archbishop Óscar Romero and Che Guevara—their overall strategy is oriented toward creating a new Latin Canadian identity in the present rather than seeking to preserve those of the past, thus embodying the culturally specific, self-determined form of modernity that Taylor and Mignolo advocate.

SEEDS OF CULTURE: CASA MAÍZ AND COMMUNITY-BASED ARTS

Located in an office building in Toronto's Finch/Keele area, Casa Maíz is more than a community centre. Since its founding in 2002 by Salvadoran Canadian lawyer Juan Carranza and his colleagues, the organization has sought to foster community development through the arts. Initially, Casa Maíz simply sought to provide a space for various community groups to meet and arrange their own activities. More recently, however, the centre has focused on organizing events—such as musical performances, poetry readings, and theatrical productions—and also on reaching out to youth through summer arts camps and after-school workshops. According to Pedro Cabezas, who served as director from 2011 to the beginning of 2013, the centre is something of a meeting place for people from different Latin American communities. "From the very beginning, Casa Maíz has provided a space for community theatre," he says. "Many groups have gotten their start here, only to go their own way later, to seek new venues for rehearsal and performance. It's a very organic process. We provide the space for connection, and our focus on community meanwhile informs the ethos of the groups that share their work here." Cabezas notes that the artistic groups that have developed around Casa Maíz are more focused on internal community development than outreach into the wider Canadian community. "There are some Latin American arts groups, Aluna Theatre for example, that seek to engage with mainstream Canadian audiences. But at Casa Maíz we are more interested in creating a safe space to support our own cultural and linguistic identities," he says. That said, while the centre does not actively seek involvement from people outside of Latin American communities, any interested groups or individuals who find their way there are welcomed, and during the past year the centre has hosted some events aimed at a multicultural, rather than a strictly Latin American, audience. "We seek to provide opportunities for people to do folk arts, for folk dance groups. The theatre groups are open to everyone and don't require specialized training; anyone can come and learn to act," Cabezas explains.

Although Casa Maíz does not actively engage with mainstream Canadian audiences, Cabezas envisions it as offering a significant contribution to the diversity of Toronto. "This city's cultural wealth comes from the sum of its many parts," he says. He adds that the emphasis on fostering a strong sense of cultural identity within the Latin American community is essential due to the ongoing discrimination that Latino Canadians continue to face. "Unfortunately, many Latino Canadians have a negative self-image about their culture due to certain social stigmas associated with us, like high rates of gang membership and low university enrolments. Part of our mission is to break down these stereotypes and focus on the good things our communities offer Toronto—our literature, dance, theatre, and also our political activism." Regarding this last item, Cabezas suggests that shared political concerns within the home and host countries serve as a unifying factor among different Latin American diasporic groups. Another challenge faced by Toronto's Latin American community is one that can be found in many diasporic groups. "I think that in Toronto there exists an atomization of various Latin American communities (such as Chilean, Colombian, Uruguayan, or Salvadoran Canadians) that come together on the basis of nationality," Cabezas says.

> But, there are other instances when people break out of these communities and come together as Latin Americans. Sometimes the need for funding leads to these alliances, as Casa Maíz currently receives no government funding. Other times alliances form on the basis of

shared political concerns, like human rights abuses related to mineral extraction in many Latin American countries—abuses in which Canadian mining companies have been found complicit.

Researching the global phenomena of migration and diaspora, Robin Cohen suggests that some of the characteristics of diaspora include a strong sense of collective memory and an idealization of a supposed ancestral home (182). Cabezas acknowledges that this tendency toward nostalgia and idealization is common within Toronto's Latin American communities. "It's so easy to create an imaginary sense of what your homeland is like. For example, if you left El Salvador in the '80s but then go back and see how everything has changed, you are left with nostalgia. Because of this, people struggle to remain connected to their countries, to stay connected with the political and social structures back home." However, he asserts that these communities have gone beyond this nostalgia and worked to remain engaged with the current realities in both homeland and host nation. Sometimes, this does occur at the level of a single nationality, such as a group of Uruguayan Canadians who have formed an organization at Casa Maíz that seeks to provide moral and financial support for former Uruguayan political prisoners still residing in their home country. At other times, though, people of various nationalities have organized events around a common political concern, such as migration and the threat of deportation. "Communities try to hold onto their roots, but they also learn that the world is a much bigger place than they might have thought initially," Cabezas says. "They learn about other cultures and develop an integrated community consciousness not restricted by nationalistic parameters. We are seeking to develop a hybrid, pan–Latin American identity that experiences more solidarity." Indeed, the very name of the centre suggests this type of integration, as *maíz* is a staple agricultural product throughout the Americas. In this way, Casa Maíz might be viewed as an organization that seeks to foster the kind of decolonizing form of modernity that Mignolo describes—one that is based on individuals' and groups' own visions of their historical experiences, cultural identities, and political realities.

All three theatre groups to be discussed in this investigation made their start at Casa Maíz, and while they have taken their work well beyond this small space, it remains a home base to which they repeatedly return. The members of the five-year-old Grupo Teatro Libre continue to rehearse there weekly, and it was also the setting for one of their most recent productions, *El amigo imaginario* (Imaginary Friend). Meanwhile, the three-year-old Double Double Performing Arts has returned there each November since its inception to present *Calaveras de Posada*, a comic performance based on the Mexican Day of the Dead ritual. By fostering connections between Latin American Torontonians of different nationalities, socio-economic backgrounds, and places of residence, this centre has provided a fertile ground from which the cultural seeds of these community theatres have grown.

DOUBLE DOUBLE PERFORMING ARTS: FROM THE GRAVEYARD TO THE PULPIT

With a long ponytail, paint-stained overalls, and a gentle manner, Oscar Ortiz has the air of a wandering bard, a beatnik artist who follows whatever path life happens to place before him. Though he has spent most of his life in Mexico, his curiosity and desire to know the world have also led him to Europe, North Africa, the United States, and now Toronto, which he visited by chance in 2010 and then decided to make his home—if not permanently, then at least long enough to have an impact on the cultural life of the Latin American community. "In Toronto, many people have the desire to do theatre, but the conditions are difficult. People have to earn their living, work, and study. Theatre demands time, discipline, and commitment," Ortiz says. "The desire is here, but for people in low-income immigrant communities, life gets in the way. But, reality can always be transformed, and we are rising to the challenge."

Ortiz's interest in community-based, non-commercial theatre began in his boyhood in San Luis Potosí, Mexico. "There was theatre in the cultural centres near where I grew up, and I became interested just out of curiosity. When I was a teenager my father allowed me the chance to study theatre as an after-school activity. From there, I just became more and more interested and continued to study informally." As he grew older and became more involved, he came to know many well-known figures from Mexican theatre, including the playwright Emilio Carballido. He began studying the work of artists known for emphasizing collective artistic creation and social criticism—people like Augusto Boal, the world-renowned founder of Theatre of the Oppressed, as well as Osvaldo Dragún, who worked in political theatre in Argentina; Enrique Buenaventura, founder of socially conscious Nuevo Teatro Colombiano; and Santiago García, another Colombian playwright and director. He also became interested in US-based Chicano theatre, which grew up around the figure of César Chávez, who led the Chicano workers' rights movement in the '60s and '70s.

Although Ortiz studied informally, he eventually had the opportunity to meet many of his masters at conferences and workshops. During the '90s, he first became involved with a Belgian theatre company that was working in Mexico. With them, he managed to travel to Europe and North Africa, where he learned completely different techniques, such as pantomime and silent theatre. This opened up many doors for Ortiz, garnering him invitations to collaborate with groups in many countries including the US and Canada. "I first came here for an international theatre festival in Quebec. I was passing through Toronto, just checking it out . . . and somehow I ended up staying." Quickly making new connections, he soon received an invitation from Toronto's Harbourfront Centre to prepare a production in honour of the Mexican Day of the Dead tradition. His new acquaintances helped him to organize a team of Mexican Canadian actors; they held rehearsals at Casa Maíz and prepared *Calaveras de Posada*, a colourful, satirical re-enactment of the Mexican Day of the Dead from the perspective of the deceased themselves. Beginning with an exaggeratedly solemn funeral procession, the play quickly morphs into a frenetic party in which people recount the stories of their lives and deaths, mocking themselves and one another in the process. Making use of *calaveritas*—rhyming couplets that satirize some aspect of a person's appearance, life, or social class—the play engages with the audience and encourages their participation.

One of the challenges faced by Ortiz in this production was that of working with professional and amateur actors simultaneously. "Obviously, working with trained actors is easier because with them, one only needs to direct . . . With beginners it is necessary to train the actor first, and then to direct. It's a question of time and patience. The actor needs to be driven and have a strong taste for dramatic art." After completing *Calaveras de Posada*—which went on to be presented at the Fêtes internationales du théâtre in Salaberry-de-Valleyfield, Quebec, in April 2011, and has since been performed at Casa Maíz each November—Ortiz took a step back to evaluate the situation.

> After the success of this production, I found that I had to ask myself, "What type of theatre is needed in Toronto? What kind of audiences are we trying to reach?" I realized that just as we need to train actors, we also need to train the audience, challenging them while also reaching out to them through stories that they can relate to. We need a message that strengthens identities, that relates to where we've come from and where we are going. Meanwhile, we need to recognize that while most of our audience is Spanish-speaking, we also have English speakers who are interested in learning about Latin American culture, and they need to be thought of as well.

Drawing on his interest in Chicano theatre, Ortiz chose for his second production Carlos Morton's *Johnny Tenorio*, a Mexican American twist on the Don Juan story. "This play deals with the *machismo* that still exists in Latin American cultures," Ortiz explains. "However, it also touches upon themes of identity, spirituality, and the experience of migration—Tenorio is an immigrant child who experiences racism and bullying in school, then grows up to be a womanizer." Enrique Castro, who considers *Johnny Tenorio* his favourite production since beginning his theatrical endeavours, still does not know how Ortiz managed to do it. "I have so much respect for Oscar, who is humble and very capable. When he started working on *Johnny Tenorio*, I never believed that the play was going to happen. He started with nothing—no production team, no actors, nothing . . . and in two months he had a show." Seeking to reach a bilingual audience while remaining true to its Chicano roots, the play was presented in "Spanglish" as part of the twentieth Festival of Images and Words at York University's Glendon Campus in 2011. While *Calaveras de Posada* had a Mexican cast of actors, the production team for *Johnny Tenorio* was drawn from many cultures, all of whom rose to the challenge of playing Mexican American actors. "People come to Canada for many reasons," Ortiz says. "Some due to exile, some for work . . . We Latin Americans come from many different cultures and backgrounds, but we have enough in common to have a sense of a shared identity." Indeed, Ortiz is not the first theatre artist in Canada to engage with Chicano Theatre. As Michelle Habell-Pallán observes in her essay on Chilean Canadian Carmen Aguirre's *¿Qué Pasa Con La Raza, Eh?*, invocations of Chicano culture attempt to "activate new social relations between Latino youth in the United States and Canada by thinking beyond the nation and employing popular Chicano music and images . . . The ease with which Chicano themes speak to their situation demonstrates their experience as being part of a larger North American context" ("Don't Call Us" 185). Habell-Pallán is quick to clarify that she does not see Chicano culture as representing a larger Latin Canadian identity, as it is itself situated in a specific place and historical moment. However, she does see Chicano identity as perhaps serving as a kind of model for new social and cultural possibilities of Latin American identities—ones that are inclusive and that transcend the nation. It is this model that Ortiz has picked up on in transitioning his group from a Mexican to a Latin American focus—one that Double Double's actors have readily embraced.

Poet and visual artist Maria Elena Mesa, who has recently joined Double Double as an actor and scenographer, adds that for her the concept of a nation does not hold too much relevance, as there are many cultural differences within any nation, including her native Colombia. "There is such a great diversity of people in this world, but the cultures do have certain commonalities in terms of aesthetics and artistic language. Meanwhile, there is a widespread shared interest in the theme of human rights and the question of how to express a political message through the arts." It is this political message and concern for human rights that fuelled Double Double's third production, *M.O.A.R.*

After meeting Rodolfo Molina, a Salvadoran Canadian, former *campesino*, and devout Catholic who continues to draw inspiration from Archbishop Óscar Romero's life and legacy, Ortiz initiated the project. Drawing on two plays based on Romero's life—Costa Rican playwright Samuel Rovinski's *El martirio del pastor* and Carlos Morton's *The Savior*—Ortiz and Enrique Castro created a new theatrical adaptation and began rehearsing with a small team of actors from El Salvador, Colombia, Mexico, and the United States. Beginning with a disturbing rendition of Romero's death through a grotesque parody of the Last Supper, the play narrates the priest's gradual conversion, inspired by his Jesuit friend Rutilio Grande, from a quiet, conservative intellectual to a fighter for the rights of landless peasants in the face of growing oppression. While depicting Romero's spiritual journey and internal struggles with fear and self-doubt, the play also reveals the corruption of the Salvadoran government during this time, the drastic social inequality, the brutality of the military (particularly through the figure of Major Roberto D'Abuisson, who ordered and planned Romero's assassination), and the complicity of foreign media in social injustice. "Most Latinos know the story of Óscar Romero—an important church leader who underwent a complete spiritual and ethical transformation in the last three years of his life," Ortiz explains. "The question that follows, then, is just what significance this story has in the present moment?" After giving the idea some thought, he concluded that Romero's message is as relevant as ever in the twenty-first century. "There is so much happening in the present moment that is worthy of denunciation, here in Canada and in our countries of origin. We need to maintain the same faith and trust in the 'God of Change' that Romero believed in."

Double Double presented *M.O.A.R.* as part of the twenty-first Festival of Images and Words in October 2012, as well as at Toronto's Holy Trinity Anglican Church in April 2013, and Ortiz is currently seeking further opportunities for the development and presentation of the work. For the actors, the experience has been fulfilling personally and professionally. Enrique Castro, who plays Romero, found the role challenging as he is not himself a Christian, but he admires the archbishop for his courage and his message. "The work that some priests achieved in El Salvador with liberation theology was amazing.

Romero in the last three years of his life lived more fully than he had in the previous sixty, and it's a privilege to tell his story through theatre. But, his are tough shoes to fill." For Colombian Canadian Jose Antonio Wesso, who works in home renovation and had never acted before meeting Ortiz, the chance to do theatre has been personally transformative. "It has changed my life completely, allowing me to experience completely different kinds of communities and friendships at a deep level." Having been involved in political struggles in rural regions of Colombia, he found it easy to relate to his role as a radicalized peasant who fights for justice under the guidance of Father Rutilio Grande and later Archbishop Romero. "For me, Monseñor Romero has been a great example to us, urging us not to be afraid of change, of defending a noble cause, to recognize our flaws, and to live according to our ideals without expecting earthly glory."

Through these three productions—*Calaveras de Posada, Johnny Tenorio,* and *M.O.A.R.*—Double Double Performing Arts has developed from a Mexican Canadian theatre group focused on exploring one nation's cultural traditions to a Latin American group interested in provoking thought and action with regard to more universal social concerns. Originating in the community around Casa Maíz, it has remained grounded in its Latin American identity; meanwhile, it has reached out to Spanish-, English-, and French-speaking audiences and continues to seek new ways to share the group's message. For Ortiz, future projects include reaching out to youth, both as audiences and potential participants in theatrical production. While Ortiz does not know how long he will stay in Toronto (particularly since his family is still residing in Mexico), he believes that there is much work to be done in Canada's growing Latin American community. "Latin American artists need to establish our own positions here, to work in socio-cultural community development through art, and always to respond to our personal convictions and the needs of the human being—no matter what."

THE APUS COOP: BREATHING NEW LIFE INTO AN OLD "CLI_CHE"

Che Guevara remains one of the most seminal Latin American figures of the twentieth century; however, many have pointed out the irony of the way in which contemporary capitalist culture has absorbed his image (as his ubiquitous presence on T-shirts throughout the world suggests). It is this irony that has provided the inspiration for *cli_CHE*, the Apus Coop's first theatrical production, which was staged in the fall of 2012 as a series of open rehearsals at Toronto's Parroquia San Lorenzo, a Latin American Anglican church devoted to liberation theology. Based on Augusto Boal's *A Lua Pequena e a Caminhada Perigosa*, this play is "an adaptation of an adaptation" that tells the story of Guevara's execution in Bolivia. However, in the Apus Coop's version, the play is narrated from the perspective of the three principal women in Guevara's life—his two wives, Hilda Gadea and Aleida March, and his most well-known lover, a revolutionary who went by the name of Tania. By presenting Guevara's story from this perspective, the group seeks to humanize Che Guevara and reveal different, lesser-known aspects of his life and character without minimizing his historical contributions as a revolutionary leader. "*cli_CHE* was actually not our first option," states Tristan Castro Pozo, a Peruvian Canadian theatre artist who founded the Apus Coop at the beginning of 2012. Like Oscar Ortiz, he finds that the instability and uncertainty of the Latin American immigrant experience in Canada does not create the most fertile ground for artistic work. "We had a very hard time getting started, not due to a lack of interest but due to a lack of people's ability to make the necessary volunteer commitment," he explains. "We actually abandoned our first planned theatre project after five months of work. Thinking about this lack of volunteerism, it occurred to us that Che Guevara might be considered the biggest volunteer of the twentieth century, and we decided to organize our project around him." Castro Pozo knew that this was a daring proposal that would not be received well by all in Toronto's Latin American circles—particularly in the Cuban community, who claim a certain ownership of Che's historical legacy and possibly would not agree with the image presented in *cli_CHE*, and also among Colombian Canadians, some of whom identify Che's image with guerrilla warfare and the systemic violence in their country (Castro Pozo). Nevertheless, Castro Pozo eventually found a team of actors from Toronto and Hamilton willing to make the commitment to the project. While rehearsals were initially held at Casa Maíz, Castro Pozo eventually moved the group to the Parroquia San Lorenzo. By staging the play in this venue, Castro Pozo affirms the alignment between Guevara's humanist principles and those Christian ones of liberation theology, a movement that strives to apply the gospel message to the lived experiences of the poor and oppressed. Meanwhile, by presenting the play in English, the group hopes to take their message beyond the limits of the Latin American community and to reach mainstream audiences. In this way, Castro Pozo pays homage to his greatest influence, Augusto Boal.

"I grew up with a theatre background," he explains. "My father is a theatre director and my mother studied at the Escuela Nacional de Teatro in Lima. In 1989, I made my start by working with two older cousins on a production of Oscar Wilde's *The Importance of Being Earnest*. After that, I became aware of the issues facing the gay community in Lima (during the early nineties little was known about HIV). Meanwhile, after working in a mental hospital, I saw a correlation between psychotherapy and theatre." Castro Pozo's interests in social issues regarding gay rights and mental illness led him to study psychodrama and then Boal's Theatre of the Oppressed. "For over a decade I was involved in artistic activism with the Theatre of the Oppressed movement in Brazil," he says. "After a while, though, I realized that some of those techniques were being reified, and there seemed to be a sameness and reproducibility among the facilitators that, for me, lessened the interpersonal human experience of the process." While Castro Pozo still believes that the Boalean method is a good way of empowering communities, he no longer uses a strict Theatre of the Oppressed model for his workshops. "Instead, we draw on Boal's inspiration by combining different elements and finding out what works," he says.

For Enrique Castro, who has been involved with the Apus Coop since its foundation in early 2012, Tristan Castro Pozo's method is completely unique and has been the most effective one that he has experienced for his own personal growth and training as an actor. "Tristan is absolutely amazing," Castro says. "His primary way of teaching is through theatre games, and I've never seen him do the same game twice. I come to the rehearsals and have lots of fun with these games, and in the process I learn how to do theatre." Castro adds that when he first began working with the Apus Coop, he was not familiar with the concept of "full inclusion" in theatre. "At one point there was a participant who could not pronounce a certain line in English. Tristan decided that our only option was to change the line so that the actor would be able to say it. When I expressed concern that this would change the work's meaning, Tristan replied that it would not change the fact that the actor was participating. This is a beautiful principle." While Castro credits many Toronto-based directors as having trained him in socially conscious theatre, he cites Tristan Castro Pozo as the most informative. "You can do this kind of theatre with anyone. I'd like to take this into schools and get young people involved, to put on a play about the difficulties that they are having in school. There's a real instrument for change in our hands," he says.

Castro Pozo likewise stresses that his method of doing theatre involves more than fun and games. "Eugenio Barba has said that rehearsals lie in between actors' desires and the real demands of appearing on stage," he says. "I'm open to working with people from many different backgrounds, but we're progressively more aware that this implies learning from each other . . . This kind of work requires discipline and a learning commitment." Like Double Double, Apus has reached out to Latin Americans of many national, cultural, and socio-economic backgrounds; it seeks to provide a space for non-professional actors to learn the craft of theatre and produce artistic works with a social message. Meanwhile, it faces similar challenges—coping with a lack of funding, a lack of stability in actor participation, and the challenge of reaching and building audiences. While both groups look to establish Latin American communities as their point of departure, the Apus Coop has expressed an extensive interest in going beyond those communities, presenting their work in English and ultimately taking it to the streets and other public spaces. Although they are a new group, their current work on *cli_CHE* has drawn a serious response that will enable Apus to create a lasting space for itself on the Latina/o Canadian artistic scene. "The group is amazing," Enrique Castro says. "We have someone who comes twice a week from Hamilton to Toronto, and she says that nothing can stop her from attending these rehearsals."

GRUPO TEATRO LIBRE: "EVERYONE IS A DIRECTOR"

One of the main challenges facing any theatre company, but especially a community-based one, is that of sustainability. For both Apus and Double Double, which were formed within the past three years, sustainability remains a concern for the actors, directors, and public alike. A clear example of this problem can be seen in the case of Teatro Crisálida, which, during its six-year existence, led theatre workshops that trained over two hundred and fifty participants and put on a number of classic Hispanic productions, culminating in a month-long festival in Toronto in April 2011.[1] While many Toronto-based theatre practitioners—Enrique Castro being one of them—credit this group as having considerable influence on their own artistic and personal development, all the beauty and solidarity that was Crisálida came to an end in late 2011 when the group's artistic director moved to Montreal. However, Grupo Teatro Libre—founded in 2008 and comprised largely of Crisálida participants who wanted to do more politically themed projects—has managed to overcome this challenge in the most logical way possible: they have no artistic director. "We want our group to be sustainable," says Mexican-born theatre artist Luis Rojas. "That means that our collective has to be larger than any one of its individual members. Everyone has to be a director." Therefore, while each production that Grupo Teatro Libre puts on has its director, there is no artistic director to the organization as a whole, which is organized and run in a co-operative fashion. "We have our different roles, and we respect

---

1   On this point, see my article "Performing Communities."

one another's roles in the collaborative process, but each group member has as much weight as any other," states another actor from the group (Jacome).

Founded in 2008 by Uruguayan director Richard Rodríguez and a small group of actors (also from Uruguay), Grupo Teatro Libre (GTL) is widely considered to be the first Latin American theatre group in Toronto to focus strongly on relaying political and social messages to its audiences. "If there's anyone who boosted Latin American theatre in Toronto, it was Richard Rodríguez," states Enrique Castro, a former member of GTL. "The people at Crisálida were mostly interested in doing theatre as a kind of entertainment; Rodríguez and his circle were more intent on doing theatre with a political message." One of their first productions, for example, was of Mario Benedetti's *Pedro y el Capitán*, a dialogue between a torturer and his captor. Set in an unnamed terrorist state, this play speaks to the universal horror of oppression and made a deep impression on the audience members—some of them former political prisoners. Other early works included Florencio Sánchez's *En familia* and Ariel Mastandrea's *¡Oh Sarah!* Eventually, Rodríguez moved back to Uruguay; however, the group's democratic, open structure, as well as its uncompromising commitment to quality, allowed it to continue and to flourish. Like the other groups discussed in this article, it grew to transcend nationalistic confines and is now a multicultural Latin American group that, though completely non-profit, strives to cultivate a high level of quality and a reputation for professionalism. Since 2008, GTL has presented eight plays, all of them works by Latin American playwrights and all of them presented in Spanish, generally without subtitles. "We are currently questioning our commitment to presenting Latin American works only," states Rojas. "We'd maybe like to include the work of Dario Fo, who is Italian but aligns with our mission in that he is a playwright of protest." However, while the group is giving some consideration to presenting works by non–Latin American authors, they remain committed to the use of the Spanish language. Although GTL used surtitles for a while, they eventually stopped when they realized that they were not particularly necessary for the company's audiences and that they put a great deal of pressure on the actors to conform strictly to the script without engaging in any improvisation. "Our language empowers us," says actor Jorge Henríquez. "There are many people in our audiences who really don't understand English, and we need to recognize and include these people. This is part of our ideological message."

When asked about the multicultural Latin American nature of GTL, the group members reply that they have found it to be a fruitful experience. Although the group was founded strictly by Uruguayans, the group quickly grew to include many nationalities. In *Pedro y el Capitán*, for example, the two roles were played by Mexicans. "In this group Uruguayans learn to speak Mexican Spanish, and Mexicans come to speak Colombian," says Uruguayan Canadian Alba Agosto, who is a veteran member of the group. "Each production is an educational experience in which we travel to different countries," says Luis Rojas. "Our cultures are so different, and yet similar all the same. My vocabulary has grown considerably, and I think a lot of us have found that through this process our identities expand toward a more universal culture." At the moment, GTL's thirteen active members are immersed in two projects: Uruguayan playwright Rafael Pence's *Causa y Efecto*, which they are planning to present in April 2013, and *El amigo imaginario*, a laboratory project in which the actors worked collectively to create a series of short sketches featuring one, two, or three actors. Beginning with discussions of imaginary friends that the actors interacted with as children, the workshop led them to explore the concepts of interior dialogue and the complex, multi-faceted relationship between the imagining subject and the imagined friend who, in Alba Agosto's one-woman show, are ultimately barely distinguishable. This type of experimental theatre, new for GTL, has been of great value. "The experience and new knowledge that we've gained have led these little theatrical productions to touch on great themes of democracy, justice, solidarity, respect for human rights, and our fundamental objective of poetic, imaginative creation," says Rojas. In deciding where to present *El amigo imaginario*, the members of GTL determined that Casa Maíz was itself the ideal location. They converted the space into five small stages alternately accentuated by sound and lighting. In this way, the audience, who walked among the stages watching each sketch, became participants in the production rather than mere spectators, as the "fourth wall" between actors and audience was broken. For future projects GTL plans to continue this experimental approach, which allows the actors to reflect critically and creatively about their own lived experiences as migrants. "This is a way of keeping alive the memory of our collective history and also maintaining our awareness of the current realities in our countries of origin," Rojas explains.

It could be argued that of the three groups in this investigation, Grupo Teatro Libre is the most traditional, as up until this year it has generally staged established plays rather than relying extensively on adaptation and collective creation. It is also the group that has stood the test of time and established itself most firmly in the community. "The fact that we are a community theatre does not entail that we're not professional," Rojas states. "We are a non-profit organization, but we are professionals in that we are always trying to develop our abilities and advance to the next level." Its firm commitment to the use of Spanish—in general disavowing the use of surtitles—is also noteworthy and aligns clearly with Casa Maíz's underlying philosophy. It seeks to provide a safe space in which Latin American communities may live their reality without experiencing the pressure to share their stories in a foreign language and fit themselves neatly into multicultural Canadian boxes. This philosophy is considerably different from that of both the Apus Coop and Double Double Performing Arts, which have included the English language into their work and are currently striving to reach non-Latino as well as Latino audiences. But while there are certain obvious differences among the three groups, these are outweighed by their similarities: their commitment to offering audiences a socio-political message rather than mere entertainment, their common challenges of funding and sustainability, and their conscious cultivation of a new Latin American identity that transcends national borders and draws on shared experiences to create something distinctly new. And, while some of these aims are shared by other Latin Canadian theatre companies, such as Aluna Theatre and Alameda Theatre Company, they are unique because they provide a space for recent migrants—some of them seasoned theatre professionals, but others who are teachers, construction workers, manufacturers, and retired people—to experience the transformative power of theatre.

CONCLUSION

Throughout this essay, I have argued that the growth of Latin American community theatre in Toronto over the past several years might be interpreted more broadly as the development of a new, self-determined, pan–Latin American identity that refuses to be contained by the tidy categories offered by paradigms such as national identity or even multiculturalism. In contrast to these paradigms, I have instead invoked other social imaginaries, such as diaspora. According to Robin Cohen, members of diasporic groups often have a troubled relationship with their host nation and as a result develop a strong ethnic consciousness, solidarity with co-ethnic members in other countries, and the development of a return movement toward their homeland (182). Even a brief glance at Toronto's Latin American diasporas reveals some of these phenomena: Grupo Teatro Libre's commitment to the Spanish language and Latin American authors might be construed as a strong ethnic consciousness, while all of the groups' desires to maintain and develop an awareness of current political issues in their home countries can be seen as a kind of return movement home.

Nevertheless, Cohen's concept of a diaspora is not adequate to characterize the forms of collective consciousness that these three theatre groups are cultivating. The pan–Latin American identity celebrated by these groups might be viewed as a symptom of the troubled relationship that Cohen describes and which Pedro Cabezas has signalled as affecting these communities in Toronto (in a society where Latin Americans of all nationalities have faced prejudice and discrimination, it makes sense to seek strength in numbers). On the other hand, Toronto's artistic communities appear to be motivated by positive factors much more strongly than negative ones, such as the desire to celebrate their roots while creating new ties in the host country. In this way, I believe that Taylor's concept of cultural modernity along with Mignolo's decolonial revisioning of *latinidad* provide some insight into the processes that are occurring. As Mignolo argues, "The most radical struggles in the twenty-first century will take place on the battlefield of logic and reason. The marginalization of Fidel Castro and the defeat of Salvador Allende are only two examples of how the global designs of an expanding capitalism operate against any possibility that might inhibit its expansion" (*Idea* 100). The formation of alliances such as ALBA and CELAC since the publication of Mignolo's 2005 book *The Idea of Latin America* suggests that many groups of people throughout the western hemisphere are indeed challenging the logic of capitalism and colonialism, along with the nation-bound sense of identity that accompanies them, and seeking to establish different modes of social, economic, and political organization.

Looking at the Canadian context, the cultural and political integration of Latin Americans that occurs in a centre such as Casa Maíz might be interpreted as a parallel process occurring through the medium of artistic production. As for the theatre groups themselves, they have demonstrated a commitment to breathing new life into old cultural tropes (such as the Day of the Dead) and political ones (like Che Guevara), seeking to explore their old meanings and discover new ones. Group members have sought to enrich their own cultural identity through contact with others, often at the level of their common yet unquestionably diverse Spanish language. They also have reached out to their communities in several ways, resourcefully overcoming many financial and circumstantial obstacles to achieve their artistic goals. Meanwhile, through all of their efforts, they have maintained an attitude of openness and inclusion, eagerly seeking to incorporate anyone who demonstrates the appropriate level of discipline and commitment. The enthusiasm that these three theatre groups have generated suggests that this is only the beginning of what will most certainly be a continued flourishing of community-based theatre by Latina/o Canadians in Toronto, and it is exciting to speculate about what new projects and community identities the future is sure to bring.

THE BILINGUAL PERFORMANCE THEATRE OF ALBERTO KURAPEL

HUGH HAZELTON

The Chilean Canadian playwright Alberto Kurapel wrote seven bilingual plays, in which Spanish and French were spoken consecutively, during the twenty-two years that he lived in Quebec. An analysis of the experimental techniques and strategies employed in the first three of his works, all of them relatively short, will reveal how Kurapel put his overall aesthetic into practice and what role exile, language, and the bilingual text played in their development. The last four of his bilingual works, which are longer and more discursive, will also be examined in order to see where he took the multilingual aspect of his work before finally turning to unilingual theatre productions in the mid-1990s, prior to his return to Chile, where he now lives.

Kurapel is one of the foremost innovators in recent Latin American theatre, and much of his most cutting-edge work was created while he was living and working in Quebec. He arrived in Montreal in 1974, a year after General Augusto Pinochet's *coup d'état* against the government of President Salvador Allende of Chile on 11 September 1973, and moved back to Chile in 1996. Although he was already an experienced actor and performer when he left Santiago, it was in Quebec that he developed his concept of "teatro-performance," or "post-teatro," a dramatic form that went beyond the bounds of conventional drama in terms of its conception, objectives, focus, and use of mixed media. Exile, in all its manifestations—from nostalgia to alienation—was the driving force of his work. Indeed, the dedicated nucleus of actor-performers in his plays, especially his wife Susana Cáceres and the actress Marinea Méndez, coalesced into the Compagnie des Arts Exilio, a theatre company devoted to his work. Kurapel, who was already well known in Quebec as a singer-songwriter and poet, received a good deal of notice in Canada, and his work was the subject of a number of critical studies. He also translated several plays by Quebec dramatists into Spanish, including Denise Boucher's *Les fées ont soif,* which was produced in Caracas in 1985 (Walker 83). By the mid-1990s, he had the highest profile in the province of any Latin American artist. Since his return to Chile, he has received international recognition: his plays have toured in Latin America, Europe, and the United States, and he has been a professor of theatre at the Chilean National Theatre School and several universities in Santiago, where he continues his work as a poet, playwright, singer-songwriter, actor-performer, director, critic, and professor.

Kurapel has written extensively about the theory and development of his work, as well as about autobiographical aspects of his life in both Chile and Canada, particularly with reference to his years in Montreal. This wealth of material, a "metatheatrical discourse"[1] (Faúndez Carreño, "Alberto Kurapel" 6) that consists of three collections of essays and numerous articles and interviews, also forms and shapes the persona and ethos that underlie his work, for he is not just a playwright but also invariably the principal actor-performer and driving force of his performance theatre pieces. His creative work amounts (at last count) to nine LPs, seven books of poetry, and over twenty works of performance theatre. It is the work of a true artistic explorer, obsessed with discovery and innovation, who has always preferred to find his own path rather than to follow established ways.

Alberto Kurapel, originally named Alberto Sendra (Faúndez Carreño, "Alberto Kurapel" 11), was born in 1946 in Santiago and grew up in a working-class family in the nearby city of Maipú. He remembers always being interested in the theatre in his childhood, especially the grotesque "teatro de esperpento" of the Spanish playwright Ramón María del Valle-Inclán and the baroque plays of Pedro Calderón de la Barca, and by the age of eleven he was already writing radio plays and poems (Kurapel, Personal interview). He was also partially of Mapuche ancestry and, as he grew up, was curious to find out more about his Aboriginal forebears. As a teenager he travelled to

---

1   This and all other translations are by the author of the present study.

Temuco, in south-central Chile, which is to this day the centre of traditional Mapuche culture, lived with the people there, and became close to a *machi* or wise woman. The woman's niece, impressed by his singing abilities, gave him a Mapuche name made up of two words in their language, Mapuzugun: *kura*, meaning "stone," and *pel*, or "throat" (Kurapel, *El actor-performer* 83). It was the name he took on permanently, and a cultural heritage with which he would deeply identify for the rest of his life. Several years later he won a scholarship to go to Memphis, Tennessee, as an exchange student, where he discovered Afro American and underground culture and became interested in American literature and theatre (Kurapel, Personal interview).

In 1964 Kurapel enrolled in theatre studies at the University of Chile in Santiago and went on to become an actor at the Theatre Institute at the same university, appearing in a variety of plays by Chilean and classical playwrights, including García Lorca and Molière (Walker 83), and also acting in films, radio, and even a children's show on television. However, it was experimental theatre, including the Living Theatre and the work of Megan Terry and the Open Theatre, that most interested him, and he acted in Terry's play *Viet Rock*, which was produced in Santiago and directed by the poet and songwriter Víctor Jara (Kurapel, Personal interview). During the leftist years of Salvador Allende's presidency, from 1970 to 1973, Kurapel was an active supporter of social change, especially through his music and songs, which he played in union halls, political gatherings, and community events in the *poblaciones* or shanty towns of Santiago. His songs and lyrics ran parallel to the new activist music that Pablo Milanés, Víctor Jara, Atahualpa Yupanqui, Daniel Viglietti, Chico Buarque, and others were spreading throughout Latin America at the time (Le Blanc 4, 16). He refused, however, to join any political party, an independent position that was to isolate him to some extent as the years went by. After the *coup d'état* he was forced to leave the theatre and acting and finally, in 1974, under the threat of death, he took refuge in the Canadian embassy (the only one accepting refugees at the time) and was flown out to Montreal (Kurapel, Personal interview).

Although he lived his early years in Quebec in poverty and isolation, Kurapel showed remarkable resilience and artistic focus: he was intent on continuing to express his vision of the world, even in an alien environment. He is essentially a multi-faceted artist who creates from a unified conceptual and philosophical basis and works in four overlapping areas: music, theatre, poetry, and the essay. Kurapel continued his artistic career as a singer-song-writer in Quebec almost immediately after arriving, incorporating themes of exile and alienation into his moving and passionate songs of mourning, suffering, resistance, and solidarity and infusing them with his own poetic voice. These themes would recur in his poetry and plays. There was a great deal of support and sympathy with the Chilean exile community at the time in Quebec, and the Quebec public opened itself to Chilean culture. Kurapel spoke English, but quickly learned French and immersed himself in Quebec culture, with which he found much in common. He was also intent on using the translation of his lyrics as a bridge to Quebec and English Canadian audiences, and was not satisfied with isolating himself within his own language.

Kurapel had always been fascinated by Mapuche musical traditions, as well as folk music, dance, and songs from rural Chile, and eventually wrote a biography of Margot Loyola, one of the great contemporary proponents and interpreters of Chilean folk music. Even in Quebec, he often appeared in a poncho and country clothing and played a Mapuche drum. As the Chilean Canadian theatre director Gastón Iturra has observed, the principal concern of Chileans in Montreal in the 1970s "n'était pas l'intégration, mais la volonté de faire connaître notre culture" (qtd. in Pozo 246). It is remarkable how single-mindedly Kurapel persevered with his musical creations, singing wherever he could, from Janou Saint-Denis's Place aux poètes, the longest-running series of poetry readings in Montreal, to Radio-Canada. He toured through Quebec and into English Canada, playing in meeting halls, CÉGEPs, universities, and any kind of venue that he could find, essentially extending the pattern of his musical activities in Chile in the early 1970s; eventually he also sang abroad, in the United States, Spain, and France (Le Blanc 38). "Alberto Kurapel est un poète-chanteur marginal, dans toute l'acceptation du mot," writes Huguette Le Blanc, who published a study of his work as a singer-composer, *Alberto Kurapel. Chant et poésie d'exil*, in 1983. "Ces pensées se reflètent dans toute son oeuvre et dans sa conduite indomptable. Obstiné.

Arrogant. Force qui ne se soumet pas et qui parcourt tous les chemins, le plus souvent en empruntant les plus durs" (38). Within a period of fifteen years Kurapel brought out six independently produced albums, all of original work in Spanish, but accompanied by French and English translations of his songs. On the first four albums he sang solo; the following three included Andean instruments, electric guitar, and synthesizers as backup, and included songs sung in French. The last two albums, *Guerrilla* and *Confidencial/Urgent*, were produced by his theatre group, La Compagnie des Arts Exilio, which Kurapel founded in 1981, and the very last of them consisted of poems by Quebec writers translated into French and set to his own music. A number of these compositions and translations would later be used in his plays.

Toward the mid-1980s, Kurapel began to shift from music to poetry and published five books of poems, two in bilingual Spanish-French format with a micro-press, Les Éditions du Trottoir, and three in French (with some Spanish) with the major Quebec poetry publisher Les Écrits des Forges. These collections at first continued along the main thematic lines as his songs, though in a more personal voice; the alienation of the speaker is now more desperate and embittered, at times even enraged by what he witnesses and what is taking place in the world around him. References are made increasingly to life in Montreal, with its own injustice, marginalization, and dehumanization: one book, *Berri-UQÀM*, is a series of poems based on scenes from the Métro as experienced by the musicians who play at the various stations. Quebec writers are now mentioned as well, especially Patrick Straram, le Bison Ravi, a French writer and cultural figure who became a close friend; in fact, for years Kurapel added a pseudonym to his name similar to Straram's: "Alberto Kurapel, le Guanaco gaucho" (notice the fusion of the French definite article with the Spanish sobriquet). All five books were translated by the distinguished literary translator Jean Antonin Billard, a long-time friend of Straram's who took an early interest in Kurapel's work. By the end of the 1980s, Kurapel was well known in Quebec and was the only poet of Latin American origin included in La Nuit de la poésie in 1991, the mega-event of Quebec poetry, held only once every decade, and filmed as a documentary by Jean-Claude Labrecque and Jean-Pierre Masse. In the years since his return to Chile, Kurapel has continued to publish books of poetry, but has only brought out one CD of his songs.

Kurapel's performance works, however, were the very marrow of his artistic vision. He has a vast knowledge of theatre, from the Greek classics to the most cutting-edge work of the present day and, in addition to his background and training in the field, continued to read voraciously on it while he was in Montreal (Kurapel, *El actor-performer* 225). A number of other Chilean and Latin American refugees and exiles were also working in theatre and film in the city. Filmmakers such as Jorge Fajardo and Marilú Mallet were both making films with the National Film Board, while Rodrigo González, Enrique Sandoval, and Miguel Retamal began writing their own plays; directors such as Gastón Iturra presented works on stage, and a nucleus of experienced, semi-professional actors such as Margarita Gutiérrez, José Venegas, Manuel Aránguiz, and Lucie Lapointe worked with a variety of playwrights and directors. Eventually, Kurapel even appeared in a feature film, *Noces de papier*, directed by Michel Brault, in which Manuel Aránguiz played opposite Geneviève Bujold in the story of a marriage of convenience between a Quebec woman and a refugee. Within a few years, a number of different theatre companies had formed and were actively presenting plays in Spanish in Montreal. In addition, many more Chilean writers were active in publishing prose—especially short stories—and poetry in the small Spanish-language newspapers and reviews that sprouted up, as well as in book form with micro-presses founded by Latin American immigrants and interested locals. *Peñas* (political and cultural community parties) were frequent, as were poetry readings. Some of these events, especially in the early years after the *coup d'état*, were organized by specific political parties to which the participants still belonged. Kurapel's theatre work stood out from this scene, however, for several reasons. His plays, which he referred to as performance theatre, were more experimental and avant-garde than those of most of the other writers—though Rodrigo González's plays, especially his collective work, was also highly innovative and had great imaginative fluidity. In addition, Kurapel was determined to find a stable, permanent place in which to produce his theatre and wanted his work to be completely bilingual, not just presented in either Spanish or French. His vision of bilingualism, from the outset, was to write plays in both Spanish and French at once, so that individual words, sentences, and blocks of speech would be given alternately in each language throughout the play. All but one of the titles of his plays are actually fusions of the two languages, without translation, so that only a person conversant with both can fully understand them.

Kurapel rejected the Aristotelian tradition of theatre as being a story told within a unified time frame, with a clear introduction, development, and denouement, in which actors would portray certain specific characters with which the audience could identify—and which he believed had turned theatre in Chile into an empty entertainment exercise for the bourgeoisie. He wanted to combine the spontaneous activity of the performance or happening with a rigorously planned theatrical event that dealt with archetypes more than individual characters and broke down the barriers between actors and audience. In order to do so, hieratic masks, gestures, rituals, and stage sets were to be as important as words, while multimedia elements such as photos, slides, film clips, recorded music, sounds, and voices were fundamental to creating the overall experience. In *El actor-performer*, his memoir published in Chile in 2010, he writes of what he wanted to take from the performance aesthetic that had been developing ever since the days of Hugo Ball and the Dadaists at the Cabaret Voltaire in Zurich—and of how he wanted to go beyond it. He was drawn to it by

> the great advances that had been made in abolishing a certain sense of stagnation and commercialization of legalized theatre, destroying the hierarchy of Institution-Producer-Director-Actor-Stage Designer. The way it valued *process* over result, the new approach it took toward development, the unexpected mobility of the climax, its unusualness, were essential to bringing about a new stage expression; but what I missed was the force and stage projection that was lacking in the performers. (191)

What Kurapel envisioned was a stage creation that fused the dynamism, presence, and focus of theatre with the spontaneity, inventiveness, and freedom of performances and happenings, staged not by actors, but by "actor-performers." He would define and elaborate upon this new form of event in the introductions to his plays; in the two manifestos that he wrote and included with works published in 1985 and 1994; in two expositions of his theories, combined with memoirs of his life and work, *Station artificielle*, published in Montreal in 1993, and *El actor-performer*, published in Santiago in 2010; in a detailed exposition of his aesthetics and concepts, *Estética de la insatisfacción en el teatro-performance*, published in Santiago in 2004; and in a wide range of essays and interviews that appeared in French, Spanish, and English in newspapers, theatre journals, and blogs in both North and South America, as well as Europe.

The goals and structure of Kurapel's performance theatre are, at the same time, part of the general evolution of theatre over the past three decades and a result of the idiosyncratic but highly cohesive and well-reasoned blend of elements of his own vision. Just as the performance aspect has roots in the Cabaret Voltaire and the Living Theatre, the theatrical aspect grows out of many styles: the quasi-deconstructivist, anarchic, avant-garde tradition of Alfred Jarry and the *Ubu Roi* plays; the complete integration of the body into theatrical expression advocated by Vsevolod Meyerhold (Kurapel, *El actor-performer* 22); the use of multimedia, particularly involving signs and film, first developed in the theatre by Erwin Piscator; the distancing techniques, return to ritual, use of music, and demystification of the actor proposed by Bertolt Brecht, especially in his "Short Organum"; the expansion of theatre beyond the text into gesture, installation, and spectacle found in Antonin Artaud's manifestos of the Theatre of Cruelty; the aesthetic of transparency and integration with the audience developed by Jerzy Grotowski in his Poor Theatre; and a myriad of other groundbreaking theatre techniques and theories from writers and playwrights around the world. Kurapel's theatrical creation was also distinctly Latin American, infused with Indigenous traditions, historical and cultural references, denunciations of oppression, poverty, marginalization, calls to action, collective focus among the cast, and shamanistic rituals. Kurapel's insistence that "[T]he imitation of Nature does not belong to theatrical expression" and that "[t]heatre will always be an artificial expression in constant opposition to naturalism" ("Montreal/ Santiago" 72) echoes the creationist philosophy set forth by the great Chilean twentieth-century avant-garde poet Vicente Huidobro in his classic manifesto of poetic aesthetics, "Non serviam," in 1914.

Kurapel wrote, produced, and directed his seven bilingual plays over a period of twelve years, from 1983 till 1995. All were presented by La Compagnie des Arts Exilio and published in sequence by Humanitas, a dynamic publisher of some two hundred literary works of all kinds by both Québécois and Quebec-based ethnic writers from around the world that was founded by the Romanian-born author Constantin Stoiciu in 1978. Kurapel and his theatre company eventually received funding from provincial and federal cultural agencies and his bilingual works were presented in English Canada, the US, France, Argentina, and Peru. Kurapel's first three works, *ExiTlio in pectore extrañamiento*, *Mémoire 85/Olvido 86*, and *Off-Off-Off ou Sur le toit de Pablo Neruda*, were short one-act performance theatre pieces grouped together into a single book, *3 Performances teatrales de Alberto Kurapel*. The collection was published in 1987, four years after the first theatre production of *ExiTlio in pectore extrañamiento* at the Galerie Transgression, on Bleury Street in Montreal. Amazingly, all of the major elements that characterized the performance theatre that Kurapel wrote in Quebec were already in place. The book is prefaced by an unsigned biographical portrait, including extracts from various appreciations of Kurapel's work by the critics who had seen his plays in Montreal and had been impressed by their dynamism and originality. This is followed by the "First Manifesto" of La Compagnie des Arts Exilio, underlining the fact that the exploration of the alienation of exile, in all of its many manifestations, from the exterior to the interior world, would be the foundation of the group's aesthetic, though "Mettre sur pied des activités culturelles en Exil ne signifie absolument pas faire un «Art d'Exil»" (xxi): theirs was to be a theatre *of* exile rather than *in* exile. For Kurapel, the term "exile" metaphorically included the minorities, rebels, artists, and marginalized individuals at odds with society: "[J]e me sens exilé comme des Québécois exilés, comme des artistes exilés ou comme n'importe quelle personne qui essaie de briser les barrières conventionnelles de cette société qui va être toujours exilée, marginalisée" (qtd. in Pozo 250). The entire book is bilingual, and the manifesto states directly that performance theatre is the art form that most suits the company's goals. It is also to be a deeply marginal theatre, put together of necessity with "objets trouvés" gathered up on the street and in vacant lots—including plastic milk crates for the audience to sit on (Martínez 47)—thereby combining Poor Theatre with surrealism. The group's performances are to be collective " 'mises en action' [not simply "mises en scène," or stagings] dans des dépotoirs, dans les rues, dans des edifices désaffectés, des entrepôts, des galleries d'art, des étables" (xxiii). Moreover, the (seemingly) fragmented collage or palimpsest of multimedia for which Kurapel became known is already firmly in place. A performance work is to be

«Un processus» qui se développe dans le temps et dans un ESPACE que nous transformons continuellement, où jouent le HASARD, le COLLAGE, la MUSIQUE ÉLECTROACOUSTIQUE, le CINÉMA, la VIDÉO, la CHANSON et les CONFLITS D'OBJECTIFS OPPOSÉS. (xxii)

It should be noted as well that Kurapel always accompanies publications of his plays with six to eight photos of key scenes, which emphasize the visual spectacle of his work.

ExiTlio in pectore extrañamiento establishes a pattern of action or development in which a single character, or sometimes group of characters, make their way through an unidentified, completely alien environment in search of something lost or inherently unobtainable. As befits a work that elevates gesture, ritual, costume, staging, and sets of "sculpted installations" (Kurapel, *Station artificielle* 39) in relation to the word, stage directions are elaborate and intricate. *ExiTlio* begins with instructions for the Exile, who is dressed in rags and standing in a garbage dump, to appear before superimposed slides of physical violence coupled with military marches, the sound of blows (to which he reacts as if he himself were hit), metal screeching on metal, voices speaking in various languages, television sets with static-filled screens, and the juxtaposition of violently contrasting film images. Overlooking this scene of bewildering aggression sits the impervious, hieratic, accusatory Mask (the only other character), atop a pyramid of tires. Disembodied voices—including those of a manikin, a young girl, and other unidentified people, as well as that of the Exile himself—come from off stage, sometimes as a chorus, sometimes engaging the Exile in conversation as he reflects on his condition, lost somewhere between Chile and Montreal, present simultaneously in both "an indescribable past and an incomprehensible present" (Gronemann and Sieber 283). What takes place does not follow any traditional pattern, but rather develops as a series of layered scenes; the action is also interrupted by news bulletins, songs, film clips (including one of the revolutionary Nicaraguan poet Ernesto Cardenal reading his work), and lists of cultural figures in the two countries, and the Exile himself at times breaks into poetry as he meditates out loud on his fate. Transparency is established between the actors and the audience so that the dichotomy between them is diminished: the first part of the play, for instance, ends with the Exile removing his makeup at a dressing table on stage and cleaning his hands and face with a towel. The Exile moves through a progression of psychological states and actions from disorientation to loneliness to abandonment in a no man's land corroded by guilt ("Avale tes vomissements alors!" the Mask commands) to an abject coupling with a plastic sex doll and then finally, through a slowly returning hope for revolutionary victory, arrives at a haggard, forlorn shed of hope:

> Baisent, enfilent, plantent leurs graines, font l'amour à tort et à travers les exiles.
> S'écoulent de la prison les urines d'un nouveau-né.
> Nous sommes au moins la Veille d'une Prochaine Pensée. (41)

Exile has reached its philosophical and emotional nadir, and something new is about to emerge from its contradictions.

The linguistic hybridization that characterizes Kurapel's theatre production in Montreal is also present, though still in a developing form. The stage directions in *ExiTlio* and the other two early plays are given only in Spanish, but most of the dialogue is in both Spanish and French, translated by Kurapel himself (Kurapel, "Re: otra"); no credit is given for the translation since all the original material in the play is by the author, whose multilingualism is integral to his work. Given that some dialogue, monologues, and material on film is only in Spanish and that some of the translated material doesn't quite match with the French—whether purposefully or not—it becomes apparent that Kurapel is basically writing in a hybrid language composed of both. In much the same way, his characters speak in two tongues in their new environment, giving rise to a process of repetition, linguistic self-consciousness, and even a slightly schizoid reality in which passion flows the most forcefully through the speaker's native language, while the second language often feels flat, indifferent, or remote. Sometimes, however, the French version of a passage comes first, with the original Spanish afterward, leaving the reader with the impression that the French text may in fact be the original. Although a unilingual French or Spanish speaker would understand most of the play, it is only the bilingual who can appreciate all of its subtleties, a reality that deftly subverts the intention of having a transparently bilingual text accessible to speakers of either language. Moreover, the repetition of the dialogue in two languages—one of which is native to the actors, while the other has been learned and is spoken well but with a non-native accent—inadvertently changes its rhythm, acting as a slightly distorted echo that is heard even as the action of the work progresses. At times the French translation also sounds a bit unusual, with turns of phrase that indicate it is not the work of a native speaker, adding to the sense of unfamiliarity. These elements produce a curious effect of simultaneous distancing and fusion, at once intimating the challenge and possible cultural enrichment of living in an alien culture and underlining the difficulties of exile, alienation, and adaptation. It is, in a sense, a metalanguage that carries over even into the characters' inner thoughts, which are at times enunciated in Spanish and then heard from an offstage recording in French, thus adding another linguistic signifier.

Kurapel's second play, *Mémoire 85/Olvido 86*, was the first to be presented in the abandoned Cadbury chocolate factory on Dandurand Street near the De Lorimier viaduct in Montreal's East End that was to become the company's permanent theatre space, the Espace Exilio. It is prefaced, as are all his bilingual plays, by a note explaining some of the philosophical and theatrical objectives of the play, particularly the desire to transgress theatrical norms in order to concentrate on the role of memory, which is integral to exile: "[P]our cette raison nous ANNULERONS L'ESPACE et nous supprimerons les ZONES D'ÉCLAIRAGE. [. . .] ON ANNULE LA TEMPORALITÉ. [. . .] Il faut FAIRE VIVRE les éléments concrets . . . " (50–51). The play begins with a further push toward player-audience transparency: a conversation between the actors as they get ready to begin, in which Kurapel calls them by name and asks if they're ready. The main character is now the Hanged Man, whose head and body are wrapped in strips of cloth, like a mummy, so that no facial expression is visible. The Hanged Man exists in the space between presence and absence, dead but still sentient in a world beyond any human desire, though with the memory of taking his own life, a metaphor for the emptiness of despair and suicide. Various other characters move past him in this short play, including the lovers Pedro and Pedra, El Étranger, who seems to be a voice for the Hanged Man ("La mort n'a pas de mémoire," he repeats) (66), a Secretary and a Receptionist, and Sutanomengana, an obsessive sadist who alternately cuddles a baby and compulsively applies electroshocks to torture symbolic images throughout the play, a predecessor of the obsessive figures that would occur in various of Kurapel's later plays. At one point, a third language is added: after a barrage of the sound of Latin American percussion instruments mixed with bursts of machine gun fire, the Hanged Man's voice comes in from off stage, breaking into a series of prayers from the Machitún, a Mapuche ceremony for the healing of the sick, recited in Mapuzugun. This linguistic fragment, inserted without explanation but linked to an Indigenous subtext of symbols and clothing in the play, serves as both a protective barrier and a link to the ancient people of the land, underlining the Hanged Man's isolation from the audience and his secret sources of spiritual solace. The play ends in symmetrical fashion to the transparency of its beginning, with the credits and a description of the Compagnie Exilio as a part of slides, film clips, and speeches of the Hanged Man and other characters, followed by a short poem (in Spanish only) by the Hanged Man:

Learn to live lovers

take this advice from my bones.

I don't love anyone, anyone,

anyone, anyone.

I sway back and forth, back and forth. (78)

It was with his third play, *Off-Off-Off ou Sur le toit de Pablo Neruda*, that Kurapel and the Compagnie Exilio began to achieve major recognition. Kurapel recounts how a group of theatre specialists organizing the second Festival de théâtre des Amériques appeared incognito at one of the performances, and immediately afterwards he was asked to officially participate in the festival, which included renowned directors and theatre groups from seven countries of the Americas (Díaz López). The play impressed the critics with its originality, forcefulness, and wealth of symbolism and received enthusiastic reviews in *La Presse, Jeu,* and the *Canadian Theatre Review*. "Kurapel frappe en plein coeur," wrote Jean Beaunoyer in *La Presse*. "Intégrant d'une façon magistrale la culture chilienne à la culture québécoise, mariant le français et l'espagnol, Kurapel ne craint aucune limite de son art. . . . On reçoit l'intensité d'un homme qui pousse la communication jusqu'à remettre des tracts du spectacle. Communion totale." Two years later, when the work was made into a film by Jorge Fajardo, it was also praised in *Cinema Canada* (Rackow). As Jean Antonin Billard has commented, however, the warmth of the critical reception did not necessarily entail a public success: the play was fiercely avant-garde and iconoclastic, and attendance was less than what was hoped for (Telephone interview).

Off-Off-Off was the most ambitiously experimental of the three early plays, and yet it also continued with a number of the themes, in some cases taking them even further. Although Jorge Fajardo made some changes to the film version (with the agreement of Kurapel), it nevertheless allows a closer visual analysis of Kurapel's style than the print versions of the plays can convey, even with their photos. The camera is, of course, more intimate with the scenery and performers, as well as evocative and interpretative in its own right: Fajardo is a distinguished filmmaker (and also a writer), with experience in the medium. Here it brings out the essential monochrome quality of the work. Kurapel has related in *Station artificielle* how he lacked enough money in the early years of the company to purchase even a second-hand transformer for stage lighting and had to make do with six flashlights rigged up to an electric console (63). This darkened stage, lit by intense small lights in key areas with the rest of the area left in shadow, is reproduced in the film and is heightened by the use of black and white for the costumes of the human characters. The only real colour (besides the film clips taken outdoors) comes from the bright red of the single non-human character, a chicken represented by a silhouette made of bright red neon tubing.

Off-Off-Off again threads through the anguish of exile, as Mario, a Chilean Canadian refugee, tries to reconcile the two cultures and languages inside him and, at the same time, discover what happened to a woman he loved who disappeared after the *coup d'état*. The intensity of the theatrical experience comes from the fact that, as Mayte Gómez has noted, "[I]t is not meant to offer audiences a vision of exile but to make them become subjects in the re-creation and re-production of exile itself, not just observing it but experiencing it" ("Infinite Signs" 39). In order to intensify the feeling of Mario's alienation, Kurapel isolates him on stage: the only other characters are the Pianist, a female figure who at various times performs a series of stiff, brusque, robotic arm movements and bangs on the keys at crucial moments; the Jogger, a mysterious figure who periodically enters and exits the stage as part of his run outdoors and toward the end of the play engages in a sadistic flirtation and the consequent psychic destruction of Mario; and the figure of a Latin American woman guerrilla fighter who appears at the end of the play. There are also a variety of offstage voices that provide information along the way. Mario's main source of conversation, however, is the red-tubed neon chicken, whose chief forte is repetition, whether of monosyllables or of Mario's reflections.

After the play's opening scene, revealing the stage layout, there is a gruelling sequence of fourteen slides of hooded, blindfolded women photographed against blood-stained walls as they are tortured and doused with water; this is repeated several times later on. The chief action of the play consists of Mario's reflections on life under the military regime, punctuated by his efforts to write, which he incessantly abandons, breaking his pencil in two. Each of these scenes is followed by numbered "Consciousnesses," or short quotations from a famous contemporary thinker, often recited by Mario in one language and then played back in his recorded voice in the other. At the end of each "Consciousness," Mario asks "¿Dónde está?" which could be interpreted as either "Where is he?" (the thinker) or "Where is she?" (his disappeared lover). Immediately afterwards he begins to pound at an enormous rock with a pair of pliers, an image of Sisyphean futility. These scenes alternate with exchanges between the chicken and Mario that start as conversations, then convert to lists of governmental and sports statistics, and finally destroy themselves in repeated numbers, gibberish, and monosyllables indicative of the meaning-lessness of such desiccated language. During the middle of the play, names of political and historical figures are called, each followed by a dummy corpse with the same name attached to it being thrown onto the theatre floor, after which the names of disappeared people from different parts of Latin America are read out. Despite the eloquence of many of Mario's meditations, language breaks down under the weight of grief and the sheer numbers of the dead. At the end of the play, Mario glimpses a fading photograph of the woman he loved as a female voice speaks of loss; finally Mario, now stripped naked by the Jogger, sits down on a white circular sheet and paints himself black; he then curls up in a fetal position as Rocía, a Latin American guerrilla fighter, appears speaking lines from Pablo Neruda's poem "Cataclysm"—providing a message of hope—accompanied by the strains of the *habanera* "Ausencia," which are constantly woven through the play: "Et il poussera plus d'une fleur, plus d'un pain, plus d'un homme / des mêmes racines oubliées de la peur."

With *Prométhée enchaîné selon Alberto Kurapel le Guanaco gaucho/ Prometeo encadenado según Alberto Kurapel le Guanaco gaucho*, originally published in 1989 and translated into English in 2013, Kurapel entered a second phase in this theatre production, in which language and dialogue play a far greater role than in his earlier works, and the visual and audio elements are used primarily as commentaries or backup for the linguistic component—a change made doubly complex in this work by its interplay with Aeschylus's *Prometheus Bound*. Many other writers, of course, have also written works inspired by the Greek play, especially in the Romantic era: Goethe and Byron both wrote poems celebrating Prometheus, Shelley wrote his own version of *Prometheus Unbound*, and Mary Wollstonecraft Shelley's novel *Frankenstein* is subtitled *or, The Modern Prometheus*. While it would be tempting to speculate on certain parallels between Kurapel and the Romantics, his *Prometheus* is a very different work, subverted and deconstructed from the start, yet retaining a touch of the original. Again, as with *Off-Off-Off*, the critical reception was excellent. The play was preceded by a perceptive prologue by Jorge Fajardo and contained "Notes de Mise en Action" by Kurapel. Alain Pontaut, writing in *Le Devoir*, summed up the Kurapelian *wunderkammer* of "une scène faite de décombres, de briques, de carcasses d'autos comme ici, de sol mou, de travesti et de nudité, de visages masqués, . . . de poupées aux corps de paille et de chiffon, de diapositives renvoyant l'image même du spectatcle en train de se faire, de projections de films sur le corps, . . . [de] porte-voix hurlant sous les lumières mobiles," and, although he found it somewhat of an hom-age to the work of Antonin Artaud, John Cage, and Julian Beck, declared that it contained "puisées au passé et au présent du people chilien, une poésie aigüe et fièrement douloureuse, une voix claironnante au service de la lib-erté." Interest in the work also extended to international literary and theatre criticism, and both Alfonso de Toro, a theatre specialist at the University of Leipzig and Fernando de Toro, a theatre semiologist at Carleton University in Ottawa, wrote scholarly articles about it.

Kurapel's *Prometheus* is based primarily on the word rather than on ges-tures or spectacle. Prometheus himself at times has the grandeur of the titanic rebel of Aeschylus's play, and yet he also reveals himself to be egotistical, petty, self-pitying, insecure, brutal, and debased. If he were simply a character with an individual personality, as he might be in a traditional drama, it could be said that Kurapel humanizes him. However, Kurapel has added a much more complex layer onto the work: Zeus, "the tyrant," "authority," and "dictator" is also a stand-in here for Augusto Pinochet, and Prometheus is tortured by his own sycophantic relationship with him. Pinochet's name is never mentioned, but the parallels are evident in the wording and treatment of the charac-ter. Aeschylus's Prometheus initially supported the gods' revolt against the titans in the hopes of a new order and only regrets Zeus's treachery; Kurapel's Prometheus, however, though embittered, still feels both an attraction and repulsion toward the tyrant's power. Whereas the original Prometheus rages nobly while chained for eons to a peak in the Caucasus, Kurapel's anti-hero, attached to a broken-down car, periodically unchains himself, walks around and interacts with other characters, and then chains himself up again: it is he who pathetically and repeatedly chooses his bondage. Jorge Fajardo compares Kurapel's Prometheus to the Chilean bourgeoisie, which simultaneously regrets and defends its alliance with Pinochet.

> On a fait confiance à Prométhée, . . . comme le peuple chilien à la bourgeoisie dirigeante. Mais peu à peu ce Prométhée "montre une autre face"; ses ambitions cachées, sa nostalgie d'être avec les puissants. Peu à peu il se voit obligé de s'expliquer, de se justifier, de crier contre le tyran, de dénoncer sa propre complicité avec lui, de reconnaître que dans le fond il n'est pas pire que le tyran, de se lamenter dans son immobilité tragique, de mépriser et enchaîner son people pour lequel il a risqué sa vie, pour terminer travesti, rendant homage dans cette condition au Che Guevara, et finir par nier tout ce qu'il a été jusqu'à ce moment. (35)

When Io, the young woman whom Zeus has seduced, reminds Prometheus that he also has slept with the god, Prometheus tries and fails to copulate with her, and then kicks and slaps her. He has surrendered himself to the god, both physically and psychologically, and his torture is internalized. Gradually he reveals his own posturing and hypocrisy as he slowly collapses into the most abject humiliation. Even his gift of fire and the arts to humankind in retrospect seems a hollow act of charity, motivated by condescension rather than true goodwill.

The mixed media elements of the play are more centred and less fragmented than in previous works: the strains of Brahms's First Symphony, intertwined with the Mexican *corrido* "Marieta," a folk ballad of the Revolution, periodically float to the surface; there is the acoustic buzzing of the horsefly that pursues

Io and the thunderclaps announcing Prometheus's descent into Tartarus; certain film clips comment on suffering and militarism; and the slides, which
consist solely of paintings by the Chilean surrealist Roberto Matta, as Alfonso
de Toro has pointed out, are perfectly calibrated parallel commentaries on the
action and emotions of the play ("Transversalidad" 248–50). Near the end,
there is also the customary text by another author, in this case a poem by the
Salvadoran revolutionary poet Roque Dalton comparing Che Guevara to Jesus
Christ, which has been set to music by Kurapel himself and, in a devastating
comment on Prometheus's credibility, is lip-synched by him in drag. There is
also the customary transparency and suspension of theatrical artifice of the
play, especially at the beginning in which Prometheus himself announces the
setting and lighting of the play, describes his costume, and announces what
his performance entails. As he suffers from the memory of his humiliation
by Zeus, Prometheus/Kurapel suddenly shouts out to the Stage Manager,
Susana Cáceres, who is also a character in the play: "Susana! Set me loose so
I can go on! Susana! Détache-moi pour que je puisse continuer!" "Set yourself
loose," she replies. "You've done it before! Détache-toi toi-même! Tu l'as déjà
fait auparavent!" (38).[2] These interstices between contrivance and supposed
reality are symmetrically balanced at the play's end, in which Prometheus/
Kurapel also describes the closing stage directions, finishing trilingually with
"Blackout, noir sec, ¡apagón!" (44).

It is language, however, that dominates in the play, for, leaving aside
the bilingual interplay, there is a constant change of tone and register in the
Spanish itself, from the grandiosity and forcefulness of the translation from
the Ancient Greek—which Kurapel has preserved in various parts of the
text, especially toward the beginning (and which, judging from certain uses
of exact phrasing, was probably based on Fernando Segundo Brieva's classic
Spanish translation from the early twentieth century)—to the more relaxed

---

2   This and the following passages from *Prometeo, encadenado* are from the author's
translation, *Prometheus Bound According to Alberto Kurapel, the Guanaco Gaucho*, published in this volume's companion anthology of plays. The Spanish has been translated
into English and the French has been left as is.

colloquialism of exchanges between the characters, the ambiguous insecurity in Prometheus's pronouncements, the coarse language of his exchanges with Io, and his monologues of self-loathing followed by sudden returns to elevated speech and nobility of feeling. Aeschylus's text itself stays on a high register, undercut at times by the passion of Prometheus's anguish; Kurapel's text, on the other hand, is in constant emotional flux, and any translation of it calls for great care in following its shifts and oscillations. "What about me? Destiny won't let me die! Moi, le destin ne me laisse pas mourir!" intones Prometheus. "My torment will continue on until the tyrant falls! Il n'y aura pas de fin à mes maux tant que le tyran ne tombera pas!" Then, after an ensuing film clip, he calls out to Io to remove his chains, and adds, "Come on, you whore! You go down for the tyrant every day, but you can't get these things off me? Voyons, putain, tu couches tous les jours avec le tyran et tu ne peux pas m'enlever ça?" (36–38).

Out of all of Kurapel's dual-language performance pieces, *Prométhée* is the work that exhibits the greatest difference between the Spanish and French texts, to the point that it truly transcends translation and confirms itself as a composite work in which an understanding of both languages is central to the text, thus fragmenting, unbalancing, and undermining the entire bilingual process. The exact reason or intention of these discrepancies does not matter: they are simply a reality of the text and enrich it in many subtle ways. Prometheus tells the Oceanids, for instance, that it was *odio* (hate) that caused dissention among the gods; in the French version, however, he says that it was *colère* (anger) that led to discord. The unilingual spectator or reader is thus left with a single interpretation, while the bilingual is aware of two. Likewise, Io's first speech to Prometheus, in verse form in Spanish, is quite different in French, in which it is left in prose. It is then immediately followed by three more lines of Spanish poetry (here translated into English) without any translation whatsoever. Speaking of Zeus, Io tells Prometheus:

> He who governs
> he who reigns
> leads and commands at his whim

constructing new laws.
Selon les nouvelles lois, celui qui règne aujourd'hui viole les droits
et règne mettant à bas les colosses des temps anciens.
That which yesterday was great and shining
disappears today
from our sight. (21)

This process, curiously, is reversed four lines later, when the Chorus of Oceanids declares:

As reckless as always! You speak rashly and I fear for your fate. Quelle audace est la tienne! L'amère adversité ne la fait pas céder. Et tes paroles s'échappent trop librement de la bouche. Mais moi je tremble, et la crainte aiguë transperce mon âme! Le sort qui t'attend me fait peur. (22)

The overall effect is to create a new level of meaning in which the two languages combine poetry and explanation and ultimately transcend themselves to fuse together into a metatext.

The last three bilingual works by Alberto Kurapel—*Carta de ajuste* (Test Pattern) *ou Nous n'avons plus besoin de calendrier, Colmenas en la sombra* (Beehives in the Shade) *ou L'espoir de l'arrière-garde,* and *La bruta interférence*—continue to focus on the word, though they contain a greater component of ritual and visual symbol than *Prométhée*. Kurapel has now hit his stride and firmly established the pattern of his plays. The use of multimedia techniques is now closely integrated with the text with fewer odd or jarring juxtapositions. Overall, the bilingual aspect is increasingly normalized and the discrepancies, intentional or not, between the Spanish and French versions are fewer, and in fact are eliminated in the last two plays, which were professionally translated into French by Jean Antonin Billard. However, each play deals with an additional use of language that either unites or isolates the characters. *Carta de ajuste*, published in 1991, follows the wanderings of a ragged Blind Man, who evidently lost his eyesight after witnessing a nuclear explosion; a talking flea named Miss Pulga that he carries in a matchbox on his shoulder; and a woman who serves as his *lazarillo*, or guide, as they wander across a post-apocalyptic wasteland and conjure up memories of their former existence in Quebec. The characters periodically pause to rest and create a series of circus-like sketches based on translation and poetry, which are underlying metaphors in the play for the healing force of human interaction, "[D]es écritures qui sont devenues/ des chemins/ dans des futurs dépouvus de/ Temps" (130). These sequences consist of video images of a Quebec poet, followed by his or her offstage voice speaking about the importance of translation both in the poet's own life and in the world; there is then a poem by the author and its translation into Spanish, one of which is sung by the Blind Man. A large part of the dialogue is in poetic form, often on the subject of translation: "En traduisant nous nous traduisons en traducteurs pour finir en une autre traduction" (62). These scenes are punctuated by recollections of having seen various Quebec and Latin American poets, filmmakers, and writers in the streets of Montreal before the destruction, as well as by sessions of Katajjaq, or Inuit throat singing—a further method of achieving linguistic intimacy—among the characters. At the end of the play, the characters, comforted by their shared memories, translations, and poetry, each disappear into their own coffin. Though the end is as bleak as the others in Kurapel's plays, the manifest power of art, translation, and human emotion to mitigate the desolation sets the work apart.

In *Colmenas en la sombra*, published in 1994 as part of a projected trilogy, Kurapel shifts the focus to the Indigenous world in Latin America and to the techniques of spectacle. The play deals with a group of political prisoners who try to displace their suffering by playing out episodes of Latin American history and put on a spontaneous theatre version of the Conquest of Mexico, complete with Aztec gods such as Quetzalcóatl and characters from colonial traditions such as La Llorona. The scenario, of course, allows Kurapel to create a second play within the play that comments and parallels the first one and provides the opportunity for double transparency. Eventually Drolox, their torturer and executioner, appears, attired in a suit filled with odd protuberances and with his head encased in a large glass ball. The play now becomes trilingual, because Drolox speaks an unidentified, incomprehensible third language, evidently that of military authority, which is translated—though only into Spanish, not French—by his armed assistant. This language seems to be fully developed and Drolox even delivers a lengthy monologue in it. In a sense, it represents the reverse of the Hanged Man's monologue in Mapuzugun in *Mémoire 85/Olvido 86*: here, rather than consolation and healing, it acts as an impenetrable semiotic wall that conceals the source of fear. Finally, after ending their play on the fall of the Aztec empire with a scene of Cortés's seduction and subsequent rejection of La Malinche, the Indigenous woman who became his translator and lover and has since been vilified as a traitor in Mexico, all of the players are executed by Drolox and his soldiers. Kurapel's last bilingual play, *La bruta interférence*, returns even farther back to Indigenous mythologies of the pre-Incan cultures of the Andean countries, through which Camilo, a Chilean immigrant to Canada and his companion (or double) Camila, wander in search of Camilo's past, and Camilo finally dies as he is digging for remembered relics. The chief linguistic innovation here is the use of extremely brutal language by two Chilean plainclothes police that kill an innocent couple who are out after curfew: it is the most violence that Kurapel has included in any of his bilingual plays and contrasts drastically with the haunting sincerity of the other characters in the play.

All three of Kurapel's final bilingual plays were well-received, particularly in the academic world, which increasingly recognizes his importance in contemporary Latin American theatre. In September 1991 Kurapel returned to Santiago with La Compagnie des Arts Exilio and, with the help of grants from the United Nations Educational, Scientific, and Cultural Organization (UNESCO) and the Canadian Embassy in Santiago, held a series of performance theatre workshops (a process described in Susana Cáceres's book *L'éveil. Théâtre performance et créativité*), which culminated the following year in staging the first production of *Colmenas en la sombra* at the Tercer Encuentro Internacional sobre Teatro Latinoamericano (Third International Congress on Latin American Theatre) at the University of Santiago (Kurapel, "Montreal/Santiago" 72). The production was a great success: it received five reviews, including two in Chile's largest newspaper, *El Mercurio*, and re-established Kurapel's presence on the Chilean theatre scene. Four years later,

Kurapel returned definitively to Chile, where "he continues his exile" (Kurapel, "Alberto Kurapel"), teaching at several universities, and eventually becoming a professor of New Tendencies in Theatre at the University of the Americas in Santiago. He received the Premio del Consejo del Libro en Teatro (the Chilean National Book Award for Theatre) in 2001, and his work has now been produced in eleven countries on three continents. In June 2011, an international colloquium on his work was held at the University of Chile, and he has given numerous papers and talks throughout Latin America. He also appeared as Claudius in a freely interpreted ("liberamente tratto") film version of Hamlet by the Italian director Michele Truglio in 2001 ("i AM LET On").

Since his return to Chile, Kurapel has published a number of new works. *10 Obras inéditas: teatro-performance* (10 Unpublished Works: Performance Theatre), with a prologue by Fernando de Toro, came out with Humanitas in 1999. It contains shorter plays in Spanish only, written between 1988 and 1997, most of them while Kurapel was in Quebec. Many of the plays are either on Chilean themes, such as the mythological creature El Trauco, said to seduce young girls in the forests of the island of Chiloé, or deal with surrealistic, more intimate situations involving two or three characters, and his customary theatre techniques are used, but much more sparingly. The two final plays, *Círculo en la luna* (Circle in the Moon) and *Antes del próximo año* (Before Next Year), complete the projected trilogy, *América desvelada* (Insomniac America), which he initiated with *Colmenas en la sombra*. Kurapel has also published two books of poetry and two further collections of plays, all in Spanish. Yet, as can be seen in his memoir, *El actor-performer*, published fourteen years after leaving Montreal but dealing mostly with his life there, as well as in other works, the bilingual plays that he wrote while in Quebec are still the centrepiece and defining experience of his work.

MOVING FROM REALISM TO HIP-HOP REAL: TRANSNATIONAL AESTHETICS IN CANADIAN LATINA/O PERFORMANCE

RAMÓN H. RIVERA-SERVERA[1]

Carmen Aguirre's groundbreaking play about Latina/o Canadian experience, *¿Qué Pasa Con La Raza, Eh?* is perhaps the best-known example of Latina/o Canadian theatre in the United States.[2] *Qué Pasa* has circulated in theatre scholarship and classrooms in the US as a testament to the development of a specifically Latina/o theatre in Canada; as an example of the political and aesthetic goals of such a theatre; and as evidence of the shared cultural and artistic codes and conventions between US and Canadian *latinidades*, or public enactments of *latinidad*. To date, critical assessments of this piece have followed a fairly conventional approach in the United States and Canada that advocates for the political inclusion of Latina/o perspectives into mainstream theatre while also celebrating the ways in which Latina/o theatre practice

---

1 I first presented a version of this essay at the New Canadian Realisms Conference organized by Kim Solga and Roberta Barker at Dalhousie University in Halifax, Nova Scotia, 27–29 January 2011. I did so in response to their call to rethink the now all-too-common assumption of theatrical realism as an inherently conservative aesthetic.

2 Guillermo Verdecchia's 1993 one-person play, *Fronteras Americanas*, is perhaps the only other Latina/o Canadian play readily recognizable in US Latina/o theatre scholarship. See Verdecchia, *Fronteras Americanas* in the companion anthology to this collection of essays.

may challenge mainstream theatre's adherence to theatrical realism and the ideological assumptions such practice upholds. I want, in turn, to challenge these conventional approaches. I want to invite scholars of Latina/o Canadian theatre to re-engage with theatrical realism and to produce a more nuanced reading of the interrelationship between aesthetics and politics in Latina/o Canadian theatre.

In this essay, focused as it is on one of the most recognizable examples of Latina/o Canadian theatre, I position *Qué Pasa* as a participant in what Canadian theatre scholars Kim Solga and Roberta Barker have termed "new Canadian realisms": a critical and productive engagement with theatrical realism that acknowledges its dominance of mainstream theatre institutions in Canada and its reliance on hegemonic ideologies of race, gender, sexuality, and nation.[3] I want to propose *Qué Pasa* as an example of how a theatrical realism done otherwise—from feminist, queer, ethnically, and racially affirming, and even post-colonial and critically nationalist ways—can contribute to an emancipatory politics of representation. I posit that realism can indeed be done progressively, even politically, for a Latina/o Canadian and Canadian public.

As I will explain below, one of the most visible engagements with *Qué Pasa* in the United States focuses on the ways in which US Latina/o cultural material is successfully imported and applied to Latina/o Canadian contexts. However, in order to buttress my argument about how theatrical realism done otherwise may provide rich aesthetic options for Latina/o Canadian theatre, I must also launch a critique against an all-too-easy correlation between US Latina/o aesthetics and efficacious progressive politics in Canada. I understand this move as one that takes us from a reliance on an analogic relationship between US and Canadian *latinidades* and into a more carefully situated comparative analysis. That is, I understand the tendency toward anti-realist aesthetics in Latina/o Canadian theatre, and in *Qué Pasa* in particular, as emergent from a critical understanding of the exclusionary and discriminatory history of realism, but also as resulting from the transnational import of affirmatively Latina/o cultural and theatrical practices from the

---

3   See Barker and Solga.

United States. In the case of *Qué Pasa*, Chicana/o popular culture represents the most visible of these imports.

I will turn to Aguirre's play to outline the ways realist codes and conventions are both challenged and deployed in telling the story of Latina/o Canadians in Vancouver. I argue that theatrical realism, an aesthetic generally understood to be unfit for politically progressive Latina/o work, can indeed be put to surprisingly good work. In order to do so, I will turn to representational traditions, historical and contemporary, that have approached *latinidad* across the border in the United States. I suggest that Latina/o Canadian theatre and most other forms of representation of Latinas/os in Canada need to be understood in conversation with the history of Latina/o representation in the United States. This is not a substitution of Canadian context for that of the United States, but a recognition of the interconnections and influences representations of Latinas/os in the United States—in the theatre, but most significantly in the media—have had in the reception of Latinas/os in Canadian contexts. As well, I want to suggest that Aguirre's *Qué Pasa* evidences the ways in which US Latina/o theatre and other cultural practices have also influenced the conceptualization, production, and aesthetics of *latinidad* in Canada. Throughout, I want to suggest that Latina/o Canadian theatrical aesthetics and scholarship about them needs to be understood outside the paradigm of a nationally bound Canadian theatre studies and more in concert with the circuits of travel that characterize the presence of Latina/o communities and cultures on Canadian soil. However, I also insist that the transnational approach ought to remain grounded in the specificities of the local situation.

TRANSNATIONAL CIRCUITS: LATINA/O REALNESS AND REALISM

For the reader interested in the aesthetics and politics of Latina/o Canadian theatre, my focus on Aguirre's play might seem an odd choice for advancing an argument about theatrical realism done otherwise. The 1999 ensemble piece, developed out of Theatre of the Oppressed exercises with a diverse group of Canadian Latinas/os about their experiences arriving and/or living in Vancouver, has been frequently upheld in Latina/o theatre and performance criticism, most notably the work of Chicana/o studies scholar Michelle Habell-Pallán,[4] as exemplary of the "new" phenomenon of Latina/o Canadian theatre. Habell-Pallán and others[5] have lauded the piece for its sketch-comedy style and structure; its incorporation of US Latina/o popular culture (from Chicano hip hop and rock 'n' roll to the rhetoric of migrant activism); and its savvy juxtaposition of hopeful dreams of a "better life" with the stark, and at times violent, realities of a marginal Latina/o life in Canada. The analyses tend to imply that the transnational cultural imports from the United States serve as representational frameworks that at once defamiliarize audiences from the representational optic of the Canadian mainstream (which I will identify as including theatrical realism below) and allow for a closer and demystified look at Latina/o Canadian reality.

Qué Pasa interweaves the stories of a group of Latina/o "characters" and their real-life accounts of the pleasures and pains of living, loving, and struggling for a better life in Canada. Starting with an opening scene about northbound border crossings between Mexico and the US en route to Canada and closing with a scene of communal celebration of inter- or pan-Latino solidarity, *Qué Pasa* focuses on a group of young Latinos in their twenties and early thirties of Guatemalan, Salvadoran, Chilean, Mexican, and mixed Latino and Anglo Canadian descent brought together by the impending deportation of an undocumented Guatemalan farm worker (Rata) and the planning of his marriage of convenience to Latina hippie and environmentalist Dandelion (Rocio). As this narrative develops, we are presented with stories of student activism, inter-Latino and inter-ethnic dating, and the daily hustle of finding community in the city of Vancouver.

While the piece seems to work primarily toward inter-Latino conviviality, it also stages the tensions in assuming such a communitarian formation. For

---

4   See Habell-Pallán's performance review of *¿Qué Pasa Con La Raza, Eh?*, " 'Don't Call Us Hispanic,' " and "Epilogue."

5   See also Verdecchia, " 'We Win.' "

example, in one of the most emotionally heightened moments of the piece, Rata introduces his friend Julio to the rest of the community without realizing he used to be a torturer for the anti-communist forces in Guatemala. Sombra, a young woman in search of her "disappeared" Guatemalan parents, recognizes Julio as one of the culprits of her personal trauma. The group rallies behind Sombra and their confrontation and literal beating of Julio serves as an important pause to the more celebratory narrative of community.[6]

I will return to the scene above at the end of this essay as an example of how realism introduces a potentiality of representation not easily achieved through other means. However, theatrical realism per se does not figure in published evaluations of the piece. In fact, most discussions of *Qué Pasa* as a specifically Latina/o intervention rehearse the idea of experimental aesthetics, hip-hop theatre specifically, as key to the assertive figuration of *latinidad* onto the Canadian stage. The argument goes something like this: In developing theatrical practices that could most appropriately get to the "reality" of Canadian Latina/o experience, *Qué Pasa* bypasses theatrical realism in favour of hip-hop "realness." Habell-Pallán examines in particular "the way the themes, iconography, and sounds of Chicano popular culture resonate in the northern reaches of the hemisphere within a framework of what scholar Angie Chabram-Dernersesian calls a critical transnationalism" (" 'Don't Call Us Hispanic' " 175). In citing feminist Chicana/o studies scholar Chabram-Dernersesian's concept, Habell-Pallán means to focus the cultural and political connections established by people of colour across the American hemisphere. That is, while the experiences of Canadian Latinas/os are fundamentally different from that of Latinas/os in the United States, the cultural production of one group may be significant or productive for the other's articulation of their experience. In the case of *Qué Pasa* it is the performance aesthetics of a US *latinidad* that grounds a critical transnationalism reaching Latina/o Canadian contexts.

The possibility of connection across national boundaries facilitated by aesthetic borrowings and enabled through minoritarian networks not necessarily

---

6   I develop a discussion of inter-Latina/o friction in *Performing Queer Latinidad*.

aligned to hegemonic national scripts yields for the Chicana/o critic a set of potentially fruitful intersections, including analogous as well as intersecting historical contexts for Latina/o life and representation across the US–Canada border. For example, Habell-Pallán discusses *Qué Pasa* along with other do-it-yourself Latina/o noir and punk projects in the US—from Marisela Norte's poetry to Luis Alfaro's performance art to the punk rock group Las Punkeras. The analogical argument between US and Canadian *latinidades* suggests that the representational politics of a Latina/o minority position relative to majoritarian Canadian or US contexts may require similar tactical, subcultural approaches to ensure viability. Punk, Chicana performance poetry, and devised community theatre emerge as similarly aligned strategies across different national contexts. On the other hand, the argument about historical convergence asserts a more concrete connection to a representational hegemony that sees no borders or boundaries. The analogical argument allows Habell-Pallán to understand the works of Alfaro, Norte, and Aguirre as challenges to the "pastoral" view of Latinos she traces back to the "Spanish Fantasy Heritage" in nineteenth-century California ("Epilogue" 206).

PICTURESQUE REALISM: SPANISH FANTASY HERITAGE

The term Spanish Fantasy Heritage was coined by journalist Carey McWilliams in the 1940s. He used it to refer to the embrace of the cultural heritage of Spain, largely promoted by a commercialized Anglo hispanophilia. He proposes that Spanish Fantasy Heritage established an "absurd dichotomy" between earlier Spanish and Mexican settler communities, who are cast as the protagonists of an idealized Spanish past, and more recent Mexican American populations, who assume the position of a less desirable mixed-race present and future (McWilliams 37). In contemporary Latina/o cultural criticism, Spanish Fantasy Heritage refers to the hegemonic representational complex that sought to make sense of the Indigenous, Spanish colonial, and Mexican national history of California after US takeover of the territory at the end of the Mexican–American War in 1848. In acts of fast-paced cultural surrogacy, the Indigenous, Spanish, and Mexican elements of California history and culture were rendered into the romantic consumable picturesque of the "mission revival culture." "Mission revival" sought to indulge in the exotic colour of the territory's otherness—its music, architecture, food, and art, even its landscape—while ignoring the history of conflict and violently implemented inequalities that made the very fantasy of California possible. These representations proliferated in painting and print media, literature, scholarship, theatre, culinary tourism, and popular entertainment in the region.[7]

Spanish Fantasy Heritage is readily identified in what theatre scholar Alberto Sandoval-Sánchez has described as the legacy of the "beautiful señoritas" in the Hollywood Western tradition where the always docile, accessible, and racially indeterminate (Spanish, Mexican, Native American) beauties become embodiments of simultaneously abject and desirable otherness.[8] It is also present in the Mexican-themed musicals of the Padua Hills Theatre players in Claremont, California. From 1931 to 1974 they staged the fantasy of a picturesque Mexican past for generations of gazing Anglo tourists who consumed both the spectacle of *latinidad* while savouring on Mexican fare served by the very performers who serenaded them in their double duty as the wait staff.[9] The role of performance is key to the production of this consumable *latinidad*, in both the representational practices and labour arrangements intimated above. Complex repertoires of dress, gesture, and attitude governed the ways in which Latina/o bodies circulated in these contexts as supposedly authentic stand-ins for their historical predecessors. That is, performing Latina/o in light of Spanish Fantasy Heritage cast performers, many of them Latinas/os, as the "real" embodiments of a fabricated past.

---

7   For an excellent historical account of these representational dynamics in the case of New Mexico and their grounding in the social and economic politics of the time, see Nieto-Phillips.

8   See Sandoval-Sánchez.

9   For an analysis of the Padua Hills Theatre players, see Arrizón, "Contemporizing Performance."

Helen Hunt Jackson's late nineteenth-century novel, *Ramona* (1884), is perhaps one of the most influential and enduring of these representations. It is also a foundational example of the material repercussions of representational practice despite the best of intentions. The novel tells the story of a mixed-race (Scottish and Native American) young woman confronting racial discrimination in the lusciously described backdrop of Southern California's Mexican colonial landscape and architecture. Published two years after her non-fiction book, *A Century of Dishonor: A Sketch of the United States Government's Dealings With Some of the Indian Tribes*, the novel was intended to extend Jackson's advocacy on behalf of Native American communities. However, despite its attempt to marshal the sentimental response of her readership toward the material betterment of an extremely marginalized community, the project propped up an industry of stereotypical representations that produced significant income on the backs of Native American and Mexican imagery and labour.[10] Since its publication in 1884, *Ramona* has inspired pageants; town, school, and street namings; and even the erection of monuments attached to a tourist industry built around the historic buildings and sites that might have served as the "real" sources for the author's "realist" fictional world. What is most significant for the purposes of this discussion is the fact that the success of *Ramona* and many other cultural products of the Spanish Fantasy Heritage tradition created by Anglos not only resulted in representational legacies that framed *latinidad* for generations to come but also supported the continued marginalization of Latinas/os as labourers and citizens by "authenticating" their "real" value through a fictive "realism." The idealized imagery of this fantasy required "Spanish" or Latina/o labour to sustain it.

What is most remarkable about the depictions of California's landscape and peoples within the aesthetic framework of the Spanish Fantasy Heritage is its reliance on a "pastoral realism" that sought to convincingly image the idealization and exoticization of Spanish/Mexican/Native American otherness. In a review of American poetry, Amy Lowell refers to "pastoral realism" in her description of Robert Frost's bucolic representation of American rurality.

---

10   See DeLyser.

She describes Frost's work as "realism touched by idealization" (134). I suggest that a similar kind of aesthetic and rhetorical idealization is at play in Spanish Fantasy Heritage as a realist mode of representation. There is an abundance of descriptive detail in the development of California's amalgamated image of idealized ethno-racial otherness that gains its aura of authority from the confidently performed aesthetics of realism: careful attention to the rendition of dress; selectively placed iconographies signalling Native America, Spain, and Mexico; a preference for meticulously specified interior domestic scenes or landscape panoramas.

The formalist investment in "realism" stands at a significant distance from the actual "reality" or "truthfulness" of its content. This is easily demonstrated in the tension between the real sites that might have served as models for the descriptive detail of Jackson's *Ramona* and the destination tourism it gave rise to and the fictional, and stereotypical, nature of her characterization and narrative. If, as Jill Dolan has stated in the context of the theatre, "realism is prescriptive in that it reifies the dominant culture's inscription of traditional power relations" (*Feminist Spectator* 84), the imposition of pastoral realism as the aesthetic infrastructure for Spanish Fantasy Heritage represents an overt intervention into the public sphere, especially as it so suddenly sought to catalogue and translate aesthetic conventions of racial, ethnic, or national otherness for the consuming gaze of "USAmerican" empire.[11]

REALISM, REALNESS, AND *LATINIDAD* IN THE THEATRE

What has all this discussion of Spanish Fantasy Heritage in California to do with new Canadian Latina/o theatre and theatrical realism, you may ask. I contend that in Habell-Pallán's interpretation of the play, *Qué Pasa* is set to

---

11   I use the term USAmerica as a gesture against imperial geographical constructions of US nationalism. I borrow the term from Gretchen Murphy's usage. See Gretchen's *Hemispheric Imaginings*.

function within a tradition of performance practice and scholarship that supposes the codes and conventions of realism, both pictorial and theatrical, to be ideologically set up against the marginal imaginaries of *latinidad*. Under this argument, *Qué Pasa*'s aesthetic intervention works explicitly against theatrical realism as an institutionalized form of mainstream Canadian theatre historically concerned with white, middle-class experience. Thus, Latina/o performance assumes an anti-realist stance that understands aesthetic experimentation as political intervention.

In reading *Qué Pasa*'s theatrical aesthetics as political praxis, Habell-Pallán draws on the long waves of a history that casts realism as suspect in present practice, especially the tradition of representational stereotype and labour marginalization characteristic of the Spanish Fantasy Heritage legacy. Her analysis focuses on "alternative" forms as challenges to more "traditional" hegemonic cultural conventions in Canada and the US. This anxiety over the aesthetics of realism, so central to the debates around feminist performance in the 1980s and 1990s, has similarly shaped the scholarship on Latina/o theatre in the United States. Performance scholar David Román has described the tendency in Latina/o theatre scholarship to focus on community-based or politically explicit performance over more commercial or mainstream theatrical forms as a "romance with the indigenous" (30). I would further argue that Latina/o theatre scholars, myself included, have favoured experimental aesthetics over theatrical realism.

In a recent essay on Wendy Wasserstein, Jill Dolan reassesses the emphasis on anti-realist Brechtian aesthetics in theatre and performance scholarship championed by materialist feminists. She does not do so to dismiss the well-founded critique of the historical biases in theatrical practice or the promise of experimental technique. Instead she invites us to entertain the political possibilities of more mainstream aesthetics and venues, realism and Broadway among them ("Feminist Performance"). Similarly, I am interested in troubling the almost commonsensical nature of this mode of anti-realist Latina/o theatrical criticism.

In closing, I will suggest a return to theatrical realism, more specifically dance realism, as a potentially significant but overlooked element in *Qué*

Pasa and in Latina/o theatre more broadly. By dance realism I wish to evoke diegetic choreography on stage. This is especially important in the case of *Qué Pasa*, which adopts the physicality of hip hop as its aesthetic framework but includes scenes where vernacular and folkloric dance belongs to the world and the action of the play.

Choreography interconnects Latina/o difference in Aguirre's play. The multiple narratives that make *Qué Pasa* an inter-Latina/o text are held together less by the narrative interconnectivity of the scenes than by an aesthetic framework "imported," as Habell-Pallán discusses it,[12] from US Latina/o contexts, especially Chicana/o cultural production in the Southwest United States. In her review of the piece, Habell-Pallán describes the aesthetic as "a mix of farce and performance art with short dance breaks between acts" (114). It is precisely these "short dance breaks" of hip-hop choreography that I now turn to in order to demystify the assumed interconnection between experimental form and efficacious representational politics. In doing so I set the stage for my brief discussion of what I understand as critical deployments of "dance realism." I am particularly interested in exploring how the staging of dance within the conventions of theatrical realism might present an alternative that offers meaningful engagements with Latina/o embodiments where the aesthetics of realism done otherwise support critical approaches to *latinidad*.

I suspect that part of the investment in hip-hop aesthetics as the framing device for this piece emerges from a real belief in its relevance to contemporary Latina/o youth. As much of the hip-hop music sampled in *Qué Pasa* (Proper Dos, K7, Crooklyn Dodgers, A Lighter Shade of Brown, and others) demonstrates, the genre has offered a critical platform for Latina/o youth in California and elsewhere to voice their disaffection with the marginality of their experience. Invested as it is in notions of "realness"—as more of an attitude or a fidelity, if you will, toward the aesthetic and the lifestyle it signifies rather than a sign of pure identity—hip-hop circulates languages of authenticity that validate poor urban youth of colour the world over as cultural agents with the ability to perform their critique and dissent toward a

---

12   Habell-Pallán uses the language of import in all three of her treatments on the piece.

majoritarian public sphere that labels them as "at-risk" elements.[13] However, the "realness" of hip hop, much like theatrical realism, is also always contextual. It depends on the particularized uses that negotiate what is now a global commercial aesthetic. The resistances and freedoms hip hop announces are always potentially compromised or confused in/as practices of consumption.

CHOREOGRAPHING *LATINIDAD*

Qué Pasa attempts to bank on the aesthetics of hip hop as an alternative to the traditions of theatrical realism. It favours hip-hop aesthetic codes as both a challenge to theatrical convention and a claim to the "realness" of the form as a grassroots vehicle for "representing" *latinidad* from within. However, in installing hip hop as an aesthetic framework without substantively interrelating form to content, *Qué Pasa* rehearses the age-old representational conflation between *latinidad* and dance.

Latinas/os have been historically stereotyped as dancing bodies. As American studies scholar Priscilla Peña Ovalle has remarked, "Latinas-in-motion have mediated the racial and sexual ideologies of mainstream US visual culture since Hollywood's formative years" (340). Ana M. López has similarly observed a historical relationship between *latinidad* and rhythm in her analysis of Hollywood music history. In both instances Latinas/os find themselves caught between "liberation and limitation" (Peña Ovalle 2) in a representational apparatus that commands their performance and the possibilities of agency that mastering movement might enable. What is key in articulating a way through the compromised political terrain of a danced *latinidad* is precisely the nuanced tactic absent from a simple citation of choreographic motif.

Originally choreographed by Barbara Bourget and directed by Aguirre herself, *Qué Pasa* positions dance as a central element of the performance

---

13   For a discussion of notions of realness and sincerity, see my discussion of reggaetón and hip hop, "Musical Trans(actions)."

aesthetic. The production notes to the published script explain that a "choreographer is absolutely necessary for the dance numbers" (54). Used as transitional markers between the three main sections of the play, the dances are described as "hip-hop with a little break-dancing thrown in and should be slick and eye-popping" (54). The notes further explain: "[I]n short, all the movement in the play should be deliberate, larger than life, polished and skillful" (54). The descriptors for the movement seem to indicate both a purposeful intentionality, a clear sense of believable motivation for its origin and direction, and an exaggerated posturing.

The expectations on the choreography vacillate between an aesthetic framework that seeks to defamiliarize, in the Brechtian sense, its audience from conventional notions of theatrical (re)presentation and a realism that advances notions of "truth" about *latinidad* as characteristic embodiment. *Qué Pasa* opens as the first verse of "Never Been to Spain (Until Now)" (a song by Chicano rock 'n' roller and Elvis parodist El Vez) comes on and the "house lights slowly start to dim" (55). Once the house goes dark the music "cuts out" and Proper Dos's rap song "Mexican Power," in "full blast," ushers the stage lights as the full ensemble cast enters dancing "over-the-top hip-hop" (55). The abrupt interjection of "over-the-top hip-hop" choreography accompanies factual information about the company projected onto slides in comic-strip-like thought bubbles, announcing the performance venue and the theatre company's name. These slides are meant to make the means of production and the strategic standpoints of the company explicit. One slide announces: "Like, did you know that none of us are actors? No? We're all like journalists and cashiers and child care workers and high school students and college students and computer geeks and so on and so on and so on" (55). The slide that follows reads: "In other words we're the real thing from the real Vancouver Latino community here to tell you some real stories based in our real selves" (55). The claims to authenticity are here couched in a strategic suspicion of the theatrical and yet reliant on theatre to achieve its truth.

The anxiety over (mis)representation is historicized in subsequent slides that announce the performer's resistance to the label Hispanic, in a repetition of El Vez's song, "[C]ause we have never been to Spain," and their preference for the designation American, " '[C]ause we are all from the Americas" (56). In this brief sequence, Latina/o actors make claim to their "realness" by breaking down the conventions of theatrical realism, literally announcing themselves as non-actors, to both celebrate their "real life" roles as non-actors and display their *latinidad* in "larger than life" hip-hop movement. Furthermore, in their dubbing for the rock 'n' roll parodist lyric they historicize the misperception of Latinos as "Spanish" in a critique that returns us full circle to the Spanish Fantasy Heritage's confused imagination of ethno-racial otherness in the US. However, the disjunction between the announcement of real Latina/o non-actors against the pastoral realism of the Spanish Fantasy Heritage and the realness set in motion by "slick and eye-popping" naturalization of *latinidad* as hip hop keeps dance in a tense, perhaps even compromised, relationship to both the possibilities of critique and the traps of stereotype. This tension is further maintained by the likelihood that the exaggeration of hip-hop movement might in its execution offer an additional layer of theatrical distance from "realness" as an easily achieved truth or simplistically rendered critique.

These tensions recur throughout the play and are not limited to the choreographed hip-hop transitions between scenes. In fact, much of the staging of dance throughout the piece showcases the tensions between dance and *latinidad* as they concern authenticity. They appear in a scene where Dandelion, known by her family as Rocío, and her aunt Mónica discourse about dating, Latin dance, and memory. In the scene, Dandelion remembers a failed date her aunt had arranged for her. Mónica attributed Dandelion's failure to her inability to treat her date in proper Latina/o fashion. She exclaims: "He's a Latin man. You have to know how to treat them." Proper treatment for Mónica entails the successful execution of Latin dance choreography. Neither Dandelion nor her date were able to dance. "He couldn't dance. You had gone on and on about what great dancers Latin men are and he couldn't even keep the most basic beat—" recalled Dandelion. Mónica responds, "Did you teach him everything I've taught you?" This failure to be properly Latin, to execute Latin dance choreography as passed down the family line, prompts the elder mentor to solicit a command performance from Dandelion, to "move like a woman." Dandelion expresses concern for her loss of skill, but her aunt dismisses the concern and reduces her account of proper choreography to Dandelion, "It's all *hips* and boobs!" (83).

The tension between *latinidad* and dance is also at the centre of the problematic closing scene where "all the dancers begin to dance like crazy" in a celebratory affirmative moment where the title phrase of the play, "Qué pasa with la raza, eh?" is repeatedly uttered by the performers in the frenzy of dancing. Here, "crazy dancing" signals community and its constitution in the heightened and chaotic rendition of hip-hop choreography. What results from the scenes outlined here is a problematic choreography of *latinidad* that proposes dance as a sign of Latina/o authenticity while relying on an aesthetic formulation of Latina/o dance that quickly defaults into stereotype. The potential intervention that choreographed movement could offer to the figurations of *latinidad* on the stage is lost in an approach to choreography that does not sufficiently approximate performance protocols in everyday life. I want to suggest below that dance realism, a diegetic presentation of dance on the stage, offers an alternative out of this impasse.

DANCE REALISMS

The other way out of this representational dilemma is modelled from within the play itself. There are moments in *Qué Pasa* where dancing along with others performs inter-Latino affiliation without reducing *latinidad* to surface ornamentation. These scenes are the least "experimental," "do-it-yourself," or "hip-hop real" of the play. In fact, these scenes approximate conventions of theatrical realism where both the choreography and the dialogue correspond to the social world of the scene.

The first scene, and perhaps the least literal in its approach to movement, takes place during the group's confrontation with Julio, the Guatemalan torturer Sombra has identified. As Julio attempts an escape he is pushed to the floor as the group encircles him and "beat him in slow motion" (100). The beating begins a mimetic action and transforms into a Chilean *cueca*, Chile's national folkloric dance characterized by fast back toe tap and individual circular floor patterns alternating with the dancing couple's approach to each other with circular motion of the arms above.

Compared to the more presentational staging of dance in *Qué Pasa*, the movement in this scene, although aestheticized, is representational in a way that approximates the motivation and meaning of the actions. While the circle dance cum beating takes place, Sombra "moves down stage and dances a solo version of the Zapateo from the cueca" (100). In this instance, the display of virtuosic and aggressive step work enhances characterization and prepares Sombra for the angry monologue that follows, in which she vents against Julio's violence toward her family and proclaims her memory of the events and the ability to tell the story as her practice of survival.

The use of the *cueca* here is also in keeping with the tradition of the *cueca sola*, a political version of the dance performed as a solo by Chilean women in front of government buildings and police stations to demand information or the return of their disappeared husbands, brothers, sons, and other family members.[14] The published play itself is offered "for the disappeared" (51). Thus, the use of dance in this scene speaks directly to the cultural and historical context addressed. There is a direct correspondence between Sombra's confrontation of Julio through a *cueca* and a genealogy of confrontations by hundreds of other women who similarly demanded justice for their disappeared.

A second scene stages a romantic social dance between Zap and Skin to the sounds of El Vez's rendition of "Fever." The scene is set up as an arranged blind date (although they know each other), and in keeping with this scenario, the dialogue offers simple flirtations. As they seek to find common ground across Latina/o difference, the couple models a more grounded version of inter-Latina/o proximity or what anthropologists Milagros Ricourt and Ruby Danta describe as *convivencia diaria*: the affectively charged quotidian exchanges out of which pan-ethnic *latinidad* is most likely to arise. The stage directions read as follows: "Zap and Skin stare at each other nervously. They giggle. Zap takes Skin's hand and slowly gets her on her feet. They giggle. They

---

14   See Bolívar.

very awkwardly begin to slow dance, until they are in a full embrace. They giggle. They break into laughter. They kiss. A slide of a child's drawing of a heart appears on the screen" (103). These are the intimacies of inter-Latino exchange lost to the presentational surface of the hip-hop framework of *Qué Pasa*. They are also truncated in the facile stereotyping of "hips and boobs" articulations of Latina/o choreographies. These are the choreographic proximities of a critical dance realism that attends to representation without losing the promise of the aesthetic to fill in where words fail. It is here where dance realism can meet the hip-hop real, dancing along with others into the awkwardness of the embrace.

TRANSNATIONAL AESTHETICS, LATINA/O HISTORY, AND LATINA/O CANADIAN THEATRE

I want to close by returning to the transnational framework with which I opened this essay. I don't want my argument for the potential usages of a critical dance realism to be understood as a dismissal of what can also be gained in the borrowings and conversations between US and Canadian Latina/o cultural materials. I also don't want to leave the reader with a sense that commercially produced cultural materials such as hip hop are politically bankrupt. My investment is less about legislating the work each of these aesthetic traditions and performance approaches might offer an affirmatively Latina/o theatre in Canada than it is about troubling the all-too-easy assumption about their universal utility. In other words, I insist that we recognize the historical legacies of Latina/o representation from Spanish Fantasy Heritage and theatrical realism to hip-hop realness and *cueca* politics. By doing so, I argue, we can carefully account for their manifestations, their potential liberations and limitations, in contemporary US and Canadian theatre.

A Latina/o Canadian theatrical criticism that takes transnationalism seriously needs to work hard to trace the deep histories of Latina/o cultural production in Canada and beyond. For example, the tendency in Latina/o theatre practice and criticism in the United States and in Canada toward

anti-realist aesthetics is rooted in the representational politics of realism modelled in the foundational (mis)characterizations of Spanish Fantasy Heritage.
However, the responses to the mainstream tradition of theatrical realism may
also default into stereotype. Without proper framing or execution, anti-realist practices may fail to offer a viable route into *latinidad*. Latina/o dance
authenticity as articulated in both hip hop and "hips and boobs" social dance
in *Qué Pasa* are examples of this potential failure. Realism, on the other hand,
may be deployed critically to Latina/o ends; the use of the *cueca* and the social
dance choreography in the romantic scene described above offer examples
where this is possible.

A transnational framework for Latina/o Canadian criticism is thus, and
quite significantly, a local one as well. That is, attending to the vastness of
cultural materials circulating under the rubric of *latinidad* and to their manifestations on stage in efforts to render Latina/o experience visible requires an
agile two-step that can account for foundational histories, transnational travel,
and local contingencies all at once. The future of Latina/o theatre criticism, in
Canada and the United States, will depend on our ability to master this dance
of realness without fetishizing any one particular move as the only real one.

FROM ABYSSAL THINKING TO LOVING IMAGINATION IN *THE TERRIBLE BUT INCOMPLETE JOURNALS OF JOHN D* BY GUILLERMO VERDECCHIA

MARTHA NANDORFY

THE NATURE OF THE BEAST: GENRE SWITCHING

This essay is based on my reading of the script of *The Terrible But Incomplete Journals of John D* and an audio recording of a live performance staged in 1998 at Performance Works in Vancouver. These texts differ from each other in the sequencing of segments, with some segments only present in the script and absent from the CD, and they are just two versions of many, illustrative of Verdecchia's fluid approach to adapting texts to audience, moment in history, and locale.[1] As the liner notes to the CD clarify: "This project was originally written for Rumble's live radio broadcast series 'Wireless Graffiti.' "

---

1   *The Noam Chomsky Lectures* and *Fronteras Americanas* were similarly adapted by updating sequences on global political events, as well as by taking into consideration the location in order to reflect local concerns and relevant references rather than touring a Toronto-centric play around the country. The preface to *Fronteras Americanas* describes the play as "a process, part of a much larger attempt to understand and invent. As such it is provisional, atado con alambre. In performance, changes were made nightly depending on my mood, the public, our location, the arrangements of the planets . . . I hope that anyone choosing to perform this text will consider the possibilities of making (respectful) changes and leaving room for personal and more current responses" (13).

Since its inception, it has been reincarnated in a number of different versions and has been shown in a variety of settings, including readings in Vancouver and Victoria, a live broadcast on CFRO Vancouver Co-op Radio from the Vancouver East Cultural Centre, and a presentation at the High Performance Rodeo in Calgary. While working with a script and an audio recording (that is necessarily a reduction of the live performance) that do not quite match might seem unnecessarily confusing, I prefer to discuss both for their individual merits and to explore how structure—based on selection of scenes, sequencing, and elimination of scenes—shapes the textual intentionality, ideology, and ultimately even the world view in each version.

The theoretical framework for my reading of the *Journals* will focus on biopolitical issues highlighted in John D's trip from Canada to Mexico, as well as in his relentless critique of neo-liberalism and of his own complicity in this global system. John D self-identifies as a "privileged Western male" (64) but at first this awareness is glib and evasive of actually relinquishing that privilege. John D suffers from a kind of double consciousness, not related to race, but rather to a rupture between intellect and affect. Most of his monologue is just that, the logorrhoea of a man who is incapable of engaging in dialogue. This inability distances him from others, making his encounters superficial and self-interested. John D's discourse clearly bifurcates his analyses of political relations from his personal relations, mainly focused on his evasion of commitment. As a way to approach both these tendencies, I will borrow the expansive concept of abyssal thinking from Portuguese sociologist Boaventura de Sousa Santos. By abyssal thinking Santos refers to a long and detailed history of Eurocentric epistemology that consistently circumscribes all things European as superior to all other cultures that it represents as savage, primitive, lawless, superstitious, and ignorant. The line that draws this circumscription is the abyssal line that is movable and no longer limited to delineating core and peripheral countries, as John D's experiences will show in both Mexico and Canada. We can therefore look at John D's journey—first to Mexico and then in relation to his life journey—through the lens of biopolitics proposed by Santos. In the first sense, John D crosses the abyssal line and the geopolitical *línea*, as the border is often referred to in the borderlands. He flies

from Toronto, a metropolitan society, from the "Western" side of the line supposedly governed by a dichotomy of regulation and emancipation, to Mexico
City, another metropolitan society that is nevertheless located in a colonial
territory governed by the dichotomy of appropriation and violence (Santos).

On a personal level, John D seems to relate the attitude I refer to as abyssal thinking to a kind of self-destructive postmodern consciousness through
which he recognizes himself as a "fucking asshole" (his ex's characterization)
(58), yet struggles to overcome this accurate and limiting identity. My reading of this drama will focus on how John D might free himself, not to just
"fuck around" as he first fantasizes (65), but to move toward a form of consciousness that must necessarily exceed Santos's epistemological analysis. At
the same time, I propose to juggle the two versions of this text—Verdecchia's
script and the Rumble Productions CD (from here on referred to simply as
the CD)—to see how they might differ in their sequencing, foregrounding
of certain details, and their denouements.[2] These aspects of the two texts I
work with are so strikingly different that I read them as ideologically and
ethically disjunctive.

This interpretive approach does however complicate the issue of genre:
what dramatic conventions do these two versions follow, challenge, and subvert? There is a considerable amount of theory and criticism on radio drama
that would be relevant to the broadcasted versions mentioned above, but the
CD I listened to is a staged performance by actor Norman Armour, accompanied by composer and performer Peggy Lee on cello, directed by Chris
Gerrard-Pinker, with set, sound, and graphic design by Andreas Kahre. The
inside of the liner notes shows a photo of a striking, geometrical set of inter-
locking wooden floors, on which Armour paces, that enclose a small sunken
space strewn with pebbles reminiscent of a Japanese garden, with the cellist
squeezed into an even smaller and sunken space; the caption of the photo

---

2   My use of the term "denouement" has nothing to do with Gustav Freytag's study of
the five-act dramatic structure, since Verdecchia's script is divided into two acts and the
live performance (at least on the CD) lacks any division. Instead, I use the term in its most
basic sense of "unfolding," that is, the clarification or resolution of the plot.

reads: "Thinking about sex all the time . . . " Verdecchia's script has copious signposts (simple indications for the director) signalling sound effects such as traffic, church bells, rain, lowing cattle, and so on, as well as snippets of music from Bach and Haydn to Cuco Sanchez (weepy bolero), Captain & Tennille, and a Muzak version of "Lucy In the Sky with Diamonds." This profusion of sound suggests that the script is written in the spirit of radio drama but that major modifications had to be made for the theatrical performance on a minimalist set dominated by the actor's monologue and supported acoustically only by cello.

Furthermore, the title of the piece invokes a journal, or a written text by John D chronicling his affairs of the "heart-penis" interspersed with rants about the alienation he feels in consumer monoculture. Yet these terrible but incomplete journals do not read as journals at all but as a dramatic script that the reader imagines hearing even without listening to the CD, thanks to the copious indications regarding sound and music. While normally the reader of a dramatic script would also visualize the imagined theatrical performance, the reception of this script tends toward the aural. The reference to journals perhaps strengthens the intertextual allusion to Dostoevsky's *Notes from Underground*, also penned by a cynical narrator who despises himself but despises others even more, puts himself first, makes women miserable, but ultimately lets the reader be the judge. The title also troubles the intentionality of the text with the unusual use of the little word "but" (prepositions can be so telling) in place of the innocuous "and." The interpretation of this shift of prepositions will have to wait for the conclusion but for now we can observe that "but" attenuates "terrible" by suggesting a possible change of fortune or direction. This makes good sense in the script but seems irrelevant in the case of the CD, as I will discuss further on.

JOHN D: WOMANIZER, CYNIC, PROPHET

John D laments that he is more than a third of the way through his life and doesn't know anything about anything (65). Given the optimistic life-expectancy rates these days, that probably makes him thirtysomething, yet he also admonishes himself to settle on the earth; "That, after all, is where adults live. And, like it or not, I am almost an adult" (62). Clearly John D is giving himself a long time to grow out of adolescence, suggesting that he infantilizes himself in order to defer certain behaviours he suspects would involve responsibility and commitment.

He identifies himself as a journalist who seems to be freelance, "[W]ho knows, maybe I'll write an article or two and make some extra cash," (54) while also working on a book. He does not say much about his writing, giving the distinct impression that he writes without passion or conviction. In fact, he explicitly states that writing or working is a form of escapism from having to think about his life, that it is a "DISTRACTION" (emphasis in original, 54). In all he says, John D shows an ironic, underground-man consciousness—never in the moment, never fully in his own skin—he contemplates himself in his despicable acts as if from outside his body. Perhaps this is how the text purports to be: the journaling allows him to distance himself as observer from himself as the observed: "It cools off a bit in the evenings now so this is when I like to write. I say I like to write but do I? Write? I'd like to. Love to. But there's nothing there. Ah, the modern condition. Nothing to say. It's the post-modern condition too. Except if it's post-modern you acknowledge it in a much more ironic way, playing all the while with your signifiers" (59). From this observation of his own—and the general—ennui, he segues into the uselessness of writing for the Canadian market and into a rant about the meaninglessness of television, the dream world of images that has presumably usurped the printed word and, with it, meaning. But he admits—in a typical play with his signifiers—that he did end up jerking off to the exercise show (59). Like the underground man, he lives in a degraded world contemplated through his own degraded vision, while still having flashes of memories about another way of seeing.

In a literary reference missing from the CD, John D apostrophizes the Mexican master of few but powerful words: "Oh Juan Rulfo: What has happened to us? Why does the world press in on us from all sides and water the ground with our blood? Why have our souls rotted?" (59). Rulfo published

one slim collection of short stories and one slim novel—*Pedro Páramo*—whose
eponym is the ultimate cynic, a *cacique* rapist-murderer, impunity incarnate,
and a harbinger of lawlessness in the current narcosphere. Presumably this
reference was omitted from the theatrical performance (and CD) since Anglo
Canadian spectators might not catch it. But Rulfo's vision of institutionalized
corruption and the betrayal of revolutionary values enriches John D's musings
on biopolitics by historically contextualizing the degradation of Mexico. He
travels to Mexico ostensibly to write about the situation there, secretly to try
and have an affair with L.[3] We know he is white, that Mexico reminds him of
this, and he wonders if he feels afraid there due to the fact of being white or
being rich (55), revealing how the abyssal line is drawn and redrawn by those
who can protect themselves from the poor. The abyssal line traverses Mexico
City separating the affluent—John D tucked safely in his taxi, hotel room, and
fine restaurants—from the disenfranchised majority he nevertheless lucidly
contemplates through windows.

As John D's thoughts dart back and forth between the political and the
personal this dichotomy leads him to make gross generalizations about himself that cause a kind of ethical paralysis. His breakup with M and accusations
from A encourage an almost morbid self-analysis: "I am a walking disaster
area. I injure people every time I turn around. Am I as horrible as all that?"
and then he quotes Dostoevsky's underground man: "(*I am a sick man . . . I
am an angry man. I am an unattractive man. I think there is something wrong
with my liver . . .*)" (51). But in this early introduction to his motives he takes
the easy way out by envisioning a binary of two extremist options: "I thought
we were using each other. I thought it was clear" and, "Clearly, the best policy is to avoid human beings at all cost" (51). To bolster the latter option, he
cites Jean-Paul Sartre toward the end of the piece, once he has reluctantly ac-
cepted to do some work with a "commie" radio collective: "Sartre was right.
Hell is other people" (66). He postures as a loner, maybe an anarchist of the
individualistic American variety. He tells R, who pesters him to join the radio

---

3   Imitating Russian literary masters, John D shows his discretion by veiling people's
identity through using only an initial in lieu of their name (including his own identity).

collective, that collectives make him break out in shingles (23). But, fortu-
nately, the journals are incomplete, and other perspectives will prevail . . . at
least in Verdecchia's script. Interestingly, Dostoevsky also defined hell in ways
that diametrically oppose Sartre's statement turned into a trite rejection of
others by John D. Thereby Verdecchia sets up two poles that pull John D in
opposite directions. Dostoevsky's challenge to rationalism based in the abyssal individualistic mind is to assert that compassion is what makes us most
human. He asks, "What is hell? I maintain that it is the suffering of being
unable to love" (312)—an insight that seems completely pertinent to John D,
who nevertheless takes a defensive attitude reductively attributed to Sartre.

John D's main problem seems to be his obsession with sex, with—as he
plainly puts it—wanting the freedom to fuck around, and not finding wom-
en who share his instrumental views of gratification. His trip to Mexico City
introduces a geopolitics based on the widespread notion immortalized in the
lyrics of country singer Toby Keith, that "There's things down here the devil
himself wouldn't do / Just remember when you let it all go / What happens
down in Mexico / Stays in Mexico," relating to a much earlier popular maxim
associated with the mid-sixteenth century amity lines: "Beyond the equator
there are no sins" (Santos).

MEXICO: INFERNAL PARADISE AND LABORATORY OF OUR FUTURE

Echoing the sentiment expressed in the Toby Keith lyrics, John D contemplates Toronto as his plane takes off for Mexico: "In an instant, I was above the
world and its consequences" (53). The day before his departure, he receives a
postcard from his partner, M: " . . . that famous Cartier-Bresson photograph,
Behind St. Lazare—the black and white of the blurry man in mid-leap. She
writes, 'It's over. M.' That's all" (52), giving him the freedom to seek pleasure
wherever the opportunity presents itself. In the script and absent from the
CD, John D has a stopover in Los Angeles, thereby adding more detail to the
transition from Canada to Mexico via the borderlands, a city he describes as

too sad: "And the whole place is like the nightmare of the 20th C. No people on the streets. Everybody indoors or in cars. Buying and selling. Consuming and sleeping and weeping silently into their expensive drinks" (53). John D, like most of us, tends to see the reality before him through his own limited experience and emotionally charged perception, in this case through a brief encounter with a man who has come to LA to find a buddy he hasn't seen in four years, and whose crumpled phone number he carries in his pocket. The man's loneliness makes John D sadder by the minute and he is relieved not to be staying in this city of *desencuentros*, but we suspect that loneliness will follow John D wherever he goes, though he tries to spin it as pride in individualism. John D likes to think that he chooses solitude because people are generally so insufferable. In this assertion of free will he resembles Dostoevsky's underground man, who relentlessly puts himself in humiliating situations just to prove to himself that the utilitarian ideas in vogue at the time are untrue, and that man has the freedom to make himself miserable instead of being driven by instinct to seek well-being.

Sad LA also serves as a contrast to Mexico City, place of exuberant chaos, diversity, abundance; a sensorial orgy of smells, sights, and sounds that John D's lens catalogues in terms of things to eat on the street, things to buy from your vehicle, and other available services. He is not, however, the wilfully ignorant tourist since he also notes that the tradesmen plying their services in the Zócalo are "all unemployed, sitting, in a long row, behind their tools and hand painted signs advertising their expertise and availability. (Three cheers for the miracles of free trade! Three cheers for the miracles of a free market!)" (54). This knowledge of geopolitics and the injustice of NAFTA would seem to carry a responsibility to write meaningful journalism by bearing witness through his first-hand experience, but John D has decided conveniently that the postmodern world is meaningless. His conscience prods him though: "What is it you want John D? What does anybody want?" (57). He admits to wanting money, and a kind of fame, "Just a little glory," but immediately his conscience asks, "And what about all those human beings living on garbage dumps and all the poor and all the hungry and what will your just a little glory do for them?" (57). Here, John D glimpses the colonial territory governed by appropriation and violence and seems aware that his own location on the other side of the abyssal line bears no connection to the possibility of emancipation for the neo-colonized.

Despite his awareness, and empathy even, John D avoids real communication, close contact, the face-to-face intimacy needed to bridge that geopolitical and biopolitical divide. In a brief but telling scene introduced by *"distant street noise and voices,"* he contemplates the possibility of a real conversation but quickly stifles this idea as if it would somehow compromise his integrity, his very being:

> I have my shoes shined. This man who bends below me earns his living shining shoes. How can that be? What kind of living is that? And what is it I feel as I climb into the chair in his little stall? We do not talk though a part of me would like to. I'd like to know where he lives. He could tell me about his children, his wife. Who his favourite wrestler is. (54)

This is very much the way a creative journalist would gather meaningful stories, directly from those who suffer the consequences of an unjust world order that they did not create, those who do not have a voice and can only tell their stories through story gatherers with access to media. "Instead: He shines my shoes. I pull the sleeves of my jacket. I hide behind sunglasses and pretend to read the newspaper. He, ten years or more my senior, a bent man in a wrinkled shirt, serves me, a white man in a clean jacket" (54). Curiously, this scene, so crucial to the theme of intimacy, is omitted from the CD, a mistake in my opinion, since it links to John D's inability to be intimate with his lovers and to the overarching theme of the drama, namely, Antonio Gramsci's insights into the connection between intimate love and the ability to love others you don't know face to face: "Gramsci said somewhere, maybe in a letter he wrote to his wife from prison, he wondered whether it was possible to love humanity, to forge links with masses of people unless one loves someone, some individual intimately . . . I should be so lucky" (63).

This thought, the fact that John D has read Gramsci and longs for such emotion, suggests that John D's callousness is a facade from behind which he struggles to reach out but cannot due to some irrational fear and force of habit. Why does he attribute this possibility of loving someone intimately to luck? Why can he not simply do it? He glimpses insights into the possible origins of these limitations: "I am distrustful like my father. Fearful like my mother. Racist like everybody else" (55). This insurmountable divide between himself and the older man who shines his shoes is symptomatic of biopower or abyssal thinking, yet John D's irritable-mind syndrome disallows him from accepting the abyssal line as natural and necessary. His consciousness struggles to free itself from what we commonly call "conscience," but every detail that enters his eyes functions as an irritant, reminiscent of a principle expressed throughout Dostoevsky's work, that suffering is the root of consciousness.

Verdecchia's script opens with John D venting against "Fucking Hippies" and though a friend of his jokingly interprets this reaction as "[a] pathological aversion to blonde dreadlocks," John D characterizes them humorously as self-indulgent, self-righteous, and cannibalistic in that they appropriate identity markers and practices from other cultures in a kind of false transculturation: blond dreadlocks, playing tablas; this stealing further concretized by the plan to "steal some food from the neighbourhood grocers" indicating a sense of entitlement parading as rebelliousness (51). This scene is absent from the CD together with another one in Mexico that resonates with the same false transcultural experiences, by which I mean the cannibalizing of other cultures to fill the Eurocentric void, all parading as the easy hybridization John D shrewdly discerns in the hippies' appropriation. Yet John D's own journalistic gaze on Mexico is not so dissimilar in its self-fulfilling/other-denying intent: "They say it's easier to get to the moon than it is to cross Mexico City at rush hour. But what do I care about traffic jams. I have dollars. I am rich. I can afford to wait in this taxi" (54).

Despite John D's growing uneasiness and even disgust with Mexico City, Mexico is also a place of hidden meanings half-glimpsed that offer him an alternate understanding and sensibility. On the one hand, it is a toxic, almost apocalyptic zone, clearly situated on the other side of the abyssal line, as Santos maps out in his analysis of how power-wealth-privilege continually draws dividing lines between itself and the other that is thereby relegated to a zone conceptualized as either hopeless or ignored as inexistent. After his initial feelings of coming fully alive in the exuberant vitality of the metropolis, John D whines, "Mexico exhausts me. The filth; the stench; the noise; the thin air; the hard empty bed in my hotel room; the black pebbles of snot I pluck from my nose; the poisonous water; the relentless push pull shove effort (to what end?); the poverty; the scarcity; the scarcity" (55). His first overwhelming impression of Mexico was diversity expressed by the long lists of sights as his taxi drives him toward his hotel. This vitality and diversity, created primarily by the ingenuity of poor people struggling to make a few pesos, is diametrically opposed to the monoculture represented by Starbucks and other corporate chains against which John D rails back in Toronto, unmusically introduced in the script by the corporatized rendition of an originally psychedelic tune:

muzak version of Lucy In The Sky With Diamonds

How I loathe Starbucks and Tea Masters and all those ubiquitous McCafés. The billboard said: Some day all cafés will be as nice as Tea Masters. We have been warned. Some day there will be nothing unique or local left in the world. Some day we will run screaming from the horror of our McLives.

What do people want? They want clean. They want neon. They want merchandise to look at so they don't get lonely while their coffee's being made. They want a place that says, "Come on in, nothing in here will surprise you." (60)

But John D doesn't quite make the connection between the sterile order and requisite lack of imagination in monoculture on the one hand and the vital diversity on the other side of the abyssal line. While in his moments of political reflection he clearly understands the geopolitical machine running the global world order, this understanding remains aloof, "above the world and its consequences" (53), instead of leading him to some personal form of intervention, even if in his sphere that would mean something as simple as conversing with a man who shines his shoes. Geopolitics becomes biopolitics. John D's inability to interact with this other is exactly what is meant by biopower: "[A] form of power that regulates social life from its interior, following it, interpreting it, absorbing it and rearticulating it. Power can achieve an effective command over the entire life of the population only when it becomes an integral, vital function that every individual embraces and reactivates this power of his or her own accord" (Hardt and Negri 23–24). John D's reflections on cafés, and corporate world order versus local community, lead him to formulate an ideal: a just, meaningful, creative space; café as microcosm:

> Give me a café with a polished zinc counter where the espresso machine is run by the owner. A café that reflects a personality, that is part of a neighbourhood, not generic, sterilized, corporate simulacra. Give me a café with sawdust on the floors and black velvet paintings of matadors on the wall. With a dog under the table. Where the guy knows your name. Give me a café where they look at you funny if you ask for a double tall foamy decaf latte with cardamom sprinkles. Like F at Calabria says, "you wanna drink it or you wanna have a bath in it?" (60)

This desire is easy enough to relate to but situates the cozy, intimate place of friendship outside the binary of moneyed monoculture/impoverished improvisation. In this reverie, John D asks not where the coffee came from but under what conditions it was grown and sold. Both sides of the abyssal line irritate him. This is one border that generates no third space and John D becomes an ironic postmodern visionary: "It won't last. Your comfy little life and comfy little garden and comfy little love. I have seen the future and it's ugly" (61). This claim to vision leads to a prophetic rant (Rick Mercer doing John of Patmos) about the coming Walmart Universe. John D's comic hyperbole parodies the hysterical lucidity of prophetic discourse, intermingling his disparate experiences, observations, and snippets of news pushed to absurd yet plausible limits:

> And the highways will be lined with enormous Arnold Schwarzenegger cows, pumped up on Bovine Growth Hormone. And it will be dangerous to get too close to them because sometimes they just explode from internal pressure. And there will be bands of nomadic people roaming the highways, stealing food from dumpsters. And something will go terribly wrong with the water because there will be no more municipal taxes because all the businesses will have disappeared and Super Wal-Mart won't pay taxes or only the barest token minimum and hardly anyone will be employed so they can't pay taxes and the water treatment facilities will break down and we'll get all sorts of terrible diseases from the middle ages like cholera and dysentery and we'll be sick as hell and they will have already dismantled Medicare so forget about that. (61)

It is in this parody of the transfixed visionary that John D ironically proclaims how First World propaganda will represent this final geopolitical Armageddon: "[W]e'll learn how Coca Cola valiantly resisted the evil peasant organizations and workers unions and brought prosperity to the people of Guatemala and we'll get by selling each other junk: old software and hand made earrings and shoe shines and t-shirts with unauthorized sports logos" (61). This is Mexico spreading north, the laboratory of our future, as Charles Bowden calls the border city of Juárez:

> At the beginning of this century, the border of México and the United States was almost a nothing to both nations. Now it is a scream that disturbs the sleep of the rulers in their various palaces. Think of Juárez as a land-locked Hong Kong in the dry desert winds. I have a hunch about Juárez, and my hunch is that this ignored place offers the real "Windows" on the coming times. The future has a way of

coming from the edges, of being created not in the central plaza but on the blurry fringes of our peripheral vision. (*Juárez* 49)

After contrasting Mexico and Europe during the invasion of the Americas over five hundred years ago when "Europe was dirty, cramped and afflicted with plague and war but here [Mexico] was light, gold and the most transparent regions of the air" (56), John D focuses on current and spreading degradation: "But now. Now. Mexico City is a portent of the future" (56). In his visionary state, John D connects what he saw in Mexico with what will come to all parts of the world (thanks to globalization), crossing current geopolitical borders and abyssal lines, while the rich, "(because there will always be rich people)," will manage to redraw the abyssal lines around "a handful of very nice islands and they'll have tons of money and their water will be ok and their food will be good and they'll have exercise bikes and Stairmasters and poor people to tend their gardens and children" (61). John D reports a local anecdote in which he shrewdly shows how the abyssal line between "First" and "Third" worlds is redrawn to divide a sardonically characterized "honourable politician and a great humanitarian" from a self-employed squeegee kid: "Our mayor was approached by one of these car window washers at a traffic light. His response? He rolled down his window and said: 'I'm not paying for that. Get away from there or I'll *run you over*' (italics mine, [meaning John D's])" (60).

This vision of a cold and heartless northern dystopia seems drained of the human possibilities John D almost inadvertently glimpses in chaotic Mexico. Amidst the grinding poverty and general degradation, Mexicans seem to have a mysteriously life-affirming connection to each other fuelled by some poetic vision that has somehow evaded the exploitative drive of the capitalist system. One of John D's self-deprecating rants is suddenly interrupted acoustically by the sound of a "*cello very light, plucked above bridge*" and the vague memory, "In the most polluted city in the world, I came across a poem for a monarch butterfly. Something like . . . *a winged tiger, / burning in your flight / tell me: what supernatural life / is painted on your wings . . .* " (55). John D lapses into Sartrean existentialism: "There is no escape here. No escape from humanity and its struggle," but now instead of seeing these other people as hell, he exclaims that "people are extraordinary," observing that they "have elaborate, elegant greetings here. They stop to eat ice-creams. They laugh, tell stories, hold hands, sing songs of lost love," that they live "as if they were perfectly ordinary . . . as if they weren't miraculous, brave, splendid," and then punctuated by the "*cello hit*" he asks: "What is my problem?" (56). What he seems to admire about Mexicans in their "crumbling, incoherent, chaotic, wilting metropolis" (56) is how they continue to relate to each other, something that John D feels disconnected from to the point of wondering, "Maybe I am nothing more than a machine in the shape of a man condemned to make notes" (54). This image of senseless function links John D's journal of disjunctive notes to Dostoevsky's *Notes from Underground* and, more tangentially for now, to Gramsci's *Prison Notebooks* but also demands audience or reader participation to help answer a series of questions he poses, all revolving around his and our inability or refusal to love: "What is my problem?" (56), "What is going on? How did we come to this? Was nobody paying attention? . . . Why do we cheat? . . . Why do I cheat? Or: Why did I cheat?" (60). While at first sight John D's notes might sound narcissistically self-absorbed and disjointed in that his musings about his own shortcomings seem arbitrarily shuffled with his impressions about places, people, and events, he slowly creeps toward an understanding not only about how the world makes us but also, perhaps more importantly, how we make the world. Despite the poetic and inspiring visions Mexico whispers, John D's emotional state infuses these with his own toxins: "Mexico keeps reminding me of myself of my condition, of our condition. Mexico City is a funhouse mirror distorting, enlarging my anxieties" (56).

Instead of trivializing or merely entertaining, Verdecchia's use of humour allows him to state glaring and unpopular truths without sounding earnest, self-righteous, or preachy. John D flounders through his changing moods and attempts at self-deception, strategically separating political critique from personal contemplation. But the prophetic rants he mockingly delivers are a true weapon. We might laugh at John D's self-indulgence, but we laugh harder at the hypocrites who serve the masters of mankind: "And flunkies like Mike Harris and Milton Friedman and David Frum and all the folk at the Fraser Institute will concoct all manner of ideological and pseudo-scientific explanations for why things are the way they are and why it must ever be thus and me, I will be old and wear my trousers rolled and— This isn't funny anymore" (61).[4]

DESIRE AND FEAR/INTIMACY AND IMAGINATION

While John D's tone and conduct bear a striking resemblance to Dostoevsky's underground man, another compelling intertextual reference that functions as an organizing principle and inspiration is Gramsci's *Prison Notebooks* and letters, similar to but more subtle than how Noam Chomsky's lectures inform Verdecchia and Daniel Brooks's play of the same name.

At first sight and listen, most of John D's journals deal with his feelings of entrapment in the relationship with M and his desire to sleep with other women. He describes this boredom with routine as a process, as something that repeats itself in the same way for the inclusive "you:" "This is how it happens."

> You are sitting at the kitchen table one morning, like any other morning, and you are leafing through a magazine, any magazine: *Canadian Forum* or *Village Voice* or *Bon Apetit* and you converse while you drink your coffee, while you scan the magazine. You venture the odd word, phrase. You make the appropriate gestures to indicate your involvement in the conversation. There is a pause. And you realize you can't remember a thing that has been said. You have no idea what you have been discussing. You have not been listening. You have not heard anything for a long time. (52)

---

4   John D's borrowing of verses from T.S. Eliot's "The Love Song of J. Alfred Prufrock"—"I grow old . . . I grow old . . . / I shall wear the bottoms of my trousers rolled"—suggests a desire for temporary respite from his acute political observations of others. At the same time, John D's mimicry draws attention to his resemblance to Prufrock's self-absorbed yet self-deprecatory meditation on aging.

The actor on the CD stresses the "You" in the last three sentences in a way that suggests the accusatory tone of John D's conscience. A similar scene plays out at a special occasion in a favourite restaurant—"You have nothing to say" (52)—making it clear that John D's vacant presence is ubiquitous and not just a temporary lapse. Accompanied by the cello growing harsher and dissonant to accentuate the next development in the process of separation, he moves from having nothing to say to the final stage: "Now / you argue about music, food, shoe laces, whether you like to dance. You begin to cultivate indifference, callousness, cruelty. You sleep with a stranger. Too late. Fatality" (52).

Routine, the little daily exchanges with his partner, seems to infuriate John D. And toward the end of the drama when he analyzes the end of the relationship he finally asks, "What is going on? How did we come to this? Was nobody paying attention," and what he calls the "64,000 dollar question," "Why do we cheat?" ironically countered by background music (in the script only) by "Captain and Tenille [sic] Love will keep us together, eq'd very flat as if played through a two inch speaker" (60), followed by the cello playing mockingly. He lists several possible responses, one being, "[W]e think it will somehow be different," after which he confronts himself asking, "Why am I using the first person plural? Is this the Royal We? Am I talking about men generally, or myself," an interrogation that leads him to ask more clearly, "Why do I cheat? Why did I cheat?" (60). Much later it dawns on him: "Because it was there. Because I wasn't paying attention. Because it was easy" (63). The problem of not paying attention becomes almost a leitmotif connecting personal and collective political failures. John D reports the incident of the mayor threatening to run down a squeegee kid as symptomatic of a larger social disorder—the inhumane reaction of the rich and powerful everywhere to the multiplying poor spilling over abyssal lines. This incident demonstrates how the abyssal line is redrawn within the realm supposedly governed by regulation and emancipation, a trend that Santos identifies as "the rise of social fascism, a social regime of extremely unequal power relations which grant to the stronger party a veto power over the life and livelihood of the weaker party." But then John D also asks, "What is going on? How did we come to this? Was nobody paying attention?" (60), thereby making a connection between his own private cheating and the mayor's arbitrary use of power, and attributing both to a lack of attention. The underlying logic connecting these seemingly disparate results of inattention eventually emerges as Gramsci's gift to John D and his audience.

Verdecchia further complicates biopolitics through gendering the power relationship between self and other, and by collapsing another abyssal line that does not concern Santos since his rational analysis deals with global politics. Verdecchia shifts John D's fevered questioning back and forth from public to private spheres, also bringing Gramsci's most personal reflections into the analysis and thereby demarcating the abyssal line separating reason from affect. How does John D's cheating on M and others relate to a kind of inattention that carries profound ethical implications for all relationships, global and personal?

Let's start with the personal, which most popular magazines—usually women's magazines—tend to discuss in a historical and political vacuum. Why do we cheat? This question prompts endless feature articles about (especially) male infidelity, and most often attribute it to male insecurity in vague ways that tend not to suggest possible resolutions for couples damaged by this behaviour. In fact, the commonsensical conclusion tends to be that people (especially philandering men) do not change and that only the deluded believe otherwise. Similarly, academic research on the subject falls short of what Verdecchia achieves to illuminate through John D's monologues. A University of Guelph study identifies two factors that predict infidelity in men: "[A] propensity for sexual excitation (becoming easily aroused by many triggers and situations) and concern about sexual performance failure" ("Sexual Anxiety"). As already noted, John D self-parodies the first factor, "a propensity for sexual excitation," by admitting to jerking off to the exercise show on TV, musing, "[T]he most exercise I get is during sex. And I'd be hard pressed to call that regular exercise" (59), and by trying to engage his penis in a futile conversation. Accompanied by cartoon music, he says, "Spent a long time looking at my penis just now. Nothing new to report . . . I was hoping for some answers. But my penis has nothing to say. You can lead a penis to the microphone but you can't make it talk" (65). He then wonders if *all* men are led by their penises and comes up with the same kind of generalizations distinguishing men and women that often characterize these discussions in both the popular and academic spheres: "I suspect men, regardless of orientation, are always led somewhere by their uninteresting tubes of skin. (Hey, look it's pointing the way!) Women? No. Women are much more in control than we are. They know penises are stupid. They know you shouldn't listen to a penis because it has very little to say that's of any importance" (65).[5] Similarly, as quoted in the news report on sexual anxiety, Robin Milhausen says that while "all kinds of things predict infidelity . . . what this study says is that when you put all of those things together, for men, personality characteristics are so strong, they bounce everything else out of the model. For women, in the face of all other variables, it's still the relationship that is the most important predictor" ("Sexual Anxiety"). So up to this point, both the psychological study and John D would seem to agree that men and women are just differently wired and that men happen to be most powerfully motivated by sexual stimuli. John D pushes this further by attributing his own infidelity to the banal fact that the opportunity just presented itself.

As to the second factor, concerns about sexual performance failure, John D exhibits no such anxiety, citing instead the allure of the unfamiliar that seems to coincide (perhaps parodically) with Freud's notion of the uncanny in how the power of the unfamiliar is unconsciously rooted in the familiar: "You meet. Something stops you: the quality of the light; maybe raindrops on hair, on a jacket, on the window pane; maybe the pitch of voice, musical, reminds you of: mother, father, ex, grade four teacher" (62). Milhausen proposes that people with anxiety about sexual performance "might choose to have sex with a partner outside of their regular relationship because they feel they have an 'out' if the encounter doesn't go well—they don't have to

---

5   The absurdity of John D's personification of his penis resonates intertextually once more with Russian literature, in this case Nikolai Gogol's satirical short story "The Nose," in which the nose of an official abandons his face and takes on a life of its own as a vexing adversary. Interestingly, a radio play based on this story was written by UK author Avanti Kumar and broadcast in Ireland in 1995.

see them again" ("Sexual Anxiety"). But in John D's case the anxiety seems not to be about physical performance but something much deeper: the fear of intimacy that disables love.[6] The flip side seems to be the rush created by physically intimate contact with a stranger: "There is a pause in the talk. A hand crosses the great distance and bisects the silence. A hand reaches over, touches the other. A finger traces the veins, the blue snakes in the skin. It begins. Always shocking, new flesh" (62).

In his self-defensive moments, John D rails against reform: "I'm too old. Too slow. Too stupid. Too lazy. I don't want change. Change what? I'm not so bad," and even attributes his behaviour to the spirit of the age: "I'm average. I'm an average, regular, straight, white, fin de siècle kind of guy" (65). But in moments of truthful lucidity, he understands what most psychological studies either miss or skirt around by separating male/female desire and motivations to place the full burden of relational dynamics on women's shoulders, while men are contemplated in isolation on the assumption that they are unable to overcome their overdetermined individualism. To repeat Milhausen's interpretation in this context: "[F]or men, personality characteristics are so strong, they bounce everything else out of the model. For women, in the face of all other variables, it's still the relationship that is the most important predictor" ("Sexual Anxiety"). Verdecchia's character does not take refuge in this gender-based exceptionalism; on the contrary, John D's conscience observes him splitting in two in order to pull off the fraud toward himself and both women: "By now you have absented yourself, you leave, someone else takes your place. You are not there to judge or decide. You no longer sustain even an intermittent mental picture of the other one, waiting, trusting. A failure of the imagination" (62).

---

6   Judging by the number of ads for over-the-counter drugs to enhance sexual stamina or to correct erectile dysfunction on radio stations specifically catering to youth, performance anxiety is likely increasing in young men. Milhausen's analysis might therefore relate accurately to this new problem plaguing youth, but Verdecchia's exploration of fear and anxiety is more compelling since it deals with the disjunction between mind, body, and spirit.

This insight about the predominance of imagination in all matters involving relationships—personal, social, global—emerges in much contemporary writing that examines the limits of reason and knowledge as data. As Charles Bowden repeats throughout his work, we do not need more research, reports, or interviews with experts; "[W]hat is needed at this moment is imagination" (*Juárez* 29), and he insists that imagination is the conduit to an understanding in the flesh, without which the other remains inscrutable and forgettable: "I began to imagine. And after I began to imagine, I argued with the things I saw in my mind. And after I tired of arguing, I finally began to see" (41). While in this context Bowden's emphasis on visual perception relates to the photographic images he contemplates of the brutal murders in Juárez, the root of the word "imagination" is "image," and suggests that only ideas embodied in images—as opposed to abstractions—can lead to meaningful contact and engagement with the other. John D's distraction in the presence of the other, whether that is his partner or the woman he is intent on seducing, signals a failure of the imagination as he admits. His imagination kicks in once M is gone and he faces his loneliness: "I imagine you are here. I imagine we take long walks together. I imagine we agree about everything" (54). But at this point, John D's imagination is limited to what has been lost.

An interesting counterpoint to John D's boredom with routine and the unremarkable gestures and words of daily life appears in the letters Gramsci wrote to his wife from prison requesting her "to write nothing but trivialities,"[7] which Christian Spurrier interprets as the very basis of the relationship: "Even in his anger, his pain at being deprived of the banal routines of family life is evident." Gramsci implores his wife to visit him: "After so many years of a life swaddled in darkness and shabby miseries, after all this, it would do me good to be able to speak to you as one friend to another. If I say this, you mustn't feel that some awful responsibility is weighing on you; all I'm thinking of is ordinary conversation, the kind one normally has between friends" (qtd. in Spurrier).

---

7   Quoted in Spurrier; Spurrier cites these words and others from Gramsci's letters without bibliographic information concerning edition or page numbers.

Gramsci's longing for ordinary conversation about trivialities contrasts dramatically with John D's inability to ever listen to the woman in front of him, whether his partner or a woman with whom he is hoping to have a brief affair. In Mexico City he looks up L for just this purpose but afterward cannot remember anything they talked about. His journaling focuses exclusively on his alter ego watching him put the moves on her while dissecting his ulterior motives and awkward, theatrical behaviour: "And I don't think I really heard anything she said. I was too distracted by her breasts and her eyes and the way she shifted in her chair adjusting her miniskirt. (Lot of miniskirts amongst a certain class of women in Mexico City). And she'd say something and smile and I'd laugh. This too energetic, too forceful a laugh" (55). John D is merciless with himself, representing his motives as contradictory in ways that suggest that he wants to have it easy while also hoping to give the impression of having admirable traits: "That kind of a laugh that I hoped would say, 'Hey, you are very clever and I am very clever and I sure do know how to enjoy myself and lets drink lots of mescal and you'll see what a carefree, reckless, responsible, intelligent, sensitive kind of good time guy I am and why don't we just go back to your place and fuck??!!' " (55). His desire to have an affair with L clearly hinges on craving to feel special and admired as he expresses in the "post-mortem" to cheating: "It is terribly exciting to be exciting again. You tell yourself: this is life" (62).

Here again the hunger for excitement contrasts with Gramsci's understanding of love rooted in the seemingly insignificant details of a shared life. Only after the breakup does John D contemplate those details, feeling the pain of their absence: "I miss you practicing those endless exercises and scales every evening from 7 to 8. / I miss your long hairs in the bathtub. / I miss the smell of your soap" (59). These lines are arranged on the page as verse, "*with cello ff strident, slightly louder than voice*," performed on the CD as discrete details, each followed by a pause for thought; the first two are potentially irritating in a different frame of mind, but the implicit meaning of these images is to bridge the gap between two individuals through signs of intimacy. Much of the *Journals* deal with the meaning of love analyzed in great detail to determine all manner of lame ulterior motives. For instance, when John

D focuses on his strongest desire—"I want you back . . . I want you. I only want you"—he immediately chastises himself on the suspicion that the root of the desire is simply comfort: "[L]ove as nepthene; love as sleeping pill; love as pain killer; love as consolation prize; love as workman's compensation." Here the monologue becomes a dialogue with himself as he struggles to define a truthful understanding of love: "So, maybe that's what it is? What do you think it is? A perfect blissful tantric union? A Jungian mandala of completion? A Sufi equation of transcendental flawlessness . . . Wake up. It's only poetry. It's only fairy tales" (64). John D then remembers that in *The Bluest Eye*, Toni Morrison says "that our love is no better than our self," meaning that love is not perfect or pure; according to John D's own interpretation of Morrison's words, he himself would therefore love selfishly, or in a cowardly way, since he is afraid of intimacy.[8]

This thinking process frees John D from the sterile and overwhelming expectations of idealized (terrifying) love that might have caused him to continually withhold intimacy. The usually strident tones of the cello accompanying his harangues now change to "*very lyrical*" and though all the verses are based on negation, the negation is positive in that it negates abstraction in favour of praxis. Instead of expecting love to do all these things, it dawns

---

8   Fear of intimacy is a frequent theme in Latina/o literatures, often linked to the migrant experience of being uprooted at an early age, of having parents damaged by state terror or grinding poverty, of trying to fit in as a kid in a new homeland that is racist. For instance, all the characters in Junot Díaz's *The Brief Wondrous Life of Oscar Wao* either struggle with the first-hand experience of having home turn into hell—in this case due to Trujillo's reign of terror over the Dominican Republic—or with the legacy of parents who have lost the capacity for intimacy, which they in turn transmit to their children even after migrating to safety. In an interview, Díaz reveals that his Pulitzer Prize–winning novel "follows the quintessential american (in lower case) narrative, which is the quest for home" followed by a series of pointed questions relevant to most Latina/o literatures: "How do people in the Americas who are historically displaced [and] historically have a very problematic relationship to lands that they've either helped colonize, colonized, or suffered colonization on—how do we make a home? How do we make a home given all those experiences and all those ruptures . . . ? Because for many of us a home isn't just a shelter. I mean, how do we find intimacy?" ("*Mil Máscaras*" 3).

on John D that he is responsible for most of them, that they cannot be delegated to love:

> Love will not solve your problems
> will not remember to take the garbage out
> will not walk the dog
> will not pay the rent
> will not save the world
> will not help you sleep
> will not vacuum all the dust balls under the couch
> Blah blah blah John Blah Blah. (64)

While this long list of mundane and quotidian things love will not do might seem insignificant, it turns out to be of utmost significance as long as it is charged with imagination. Once Gramsci started to despair because of the scant replies to his letters from his wife and sons, he put these pointed questions to them: "Was the problem that they were lazy and lacked imagination, or did they no longer care?" (Spurrier), questions that resonate with a similar intent to John D's repeated question, "Was nobody paying attention?" John D's epiphany reveals the crux of what he has been missing all along, the marrow of intimacy connecting individuals through empathy: "I cannot imagine what she must be feeling. I cannot imagine: aye, there's the rub. This consistent failure to imagine anything other than myself at the centre of a story. The inability or unwillingness, to imagine, consider, someone else's story, in this case her story: her pain, her consciousness" (65). This epiphany leads to a new emotion that strikes John D as archaic but which he nevertheless experiences and clearly identifies as "[s]hame. That's what it's called. This feeling is shame (Isn't that an emotion from a different century?) I feel shame when I talk to M" (65). The liner notes to the CD note that, "[F]aced with the collapse of his moral prevarications, he ruminates on the politics of guilt and love," but I would argue that there are significant differences between guilt and shame. His earliest reactions might seem more like guilt in their semi-conscious, physical quality: "Then, later, in the shower, I noticed. I noticed a certain constriction in my chest. Muscles contracting, like a knot, around my heart. Hardening" (62). Guilt is largely self-indulgent and paralyzing in that it causes suffering leading to either denial or self-loathing, but always focused on the self instead of on the wronged other. Shame, on the other hand, is a recognition based on a coming into consciousness about how one's actions have hurt another. In this sense, shame comes from a true awareness of a relational problem and constitutes the first step toward restitution. While much of John D's journals record him wallowing in guilt, escaping into denial, and ranting about seemingly disconnected events, there is real character development in Verdecchia's script in that John D moves from this self-indulgent mode of reflection to a potentially healing epiphany with both personal and collective implications: the simple but not so obvious insight that all relations depend on imagining the other's story.

WHAT'S IN AN ENDING?

In both the CD and script versions of *The Terrible But Incomplete Journals of John D* we see the world almost exclusively through John D's generally impotent gaze, but there is a higher intelligence at work in Verdecchia's script, distancing us from this character to contemplate him from a comic world view. This is one of the most striking differences between the two versions I have been discussing, and while there are plenty of funny moments in both, the sequencing of key moments and how each director chooses to end the piece have a huge impact on the story's intentionality. One of these key moments is a dream sequence in which John D finds himself in a café in Mexico, reunited with his beloved who chats with Gramsci himself. This sequence juxtaposes all positive elements from different sections of the *Journals* as if in some kind of cosmic convergence—an open ending full of promise. "Our hands are in a patch of sunlight on the table top," John D observes, and even this little detail contrasts with its earlier placement in a scene where such a hand belongs to a woman he selfishly and thoughtlessly wishes to seduce. Once Gramsci enters, John D records the dream sequence directly addressing M as "you" instead of distancing her through the use of the third person; furthermore, instead of arguing with her as he had always done, he agrees with her even though he initially thinks she is mistaken: "You say, very matter of fact, 'It's Gramsci. Look, it's Gramsci.' I'm thinking, 'That's not Gramsci; Gramsci's dead,' but I say, 'oh you're right. It is Gramsci' " (67). M and Gramsci yabber away in Italian "like old comrades" and John D seems to become the brunt of their good-natured jokes: "And Gramsci he keeps pointing at me and laughing . . . And I'm laughing and you're laughing and he's laughing and the place fills up with butterflies on their way back to Ontario from Michoacan and we . . . " (67). The oneiric convergence of Mexico (previously abjected Third World) and Ontario resonates through an earlier poem that John D had found miraculous "in the most polluted city in the world"—"*a winged tiger, / burning in your flight / tell me: what supernatural life / is painted on your wings . . .*" (55)—also ending in an ellipsis like Verdecchia's dream-sequence ending to the *Journals*.

This same scene occurs in the first third of the CD where it might establish Gramsci's significance, but does so too early on for the audience to grasp its implications in relation to John D's slow and painful coming into consciousness. This version ends instead with a devastating letter from M to John D in which she vents her hurt and rage and ends their relationship. It is one of the rare moments in the text when another character, significantly a woman, has a voice instead of being filtered through John D's. Taken together with the postcard, "that famous Cartier-Bresson photograph . . . of the blurry man in mid-leap," that she sends him at the beginning, we might imagine this ending to be open for M in that she finds the determination to end a hurtful relationship. But given the bitter tone of the letter, this version of the story is not healing by any stretch of the imagination. It also categorically negates John D's epiphany—"If you had any idea—but then that's the thing, you don't, you didn't, you haven't and you won't . . . Do not phone me. Do not write me. Do not ask about me"—with the soundscape dramatically underscoring the discord she feels: "*Cello plays out ending on dissonant chords repeating again and again, slowly, very slowly diminuendo and resolving to a single bass note*" (58). This abrupt ending creates a marked contrast to the ending of Verdecchia's script, which repeats the butterfly poem, thereby interweaving the insights he has gleaned about the geopolitical and the personal. Furthermore, M's letter appears in the first half of the script, leaving space for more positive developments to unfold.

The overall effect of the two endings based on sequencing leaves audiences with completely divergent interpretations. Santos's concept of post-abyssal thinking can be applied only to the version scripted by Verdecchia, since it traces John D's development from alienated self-interest, both in his dealings with women and with Mexican others, toward imagining the other's consciousness, a movement from fearful self-defence toward intimacy supported by music and sound effects: "*cello begins very light, almost tentative, enchaining phrases . . . cello plays fuller, phrases connecting more and more . . . cello plays out into . . . loon calls which continue and evolve for a minute or so*" coinciding with the migrating butterflies of the juxtaposed dream sequence (67).

The title's ambivalent "But Incomplete" diminishes the terrible aspect of the *Journals* and foreshadows Verdecchia's open ending, subtly suggestive of John D's healing through Gramsci's practical understanding of love: "Gramsci said somewhere, maybe in a letter he wrote to his wife from prison, he wondered whether it was possible to love humanity, to forge links with masses of people unless one loves someone, some individual intimately" (63). This simple insight heals the rift between John D's political insights into an alienating world system that entraps him and his repressed, but finally liberated, capacity for love. Ultimately, John D's slow transformation is ignited by the poetic visions of the everyday that he first glimpses in Mexico. All the binary oppositions created by abyssal thinking become undone once he sees the beauty, joy, freedom, and connectedness on the other side of the abyssal line. John D's journey makes him a border-crosser in the deepest sense, "[O]nce you become a border crosser, then the borders cease to exist" (Bowden, *Inferno* 124). Santos might interpret this as becoming a post-abyssal thinker:

> In sum, I argue that the metaphorical cartography of the global lines
> has outlived the literal cartography of the amity lines that separated
> the Old from the New World. Global social injustice is, therefore,
> intimately linked to global cognitive injustice. The struggle for global

social justice must, therefore, be a struggle for global cognitive justice as well. In order to succeed, this struggle requires a new kind of thinking, a post-abyssal thinking.

But thinking is not what clears up John D's confusion about any kind of struggle, personal or collective. In fact his logorrhoea recorded his disconnection from others all along, despite his incessant thinking. He is much more precise when identifying imagination—the ability to imagine someone else's story—as the key to healing the rift between self and others. And his insights into the inherent value of Mexico germinated in poetic vision, which is not simply cognitive. Gramsci's physical presence heals John D's relationship to M through laughter and through the memory of the Italian revolutionary's ruminations on the necessary connection between loving an individual and loving unknown others. Verdecchia's oneiric ending erases abyssal lines separating self from other(s) even if hegemonic power constantly redraws those lines globally. John D's journey crosses the abyssal line between poetic vision and theory into praxis and enacts Gramsci's leap into post-abyssal imagination.

HASTA LA VICTORIA SIEMPRE! THE PERSISTENT MEMORY OF REVOLUTIONARY POLITICS IN THE PLAYS OF CARMEN AGUIRRE

GUILLERMO VERDECCHIA

In his final letter to Fidel Castro, the Argentinean-born revolutionary Ernesto "Che" Guevara signed off with the phrase, "Hasta la Victoria Siempre," a clever conflation of the familiar closing "hasta siempre," or "forever yours," with the idea of unflagging commitment until victory ("Letter" 387). It might be (awkwardly) rendered as "Yours until the final victory" or "Onward to victory, always." Guevara, of course, did not live to see the final or global victory of revolutionary socialism. Nor does it seem likely that Castro, despite his extraordinary longevity, will either. However, Guevara's exhortation to persist in revolutionary struggle echoes at varying degrees of intensity in a somewhat unlikely site: the plays of various Canadian playwrights. In this essay, I will examine the persistence of revolutionary politics, specifically in the work of Chilean Canadian writer Carmen Aguirre. I will consider how a memory of revolutionary ethics and struggle operates dramatically within the plays to structure characters' responses to their circumstances, and I will also suggest a way to understand what the persistence of this memory of revolutionary struggle might mean currently through the work of philosophers Paul Ricoeur and Alain Badiou.

The political struggles that have marked Latin America since Guevara's death in 1967 have not gone unremarked upon in professional Canadian theatre. In the late '80s and early '90s, plays such as Joan MacLeod's Governor General's Literary Award–winning *Amigo's Blue Guitar*; GG nominee *The Noam Chomsky Lectures*, which I co-wrote with Daniel Brooks; Alisa Palmer's Floyd S. Chalmers Canadian Play Award–winning *A Play About the Mothers of Plaza de Mayo*; and my own *Another Country* considered the deadly political confrontations that erupted in Central America and the Southern Cone. MacLeod's play examines the emotional complexity and volatility engendered when a refugee from El Salvador's terrible civil war is sponsored by a Canadian family on BC's Gulf Coast, while *Chomsky* uses the US-sponsored terrorist war against Nicaragua as a central "case study" in its interrogation of the political economy of human rights as pursued in Canadian foreign policy, and understood and represented by the Canadian media and Toronto theatre. Palmer's play and *Another Country* turn their respective theatrical lenses to the practice of and resistance to disappearance and extra-judicial execution in Argentina's Dirty War.

In the more recent work of Rosa Laborde and Beatriz Pizano, attention shifts to the specifically revolutionary aspirations and struggles in Chile and Colombia. Laborde's celebrated play *Leo* concentrates its dramatic action at "the beginning of a new world" (15) in Chile during the heady, turbulent years of Salvador Allende's presidency (1970–'73). The play makes much of Allende's assertion that "to be young and not be revolutionary is a contradiction in terms" (27), but builds its drama out of its characters' emotional and sexual lives more so than the revolutionary aims, achievements, or failures of the Popular Unity government.[1] Latin American revolutionary struggles play a more central role in the work of Beatriz Pizano. In plays such as *For Sale, La Comunión,* and *Nohayquiensepa,* Pizano, with a team of collaborators, stages the narratives of men and women caught up in Colombia's half-century long, low-intensity conflict. Typically, Pizano and her collaborators examine the brutal consequences of paramilitary and guerrilla action, with a special focus on those displaced by this ongoing (and now only vaguely) political struggle.

---

1   For more on this, see my article "*Leo* at the Tarragon."

It is in Carmen Aguirre's work that we find the strongest echo of Guevara's call. In her work we encounter the most explicit engagement with and, indeed, endorsement of Latin American revolutionary politics. Her plays, *Chile Con Carne*, *The Refugee Hotel*, *The Trigger*, and *Blue Box*, which draw on aspects of Aguirre's life, can be read together as an extended narrative grappling with the memory of revolutionary politics and anti-Pinochetist resistance in the context of exile in Canada.[2] Before describing and analyzing these plays, some clarification of the term "revolutionary" may be helpful.

The word "revolution" has a long history and its usage has shifted over time. Many theorists and activists have considered the term, but it is primarily Guevara whose example and writing did the most to settle the sense of the term in late-twentieth-century Latin America. Prior to the late-seventeenth century, political revolution implied a cycle, an idea derived from astronomy, and signified "the restoration or renovation of an earlier lawful authority" (Williams 272). Karl Marx used the word in multiple senses, sometimes to mean the slow process of social evolution in which one class displaced another and, at other times, to mean political upheaval, quick and widespread social transformation (Wintrop 97). Since the late-nineteenth century, this last sense has become the dominant one. The twentieth-century revolutions, movements, and struggles, such as those referenced in Aguirre's work, are cataclysmic processes that aim at, in Hannah Arendt's formulation, a "*novus ordo saeclorum*" (16). In other words, they attempt not only to overthrow an old order but to establish "an entirely new story, a story never known or told before" (18). However, revolution is not only an effort to seek "a change in a government's basis of legitimacy, . . . in those principles or norms which determine its claims to its subjects' obedience" (Close 2). It is essential to the meaning of modern revolution that "violence is used to bring about the formation of a new body politic" (Arendt 25).

---

2   Aguirre and members of her family were actively involved in the anti-Pinochet resistance. Much of her involvement is described in first person in her memoir *Something Fierce: Memoirs of a Revolutionary Daughter*. The plays, of course, are also a kind of memoir.

In Latin America and elsewhere, violence in the form of armed struggle was understood to be a legitimate and necessary counter to the force or
threat of force that ultimately underpinned every state and oppressive political order. It is this explicit endorsement of armed struggle that distinguishes
Aguirre's work. Flaca in *The Refugee Hotel* explains to her husband: "I believe
in armed struggle. [. . .] I no longer believe you can talk to the enemy. I believe you must fight him" (33). Revolution is opposed to the reform of an
economic-political system, aiming instead at overthrowing it, destroying it,
and building something new in its place.

The "armed struggle" Flaca "believe[s] in" has the aim of ultimately changing "the horrifying conditions of exploitation under which the Latin American
people live" (Guevara, "Guerrilla Warfare" 73). At this point, then, there is a
theoretical parting of the ways with Arendt, who argues that revolutions can
only address "political questions" of freedom from tyranny and oppression
not "social questions" of freedom from necessity (Arendt 52–55). The often middle-class militants of the Southern Cone, inspired by the example of
Che Guevara and the success of the Cuban revolution, who chose the leftist
via armada or path of armed struggle in the 1960s and '70s, would have had
little patience with Arendt's analysis. For them, revolution meant a violent
struggle against the structural violence of poverty, misery, and class privilege.
Aguirre states the matter simply in her confessional play *Blue Box*: armed
struggle was at the root of "our attempt to create a society where the basic
human rights of food, water, health care, shelter, and dignity for all would be
met, even if it cost us our own privilege" (33). In this goal, the revolutionary
left shared ends, though not means, with the more traditional communist
and socialist parties, which, historically, have aligned with the economically
marginalized, preferring social change over continuity, wealth distribution
and social justice over economic performance, and state intervention over
free markets (Castañeda 18).

The revolutionary movements of Latin America of the 1960s represent a
move away from the control of mainstream socialist and communist parties,
as well as a distancing from or reinterpretation of traditional Marxist-Leninist
theory, which held that certain "objective" preconditions were required before

revolutionary action could be undertaken with any hope of success. But for "nearly every Latin American guerrilla movement of the 1960s" (Childs 595), including the "resistance" referenced by Aguirre in her plays, and in which she and her family participated, the example of the Cuban Revolution indicated that "it is not always necessary to wait for all conditions favourable to revolution to be present" because "the insurrection can create them" (Guevara, "Guerrilla Warfare" 71). In other words, revolutionaries no longer needed to correctly parse complex socio-economic conditions to determine the propitious moment or to wait, as Trotsky put it, for the development of a revolutionary consciousness among the oppressed, for the discontent of the "intermediate layers" of society to manifest, and for the ruling class, riven with internal conflicts to "los[e] faith in itself" (311). Guevarist theory,[3] based on the Cuban experience, suggested instead that a small and dedicated insurrectionary cell or *foco* could bring these conditions into being.

For Guevara and the leftist groups that followed his example, the objective conditions were not as important as the subjective ones, "[T]he most important being the consciousness of the possibility of victory through violent struggle against the imperialist powers and their internal allies" (Guevara qtd. in Childs 610). A group of twenty-five trained revolutionaries could act as a "small motor" that would engage the "big motor" of the masses, which would become politicized and join the ranks of the revolutionary forces (Debray 91). Kick-starting mass insurrection in this way would require revolutionary cadres fiercely dedicated to the destruction of an unjust social order and the building of a new one. Guevara describes the revolutionary or guerrilla fighter as an ascetic dedicated to the destruction of an unjust social order and, therefore, committed to the creation of something new. A revolutionary must have, according to Guevara, impeccable morality and "rigid self-control that will prevent a single excess, a single slip, whatever the circumstances" ("Guerrilla Warfare" 72). Not only does the guerrilla provide a concrete example with his own life and actions, but he should—the guerrilla is always figured as male in Guevara's writing—also be able to "give orientation in ideological problems"

---

3   As propounded by Guevara, Régis Debray, and Castro.

("Guerrilla Warfare" 73). He should have a grasp of theory, in other words. Given the hardships attendant on guerrilla warfare, revolutionaries need ideological motivation: social justice and a love of liberty are, for Guevara, the basis of this ideological commitment.

The depth of just such a commitment is felt early in *The Refugee Hotel*. This play introduces us to the Gonzalez family upon their arrival to Canada from Chile, five months after the bloody, US-supported 1973 coup that deposed the democratically elected Marxist government of Salvador Allende. The family, Flaca, Fat Jorge, and their two children, Manuelita and Joselito, encounter several other refugees in their temporary shelter, a hotel in Vancouver. Much of the play is concerned with tracking what happened to both Jorge and Flaca, and trying to understand what the recent events in their lives will mean. Fat Jorge learns in an early scene that his wife, unbeknownst to him, joined the revolutionary movement "two years ago." The timing is significant because it means that she joined only a year into Allende's presidency, when Chile appeared to be on a relatively peaceful, electoral path to socialism.[4] Of her decision to become a revolutionary, Flaca says only, "It had been easy to support Allende as long as there was no risk to take. Those days were gone and I knew we'd have to fight tooth and nail for what we'd achieved so far.

4   Confusion may arise through Aguirre's repeated use of the word "resistance." Technically, there was no resistance yet, as the *coup d'état* was still at least a year away. There were, however, revolutionary or "ultra-left" parties or groups, most of whom supported (though not without reservations) Allende's Popular Unity government, and who were prepared to (physically) defend the advances made by the Allende government. These groups, such as the MIR (*Movimiento de la Izquierda Revolucionaria* or the Revolutionary Left Movement), urged Allende to move more quickly and aggressively along the path to socialism, foreseeing a fierce reaction from the ruling classes and international capital. It would be such a group that Flaca joined. With the military coup, the aims of these groups changed. They now organized to resist Pinochet, attempting to draw the state into guerrilla war, which would eventually bring down the regime and allow for the establishment of a truly socialist Chile. "That's what us resistance members wanted," Aguirre explains in *Blue Box*, referring to the struggle against Pinochet waged by revolutionary leftist organizations in the hope of achieving "[t]he fall of an entire system"—not simply its reform or the deposition of Pinochet alone—"[t]hrough a revolution" (*Blue Box* 8).

It was an honour to be asked and when you are asked to give your life for a better world, you don't say no. You say yes." However, she had to keep her participation secret because of the oath she took when she joined, in which she swore "not to tell a soul. Not even [her] family." The oath, in fact, committed her not to "speak" even "under torture" (40). And, should the torturers "break you," she explains to an astonished Fat Jorge, "only let them do so after enough time has passed to give your comrades the opportunity to run and hide. If you break and give people away easily, you agree to be executed by the leadership" (41).

Fig. 1. Beatriz Pizano as Flaca and Juan-Carlos Velis as Fat Jorge in *The Refugee Hotel.* Much of the play is concerned with tracking what happened to both Jorge and Flaca, and trying to understand what the recent events in their lives will mean. Photo by Itai Erdal.

It is this ferocious dedication to the struggle—as Flaca says, "I would die for what I believe in. I would kill for it too" (33)—and to her fellow revolutionaries that sustains Flaca through her five months in a concentration camp and her time in exile (50). "Many stories" circulate among the "prisoners . . . about the pain [she] endure[d]" without giving anyone or any information away (60). She is, according to the Canadian "hippie," Bill (57), who has just returned from Chile and was also detained, an "example" (60), a "resistance symbol" (61), an embodiment, in female form, of the Guevarist revolutionary ideal.

Her heroism does not mean that Flaca doesn't feel sorrow or loss. She has moments of sadness in this play (as does the activist mother in *Chile Con Carne*), but she is able to move beyond these moments by actively remembering differently. By recalling her engagement in revolutionary struggle, she is able to recontextualize her experience. She recalls, for example, the comrades she was imprisoned with, and shares with others the (revolutionary) card games she learned from them, among them Mao-Mao—not to be confused with Ho Chi Minh-Ho Chi Minh (53). When necessary, at moments of intense emotion, she exercises the "rigid self-control" Guevara listed as one of the qualities of a revolutionary. In contrast, Jorge becomes melodramatic; he makes speeches, picks fights, drinks too much, and generally indulges his emotions rather than contemplating the situation and analyzing it to best understand how to apprehend it (72–75). Where others despair, "I should just kill myself," Flaca analyzes strategically: "If you kill yourself it will mean you have surrendered to the enemy" (75). Even in exile, thousands of kilometres from her comrades and the day-to-day struggle against state terror, Flaca's comportment is always guided by revolutionary standards. Like the ideal revolutionary leader Guevara described in "Socialism and Man in Cuba," "there is no life outside" the revolution for Flaca (226).

Lacking Flaca's revolutionary will and experience, Fat Jorge remains profoundly traumatized by his detention. Throughout *The Refugee Hotel*, he is troubled by a recurring nightmare of his detention and torture by the secret police. Flaca tries to reassure him, insisting "we're here now, Fat Jorge" (91), by which she means the west-end Vancouver "refugee hotel" (a synecdoche for Canada). His physical distance from the agents of state terror in the

Pinochet dictatorship makes no difference; trauma travels. He, unlike Flaca, cannot turn his thoughts or recollections in another direction. He is prey to a terrible power and enigma of memory, in Paul Ricoeur's words, "to make present an absent thing that happened previously" (*Memory* 229).

His nightmares persist through *The Refugee Hotel* and into *Chile Con Carne*, which takes place once Manuelita's family is more settled in Canada. This one-person play focuses on seven-year-old Manuelita, the young girl we first met in *The Refugee Hotel*. The play explores her attempts to navigate the two worlds she moves between: the world of Canadian primary school in the early '70s, Barbie dolls and *Charlie's Angels*, and the world of Chilean exiles—solidarity meetings, fundraisers, hunger strikes, and living with "suitcases packed," ready to return to Chile as soon as "he [Pinochet] falls" (69). In *Chile Con Carne*, Manuelita tells us that her dad still "screams in his sleep. He yells out, 'No, no!' and my mom has to shake him awake." He "dreams at night that the military's going to get him" (67). In Cathy Caruth's explanation of traumatic experience, the "painful repetition of the flashback can only be understood as the absolute inability of the mind to avoid an unpleasurable event that has not been given psychic meaning in any way" (59). Where Flaca is able to situate her suffering and sorrow within the context of an ongoing struggle of which she is a standard-bearer, Fat Jorge is unable to make any meaning of his experience. His inability to locate the originary wounding within any meaning-making paradigm ultimately undoes him.

Unlike Flaca, Fat Jorge's revolutionary politics remain notional. His political understanding lacks a concrete, embodied element; to put it in Marxist terms, there is no praxis to his politics. Guevara did not dismiss the importance of revolutionary theory, but stressed that where "one really learns is in a revolutionary war; every mistake teaches you more than a million volumes of books" (qtd. in Childs 609). Lacking the "extraordinary university of [revolutionary] experience" (609), Fat Jorge cannot frame his understanding of the suffering he has endured. This inability to re-frame is evident in his early conversations with Flaca in *The Refugee Hotel*.

When Flaca reveals her dedication to armed struggle and revolution, Fat Jorge supposes the depth of her feeling arises from "what they did to [her]."

Flaca corrects him. "No," she says. Her commitment arises from "what they're doing to the country [. . .] what they're doing in Vietnam [. . .] what they did in Guatemala" (33).[5] While Fat Jorge personalizes the situation ("[W]hat they did to you"), Flaca, exercising a dialectical praxis, uses her personal experience to deepen her theoretical understanding of revolutions. "They," the torturers who abused Flaca, by, among other violations, cutting off her nipples, become, for Flaca, a synecdoche of the imperialist forces of international capital. Fat Jorge remains grounded in an individualist paradigm, where Flaca sees the struggle structurally, as an encounter between exploiters and oppressed masses; she and her comrades as well as the soldiers who detained and tortured her are part of larger historical forces.

The issue for Flaca, as it will become for the character of Carmen in *The Trigger* and *Blue Box*, is never "what they did to [her]." To be concerned about one's own suffering instead of the suffering of political prisoners (referenced in all four of the plays), or the suffering of "dirt poor Chileans who are maids and construction workers in Argentina [. . .] who are now going to live in the shantytowns of Bariloche, the Argentinian ski resort, whose babies will freeze to death in their cribs in the middle of the night" (*Blue Box* 19) would be "bourgeois," as Carmen puts it when undertaking a similar comparison in *The Trigger*. "And bourgeois is the worst thing one can be" (46). Flaca, like

---

5   Lines cut from the published version *of The Refugee Hotel* made the difference in outlook between Fat Jorge and Flaca even more explicit. She explains that she would "give up: the white sheets and hot lunches and the symphony on Sunday afternoons" as well as "Christmas Eve dinners at The Chez Henry and lazy strolls in Vina [sic] on a hot summer day" for the revolution. For Jorge, this list comprises their life together, but Flaca is firm. "I'd give it up if it meant that the rest of the country could eat, if it meant that the rest of the country could get their vaccinations, if it meant that the rest of the country could learn how to fucking read" (Rehearsal draft). Here, Flaca could be paraphrasing Guevara in "Socialism and Man in Cuba," who argued that a revolutionary's satisfaction "is not a matter of how many kilograms of meat one has to eat or how many times a year someone can go to the beach or how many pretty things from abroad you might be able to buy with present wages" (225). Fat Jorge accuses her of a willingness to "die for others but not for us." Flaca, however, refuses the either/or terms of his argument. "Dying for a better world IS dying for us. IS dying for my children" (Rehearsal draft).

the heroic revolutionary Guevara praises in "Socialism and Man," knows "that the glorious period in which [she] happens to live is one of sacrifice." For the Cuban revolutionary and for Flaca, "[T]he task of the vanguard revolutionary is both magnificent and agonizing" (225). Lacking a powerful lived experience of solidarity in struggle, Fat Jorge knows only agony.

Manuelita understands her father's fear and agony because she also struggles with difficult memories. She remembers, for example, "[I]n Valparaíso when I came home from school and [soldiers] were in the house, checking everything. They were even in the closets." These memories determine her behaviour even now, in Canada: "So now I always check the bathtub before I go pee, just in case there's a military still in there" (*Chile* 67).

Her trauma is triggered one day at school, when "the man from the RCMP" comes to her class "to talk about safety." Picking up on the disdain of her classmates, Manuelita thinks at first that his visit is "so stupid," but then discovers that the generic "man from the RCMP" is in fact "a *huge* gringo policeman, with a gun at his side!" Though the RCMP officer has "a nice warm smile on his face," Manuelita "reads" him through her past experience: "[T]hose are the same grins they wore when they raided our house and tore my favourite doll's head off." Furthermore, her mother has explained to her "that the gringos helped to do the coup in Chile." When the officer shows the school children his gun, which "he never uses," Manuelita hears "a kid screaming real loud. A few moments go by before" she realizes she's the one screaming. She discovers "there's a puddle of pee on my seat," and runs out of class to the safety of her beloved tree "Cedar" after her teacher, "Miss Mitten," helpfully hits her on the head with her flashcards (*Chile* 73).

Though Manuelita suffers trauma like her father, she is, in contrast to Fat Jorge, able to give her wound "psychic meaning" (Caruth 59). Manuelita hasn't simply inherited trauma, she has also inherited her parents' revolutionary politics. It is, in fact, Fat Jorge whom we see teaching Manuelita the codes, language, and values of those politics. Fat Jorge, therefore, is instrumental in the development of a family memory of which Manuelita/Carmen will be the bearer. It is Fat Jorge, for example, who analyzes, in an exegesis worthy of Armand Mattelart and Ariel Dorfman's *Como Leer el Pato Donald*, the television show playing in the lobby of the refugee hotel that has virtually hypnotized his children. He comes in to find them watching *My Favorite Martian*, and although he argues the show and others like it are "designed to keep people from thinking about their world" (*Refugee* 44), he turns the premise of the show into a teachable moment around the phases of human social organization (feudalism, capitalism, socialism, etc.) according to Marxist doctrine. While Flaca provides Manuelita a powerful example, Fat Jorge provides lasting instruction. As an adult, Manuelita tells us, in the epilogue to *The Refugee Hotel*, that she "do[es] what my dad told me to do when I was a little girl: I keep my eyes and ears open" (126), implying a direct link between Fat Jorge and the telling of the very story we are presently witnessing. In important ways, then, Fat Jorge is responsible for the continuance of this revolutionary legacy.

The conflict between the seductions of mass media and the struggle for a classless society, between Martians and Barbies on the one hand and Marx and Che on the other, between the middle-class lives of her school friends and the lives of sacrifice and solidarity of Chilean exiles, plays out in all of Aguirre's work. In *Chile Con Carne*, Manuelita struggles to adapt her revolutionary heritage to her immediate context. Sometimes this struggle plays out as a strategic splitting: "At school nobody knows I dance *cueca*. [. . .] Nobody knows my dad was in jail. Nobody knows we're on the blacklist. Nobody from school, not even Lassie, comes over to my house. Nobody knows we have posters of Fidel Castro and Che Guevara on the walls. Nobody knows about the Chilean me at school" (72).

In time, however, she learns to successfully transform her family's revolutionary codes into agency and activism that serves her current situation. In *Chile Con Carne*, for example, Manuelita organizes her cousin Joselito—figured as her brother in *Refugee Hotel*—and her friends, including Lassie, "the beautiful honey-coloured girl" (64), in various projects including a crusade to save her beloved tree and refuge, Cedar, from development. This multi-dimensional campaign involves industrial sabotage (she and Joselito smash the windows of the bulldozers) and a petition, because, as the family friend Juan of the Chickens points out, "[T]o be an urban guerrilla you must use different tactics for your strategy. It's not all just molotov cocktails and burning tires for barricades" (73). *Chile Con Carne* ends with Manuelita making an explicit link to the memory of anti-Pinochetist resistance in Chile. "Calladita," another family friend whom we first meet in *Refugee Hotel*, "told me about the Mothers and Wives of the Disappeared chaining themselves to the Presidential Palace in Chile." Drawing on that gendered performance of resistance, Manuelita ties herself to her beloved tree with a rope, clutching a hand-painted sign that reads, "Keep Your Dirty Hands Off Cedar," just before the bulldozers approach to tear the tree down (*Chile* 85).

The Aguirre surrogate Manuelita/Carmen transforms even the most harrowing individual experience into social action. Aguirre's extraordinary play *The Trigger*, about rape and its reverberations through a young woman's life, was written "for the 170 victims of the Paper Bag rapist" (13), a violent sex offender who attacked women and children, including Aguirre, in the Vancouver Lower Mainland area between 1974 and 1985. In its examination of the effects of this assault, the play highlights a profound conflict between a leftist revolutionary ethic and individual needs. This conflict, however, is eventually undone or overcome through a creative ability to adapt that revolutionary legacy to new contexts and problems.

Following her rape at gunpoint, witnessed by her cousin Macarena, thirteen-year-old Carmen is taken from the police station to the hospital. As they travel to the hospital, her father tells her: "We will never talk about this. And you will not mention it to anybody. If you tell, people will point. They will shame you. They'll say terrible things about you, daughter" (39). Carmen seems to agree. Above all she cannot allow herself "to feel sorry for [her]self" because within the context of "a Chilean family living in exile that is strictly forbidden" (45). Instead, "[o]ne feels sorry for the executed. For the tortured. For the disappeared. One gives one's life for the cause. But one never gives one's life for oneself" (45–46). Nor, apparently, does one speak of personal, emotional, or psychic needs. Alone in the hospital, she repeats: "We will never talk about this," but her reasons for maintaining silence do not arise from the gendered shame her father seems to want to impose on her. Instead, she performs a political calculus, measuring her emotional needs against the sufferings and needs of others. Carmen, for example, is relieved that the rape will not be spoken of again because "now" she doesn't "have to worry about telling [her] mother who is living in Bolivia, where she hides Chilean revolutionaries in her house." The dangerous clandestine work her mother is doing is "something." What happened to Carmen, in contrast, "is nothing" (40). Though there is obviously a great deal to unpack in this expression—shame perhaps in the "worry" associated with telling her mother, a sense of not living up to her mother's example by complaining about her "petty" problems—there is, clearly, a sense that she so highly values what her mother does she does not wish to distract her with this troubling news.

While this sort of calculus may strongly suggest a dangerous denial and suppression of genuine needs, and although her family seems to have no ability to deal with the sexual violence inflicted on her, Carmen, through her persistent commitment to this revolutionary code that insists on a remembrance of the suffering of others, eventually overcomes the trauma of the attack. Immediately after her rape, Carmen attempts to apply the political models she has inherited to the rapist and event:

> I didn't see the rapist but I don't think he looks like the enemy. He's not a military man, he's not Pinochet, Rios Montt or Reagan. Or the fascist motherfuckers who tortured my uncle in Chile. He's not the hunchback man or Sasquatch. I didn't see the rapist at all. And yet I don't think he looks like the enemy. If you were to see him having a picnic in the park you wouldn't know he's the enemy. Shit. Now I don't know what the enemy looks like. (30–31)

Significantly, her thinking here indicates that she does not dismiss what happened to her as unimportant. After all, the perpetrator is now an "enemy." She recognizes, therefore, that what happened is unacceptable, wrong, something, according to the revolutionary framework in which she has been raised, to be fought. The problem, however, is that the new enemy does not fit the paradigms that she has inherited. The enemy isn't a "classic" fascist. The enemy, she begins to understand, is slipperier, more complex.

Five years after the attack, Carmen seems to have transformed it into a catalyst for a refocusing of her political energies. At eighteen, she is a disciplined early riser ("six in the morning," even on Sundays), "an avid anti-drug crusader," and "an honour roll student," who has "never had a drop of alcohol" (53). She has complemented her Marxist theory with Andrea Dworkin, in a very clear effort to theorize the gendered violence she suffered. In addition to reading radical feminist literature, she is "applying to law school AND medical school" (53). With her firm revolutionary commitment, Carmen seems to have travelled, albeit in less time, as far as Flaca from *The Refugee Hotel*, who overcame her exile and experience in a concentration camp. After "working at the cannery for many years," Flaca "put herself through school again [and] revalidated her degree" to become "one of the top professors in pedagogy at SFU" (*Refugee* 125). Indeed, it would appear that for a revolutionary "any experience is good, comrade," as Rafael, her trainer and superior in the underground, tells her in *Blue Box* (21).

The contrast with characters lacking revolutionary praxis could not be starker. Carmen's cousin Macarena, who witnessed the rape, has "dealt with it all in a very different way. Radically different. She consistently drinks to the point of no return, drugs are a way of life for her, and she belches like a truck driver." In contrast to the studious Carmen, Macarena is "basically illiterate" and "seriously contemplating working the streets." Carmen claims it is her "life's work to go to parties with [Macarena] on weekends, where I make it my chore to make sure she pukes facing down and"—in a move Dworkin might approve—"punch out guys who try to take advantage of her" (*Trigger* 53). Macarena, sadly, seems to be on the same path as Fat Jorge who, we learn at the end of *The Refugee Hotel*, "worked at the steel mill for a decade" and "drank and drank and drank." Eventually abandoned by Flaca, Fat Jorge "drank himself to death on skid row." Having "lived in the open wound" and lacking a revolutionary praxis to help him close it, make sense of it, "he died in the open wound" (*Refugee* 125).

The plays insist on the value and potency of a revolutionary outlook, of a revolutionary paradigm, to guide one in the world. A memory of revolutionary politics is, for many of Aguirre's characters, a touchstone and a framework that is not broken even by deeply traumatic experience. The ability to draw on a revolutionary paradigm, one that subsumes and transforms immediate, personal conditions and situations into an aspect of a larger historical dynamic, are key to the survival and well-being of Aguirre's characters, especially the figure of Flaca and the Aguirre surrogates, Manuelita and Carmen. Characters without a deeply lived revolutionary outlook, such as Fat Jorge and Macarena, cannot overcome the difficulties that beset them and the violence that has been inflicted upon them. The plays stage, then, the transmission of a revolutionary heritage—an embodied example of Guevara's *hasta la victoria siempre*. This memory persists within and across the plays, is transferred across generations and continents, and acts as a source of strength for those characters that are able to live with and within a revolutionary paradigm.

While the plays represent the transmission of a revolutionary impulse, they are also, at the performative level, a medium of transmission for this revolutionary heritage. If we pull back from the texts of the plays to the context of their enunciation on stages today, we might be tempted to ask what is at work in this commemoration of ideals and political models that appear to be, by contemporary standards of political engagement and activism, outmoded at best, if not completely obsolete? Does this quartet of plays signal an unproductive fixation on a lost past? It has been, after all, almost forty years since the Chilean socialist experiment was killed off, over twenty years since "the Sandinistas los[t] the elections in Nicaragua," and the failure of "the final offensive in El Salvador" (*Blue Box* 32); twenty years since "an old comrade" told the playwright herself that "it's all over" (*Blue Box* 33). These events, along with the collapse of the Soviet Union and the fall of the Berlin Wall, conclusively signalled, for some observers, the end of revolutionary ideals (if not of history itself). They ushered in what others have called the "pervasive atmosphere" (Fisher 16) of "capitalist realism," that is, "the widespread sense," the inchoate attempts represented by the recent Occupy and related movements

notwithstanding, "that not only is capitalism the only viable political and economic system, but also that it is now impossible even to *imagine* a coherent
alternative to it" (2). If that is the case, what value does Aguirre's work offer?

Some might be tempted to adjudge these plays as examples of what Wendy
Brown, revising Walter Benjamin, defined as "left melancholy." According
to Brown, "[L]eft melancholy represents not only a refusal to come to terms
with the particular character of the present, . . . it signifies, as well, a certain
narcissism with regard to one's past political attachments and identity that
exceeds any contemporary investment in political mobilization, alliance, or
transformation." These plays and their strong focus on a Guevarist revolutionary code of superhuman voluntarism might appear "attached more to a
particular political analysis or ideal—even to the failure of that ideal—than
to seizing possibilities for radical change in the present" (20). However, such
a judgment could only be sustained by ignoring the many, albeit subtle, ways
in which the revolutionary heritage these plays remember, celebrate, and
transmit is continually adapted to present conditions.

Glimpses of this adaptation can be seen in, among other plays, *Chile Con
Carne*, when, for example, Manuelita's mother tells her father "to grow up"
after she explains that some of the people doing solidarity work with them are
"from the Gay and Lesbian movement" and further explains "what gays and
lesbians are" (74). Dad blushes but Manuelita takes it in stride. "Ever since she
explained what they were, I don't make Barbie and Ken kiss at Lassie's house,"
Manuelita tells the audience. Instead, she "practice[s] with two Barbies kissing.
It doesn't look so bad" (74). With this small gesture, the conservative sexual
politics and the notorious homophobia of the Latin American revolutionary
left are deftly undermined.

Perhaps more significantly, an assessment of Aguirre's work as melancholic mistakes the character of the memory at work in these plays. What
we see here is not the enduring attachment to a lost love object characteristic of melancholia, but what Paul Ricoeur, drawing on Aristotle, has termed
anamnēsis. According to Ricoeur, Aristotilean *anamnēsis* is "active recollection" that requires "effort" (19), and is distinguished from a second modality
of memory, *mnēmē*, which refers to the simple presence of memories (17)

or the "the unexpected appearance of a memory" (26). As Ricoeur asserts, *mnēmē* "rises in the manner of an affection," such as the pity and misery of melancholia, not unlike the depression from which Fat Jorge suffers, whereas *anamnēsis* "exists in an active search" (*Memory* 17). The memory transmitted and referred to through these plays is effortful recollection. Apart from traumatic memories, the memories circulating in these plays are actions; they require voluntary effort.

There are numerous acts of deliberate recollection represented within the plays. While Fat Jorge is prey to the presence of memories (*mnēmē*) over which he has little power, Flaca constantly directs her memory, searches actively for those recollections that will serve her and further her growth. Carmen does the same. A clear example occurs in *Blue Box* when Carmen confronts the Blue Eyed Man, an agent of the Chilean security services who has been following her for days. Almost certain that her identity has been discovered, she "conjure[s] Rafael, the man who trained me in check and counter-check skills" to help her overcome her almost paralyzing fear. The precise recollection of her mentor's "fierce black eyes" saves her "from drowning in [her] terror" (21). Apart from the acts of recollection depicted or related in the plays, the plays themselves often foreground the act of recollection. *The Refugee Hotel*, for example, announces itself as a conscious recollection when the adult Manuelita tells the audience, "It was one week in the month of February. It poured with rain the whole time. It was 1974," and as she describes the decor, the lights come up to reveal the principal characters of the drama and a set that matches her description (17). Taking a step away from the worlds of the plays to look at their construction, we will notice that all four of these plays make use of split-time: Then and Now (and very strongly correlated Here and There) are clearly demarcated in these plays. Chile is There and Then, past, while Canada is Here and Now. This splitting of time-space into a binary corresponds to what Edward Said calls "the unhealable rift" (*Reflections* 173) of exile, but, more significantly here, the time structure of the plays again reveals a temporal sifting, a calculus of the lapse of time, which highlights "the rational side of recollection" (Ricoeur, *Memory* 18). This is not melancholia then, but, as Ricoeur puts it, "[A] sort of reasoning" (18), characteristic of *anamnēsis*.

Rather than melancholia as a "persistent condition, a state, indeed, a structure of desire" (Brown 20), the *anamnēsis* in Aguirre's work involves "returning to, retaking, recovering what had earlier been seen, experienced, or learned" (Ricoeur, *Memory* 27). The effort engaged throughout the plays is directed precisely against the discrediting, and indeed forgetting, of revolutionary values and politics in our present. The active search through the past for traces, fragments, moments, images, models, and examples of liberating visions and practices "moves against the current of the river Lethe" (Ricoeur, *Memory* 27).

Rather than qualify Aguirre's work as melancholic indulgence, we might valorize her insistence on these themes over almost twenty years, in several plays in multiple iterations and productions, as *fidelity*. The philosopher Alain Badiou uses precisely this term, fidelity, to identify an ethical relationship with, or a loyalty to, the past. But Badiou's fidelity is not a "general faithful disposition" (*Being and Event* 233), an aspect of the playwright's personality. Fidelity, for Badiou is, rather, a response to the eruption of an Event.[6] An Event is an occurrence that breaks with or punctures a given situation; a point at which truth, as opposed to opinion or common knowledge, interrupts or cleaves the existing order. An Event is "*situated*—it is the Event of this or that situation—and *supplementary*; thus absolutely detached from, or unrelated to, all the rules of the situation" (*Ethics* 68). In other words, an Event cannot be understood, accounted for, or named by the terms and rules of the context in which it erupts and exceeds. Events are new, and can only be encountered, according to Badiou, in four sites: politics, art, science, and love. He gives as examples of Events: the French Revolution, Schoenberg's invention of the twelve-tone scale, and the creation of Topos Theory in mathematics.

Because an Event exceeds "the anarchic debris of circulating knowledge" (*Ethics* 50), or those already known languages and methods of understanding, there is an element of "undecidability" (*Infinite Thought* 62) involved in the eruption of an Event. Events can only be determined or verified retrospectively,

---

6   I will capitalize Event when used in Badiou's sense to distinguish it from the more quotidian sense of the word.

and, therefore, a kind of a gamble has to be taken (*Infinite Thought* 62) "to decide a *new* way of being" (*Ethics* 41) in response to the Event. Precisely because the Event is "undecidable," fidelity "constructs bit by bit" or "gathers together and produces" the truth of the Event (*Ethics* 68). According to Badiou, "[N]othing places a truth but the succession, point by point, of the choices that perpetuate it" (*Logics* 401). It is the task of fidelity, then, to testify, as it were, to the truth that issues from the Event and interrupts, overthrows, the old order. In testifying, fidelity constructs the truth and defines/defends the Event *qua* Event.[7] The active search of Ricoeurian *anamnēsis* in Aguirre's work is driven by Badiou's fidelity in an effort to recover and reclaim from the past that which the present would admit only as already known and finished, if not denying its significance and value outright. Aguirre's plays, *Chile Con Carne*, *The Refugee Hotel*, *The Trigger*, and *Blue Box*, "place" the truth of the Chilean revolutionary movement and moment.

Aguirre's work is not, therefore, left melancholia. Nor is it simply an act of maintenance, the museological preservation of a history, because there is in her work an implied address to the future. Bearing witness to the historical eruption of a new truth, these works assume a responsibility to the meanings of the past and to the conduction of those meanings to other witnesses (Ricoeur, *Memory* 89). There can be no fidelity to an Event (or to the past) without assuming a charge or obligation to bring the traces and voices (and truth) of that past into the light of the present in the expectation that it will inform the future. As Manuelita says in the prologue to *The Refugee Hotel*, the hotel's "story about the past could inform [. . .] the present and illuminate [. . .] the future" (17). The continued effort to construct the truth of the Event of the Chilean revolutionary movement in Aguirre's work is a future-oriented project. There is an insistence in the dramaturgical interplay between Then and Now in these four works that implicitly "relates the being affected by the past to the potentiality-of-being turned toward the future" (Ricoeur,

---

7   It can only be justified, identified, as Event retrospectively. Previously existing language is inadequate to the task. Badiou claims, "Truths exist as exceptions to what there is" (*Logics* 4).

Memory 381). In this way, these plays in their current enunciation "struggle against the tendency to consider the past only from the angle of what is done, unchangeable, past" (Ricoeur, *Time* 216). Because the Chilean revolutionary movement failed, the Chilean Event remains incomplete, and these plays take on the task of resuscitation; they aspire "to reopen the past, to revivify its un-accomplished, cut-off—even slaughtered—possibilities" (Ricoeur, *Time* 216). By returning repeatedly to its memory, Aguirre and her plays "remain [. . .] true to the Chilean resistance" (*Blue Box* 10) and faithful to Guevara's call to persist until the final victory. Aguirre and her plays seek in the past what they hope may be found again in the future (Ricoeur, *Memory* 435).

RESTAGING, REFRAMING, REMEMBERING:
THE ROLE OF COLLECTIVE MEMORY IN GUILLERMO VERDECCHIA'S *FRONTERAS AMERICANAS*

PABLO RAMIREZ[1]

What happens when you cross two or more borders and acquire two or more sets of memories that nationalism renders incompatible? Guillermo Verdecchia addresses this question in his autobiographical one-man play, *Fronteras Americanas*. Opening to wide acclaim, even winning the prestigious Governor General's Literary Award for Drama in 1993, Guillermo Verdecchia's *Fronteras Americanas/American Borders* seemed like a timely play about the ever closer relations between Latin America and North America. With the dawning of the age of NAFTA, one theatre reviewer described "*Fronteras* [as] the perfect play for the age of globalization" (Reid). However, while goods cross borders with ease, people and memories do not. Written and performed by a Canadian Argentinian, *Fronteras Americanas* is a play about a man, Guillermo Verdecchia, who is unable to situate himself historically in either Canada or Argentina. He has no ground on which to base his identity and no compass that will help orient him.

The problem is that his memories as a Canadian Latino immigrant are unassimiable to a Canadian context. As a Latino, Verdecchia's memories,

1   I would like to thank the editors of Wilfrid Laurier University Press for granting me permission to reprint a portion of my previous essay, which appeared in *Latin American Identities After 1980*, in this volume.

as Mayte Gómez explains in her article, "Healing the Border Wound," are framed by Canada's "ideology of multiculturalism." Despite Pierre Trudeau's 1970s policy of multiculturalism and its emphasis on the existence of many cultures, Gómez claims that there are in practice only two cultures in Canada—the British and the French—that shape social norms and institutions. All other cultures, she argues, are simply categorized as "ethnic groups." Referring, in part, to the 1967 report created by the Royal Commission on Bilingualism and Biculturalism, Gómez explains the implications of this distinction: "In Canada, the British and French are called 'cultures' because they have a social impact, being the creators and safeguards of the material practice of the country. Other groups are simply 'ethnic groups', because their material practice has a limited influence outside their own communities" ("Healing").

Lacking the influence and social impact of the two dominant Canadian "cultures," Verdecchia wonders how Latinas and Latinos in Canada can sustain their identities when "there is no validation, no echo, no correlation forthcoming from the groups in which [they] participate" ("Staging Memory" 2–3). One becomes traumatized when memories have no social meaning and become mere individual acts of remembering. For Verdecchia, being a Latino in Canada becomes traumatic for two reasons. First, dominant Canadian cultures cannot or will not incorporate the memories of Latin America and the experience of migration. Second, representations of Latin America and Latinas/os that do circulate in Canada are, for the most part, stereotypes that distort and warp Latinas/os' vision of themselves and Latin America. These stereotypes form a North American collective memory about Latin America and Latinas/os. *Fronteras Americanas* confronts these issues by dramatizing how a lost, traumatized Canadian Latino can heal his "border wound" through the instantiation of a borderlands collective memory. The inadequacy of official historical discourse drives the Verdecchia character to find a space and framework that will render his memories intelligible. This journey of discovery takes him from history to nostalgia to trauma and finally to the no-place space of a borderlands collective memory. Instead of grounding his memories in nationalist history and territory, *Fronteras Americanas* uses the stage as a locus of enunciation in order to create a space for a borderlands collective memory that is accessible to a national and international audience.[2]

COLLECTIVE MEMORY AND THE BORDERLANDS' "ORIGINAL RELATION TO HISTORY"

Paraphrasing Carlos Fuentes, the character Guillermo Verdecchia[3] explains his disorientation by informing the audience that "a border is more than just a division between countries; it is also the division between cultures and memories" (Fuentes qtd. in Verdecchia, *Fronteras* 21).[4] This explanation is followed by a slide with the question, "Remember the Alamo?" Borders divide memories, and memories—the slide reminds us—become part of historical discourse. Historical discourse helps to constitute what Walter Mignolo calls a "territorial gnoseology" in which knowledge is articulated and legitimated "through the cohesion of national languages and the formation of the nation state" (*Local Histories* 11). Nations work to create a bounded relation between subject and national territory. As a result of this bounded relation, the subject comes into being as an effect of a nation's solidification of space. A person's history and sense of self therefore become intelligible within the inside-outside logic of a bounded space; one is either a native or a foreigner, an insider

---

2   In *Local Histories/Global Designs*, Walter Mignolo uses the phrase "locus of enunciation" as a part of his attempt to transform post-colonial studies from a field of study and Latin America as an object of study to sites of knowledge production. These loci of enunciation engage a border gnosis, a kind of knowledge that is produced by the intersection of two types of knowledge and two perspectives: knowledge from the perspective of modern colonialism (science, philosophy, and rhtetoric) and knowledge from the perspective of Latin American subalterns. To embrace a border gnosis is to transform the subalternized knowledges into loci of enunciation (sites of knowledge production).

3   From this point forward, unless otherwise noted, any mention of Verdecchia will refer to the character in the play.

4   Unless otherwise noted, all citations from *Fronteras Americanas* are from the 1993 Coach House edition of the book.

or an outsider. In her reading of Michel Foucault, Gilles Deleuze, and Félix Guatarri, Kathleen Kirby notes how these three theorists "criticize the solidification of space accomplished by State knowledge" and the manner in which the State works to "capture the flows and snags of escaping movements," thus "compressing mobile heterogeneities into arrested masses" (104).

For Latinas and Latinos like Verdecchia, however, their histories and memories cannot be contained within the nation's boundaries. Due to the proximity of Latin America and the role of migration, Latina/o memories and histories can only be articulated across a break. Unfortunately, because his memories do not contribute to national formation, they are not sustained by state-mediated forms of remembering and commemoration. As Verdecchia, the playwright, explains in his master's thesis, "Staging Memory," without the legitimation of the state and the support of communities, Verdecchia-the-character's memories in *Fronteras Americanas* "do not 'fit' because . . . the social spaces in which he tries to retain, organize and understand those memories are all wrong. Because there is no group interested in them, the memories in *Fronteras* float, disconnected and unstable" (2–3). Memory is social and structural and can only be sustained by a community. Memory is not simply an act of individual remembering; it is both individual and social. When memories have no social meaning, they become mere individual acts of remembering. As a result, traversing borders becomes a traumatic experience because the borderlands subject's memories embrace two or more frames of reference. The state refuses to engage another frame of reference outside of its own for fear of dissolution.

These borderlands memories need a framework for their articulation and reproduction, and this framework is known as collective memory (Crane, "Writing" 1373). It is important to keep in mind that collective memory does not determine what each individual remembers. As Iwona Irwin-Zarecka explains, collective memory is located not in individuals' memories but in the resources they share (4). These resources can run the gamut from official archives, history books, folktales, ads, songs, movies, cartoons, etc. For Amos Funkenstein, collective memory's relation to individual memory is analogous to a person's relation to language. Just as a person may use a shared language to make an individual statement, so can a person use the resources that make up collective memory to create an individual act of remembrance (Funkenstein, qtd. in Klein 133). While North American Latina/o collective memory may be described as a system that is composed of the signs, customs, languages, official histories, and myths of two or more cultures and countries, it is not simply content. Collective memory is a structure that responds to political and social upheaval and crisis by using memories and history to interpret and create the present. It provides a framework that helps to articulate how and why members of a group remember.

However, memory, as Susan Crane insists, is essentially a *historical* process that reconstructs the past in order to create a meaningful present ("Memory" 49–50). Verdecchia wants to understand his memories and experiences historically. Crane calls this desire to historicize one's past "historical consciousness," which is "an expression of collective memory, not because it is exactly shared by all of the other members of the collective but because that collective makes its articulation possible, because historical consciousness has itself become an element of collective memory" ("Writing" 1383). The play performs the articulation of a new historical consciousness in order to imagine and express a Latina/o collective memory that can function as a framework and locus of enunciation that will render Verdecchia's and other Latinos' memories intelligible both to themselves and to others. To create such a framework requires transforming the stage into a borderlands space.

A borderlands space is not a place; it cannot be confined to a border or any particular location. The borderlands is a paradigm that allows Chicanas/os to create self-representations that address cultural amnesia and trauma by representing both personal and collective meanings of loss (Velasco 319). Living between two or more cultural frames of reference requires North American Latinas/os to create a borderlands collective memory. Because a territorial gnoseology cannot accommodate their histories, memories, and experiences, US Latinas/os, Chicanas/os in particular, have formed a border gnoseology: a knowledge system that deals with two or more seemingly antithetical cultural frames of reference in order to open up possibilities of alliance and mixture that have been foreclosed by nationalism. This, of course, is no easy process.

Negotiating between two or more cultural frames of references can cause what Gloria Anzaldúa calls cultural *choques* or cultural clashes and/or shocks. In order to reside in the borderlands, the mestiza "puts history through a sieve, winnows out the lies" and "reinterprets history and, using new symbols, she shapes new myths" (82).[5]

Chicana/o artists and writers, influenced by Anzaldúa's *Borderlands/La Frontera*, have worked to attain a historical consciousness that does not depend on borders for its coherence. To achieve a historical consciousness, the borderlands subject must establish what Michael Hames-Garcia, in his reading of *Borderlands*, calls an "original relation to history": "By an 'original relation' I mean something different from a simple return to the past. An original relation to the past represents a new way of relating to the past; it responds to the needs of the present and remains dynamic, rather than traditional or custom-bound" (113). By establishing an original relation to history and rewriting loss, *Fronteras Americanas* reveals how the borderlands can be a site on which to ground collective memory and to imagine collective memory's transnational character.

FROM THE LIMITATIONS OF NATIONALISM'S HISTORY OF RETURN TO TRAUMA'S HISTORY-AS-DEPARTURE

The necessity of establishing an original relation to history becomes evident in *Fronteras* when Verdecchia attempts to use history to ground and orient himself, but to no avail. He begins with the Triassic period of the Mesozoic Era and then jumps forward to Joan of Arc, Christopher Columbus, Beethoven, Beatrix Potter, Ernest Hemingway, *West Side Story*, and ends with the 1969 Stanley Cup. As Kathleen McHugh points out, Verdecchia's historical narrative "exemplifies the seemingly arbitrary character of (any transnational) historical narration divorced from the perspective of a distinct location or nation" (171).

---

5   A mestiza is a woman of mixed Indian and Spanish heritage and ancestry.

His incoherent historical narrative marks both the power and limits of a territorial gnoseology by revealing the connection between a bounded identity and the construction of a linear, coherent historical narrative.

In Act One, Verdecchia fails to understand the limits of historical discourse and attempts to ground his memories in a national territory. Since he cannot ground himself in Canada, he designates Argentina as his true homeland. Argentina becomes the site of a nostalgic return and comes to represent the nation that will finally give him the fullness of identity that Canada has failed to provide: "After an absence of almost fifteen years I am going home. Going Home. I repeat the words softly to myself—my mantra: I am Going Home—all will be resolved, dissolved, revealed. I will claim my place in the Universe when I GO Home" (36). Verdecchia embraces nostalgia's and history's movement of return to a specific territory or point of origin. In doing so, he establishes a locus of referentiality (Argentina) for his memories.

Pointing to a place or territory as the ground for a historical narrative, however, often obscures the fact that coherency, and the nostalgia that accompanies it, are achieved through an active forgetting and editing. For example, the lack of any reference to the "disappeared" in Argentina is a conspicuous absence in the play. Even the most minimal knowledge of Argentina's political past makes it clear that his family left due to the political violence in the country. As a toddler, Verdecchia the playwright left Argentina with his family at a time when thousands of Argentineans were being "disappeared," tortured, and murdered. His family, he tells an interviewer, was not directly touched by the violence; they did, however, know several families who were (Moll). The violence of Argentina's military regime sets his family in motion and transforms Verdecchia the playwright into a borderlands subject. This past, however, is unassimilated or unincorporated in the autobiographical sections of the play. Instead, the history of political violence in Argentina haunts the play and can only manifest itself in Verdecchia's ever-present irrational fear that the Argentinean government will demand he perform his military service and conscript him.

Having escaped Argentina's period of political violence at such a young age, Verdecchia is traumatized because he is unable to grasp and understand both Argentina's traumatic past and the implications of his survival. Being both a witness and a survivor, as Cathy Caruth explains in her reading of Freud, causes trauma.[6] The person has witnessed death and survived, but it is the very act of survival that prevents a full understanding of death; this is what haunts the victim. In Verdecchia's case, he is a survivor but an uncertain witness. As we find out later in the play when Verdecchia's character recounts his trip to Chile, his return to Argentina is fuelled by the need to become a witness, but Argentina cannot fulfill this need. The Argentinian military government the playwright left as a toddler no longer exists. Instead he grasps the legacy of political violence in Latin America by moving away from a dependence on Argentina as a nostalgic locus of referentiality.

Instead of witnessing political violence in Argentina, he witnesses a shooting in Chile. He visits Chile in 1990, only one year after the Pinochet regime has fallen. However, Chile still resembles a police state for Verdecchia: "I count all the policemen, one per block it seems. What was it like under Pinochet? A policeman in every house?" (38). On his first night there, Verdecchia is awakened by gunshots. He looks down from his hotel room and sees a man writhing in pain on the sidewalk below, his shirt soaked with blood. With a telephoto lens, Verdecchia takes several photographs of this man who tries in vain to stand up. Police gather but no ambulance ever comes, and the man dies. To Verdecchia, it seems that the man dies due to police indifference.

The shooting reintroduces or rearticulates Verdecchia's traumatic past. Trauma, which is the Greek word for "wound," allows Verdecchia to finally address his "border wound." As with most cases of trauma, Verdecchia gains no immediate understanding at the time and place of the shooting. Experiencing the original event at the time and place of the event does not provide us with

---

6   I will be applying Cathy Caruth's theories of trauma to read the play. For a more in-depth look at the issue of trauma, please see Caruth's *Unclaimed Experience*. In *Beyond the Pleasure Principle*, Freud explains trauma with the following example: a man witnesses a train accident that involves the death of several passengers. He leaves the site of the accident, shaken, but otherwise fine. A few weeks later, he goes into shock. What returns to haunt the victim is not the reality of the violent event but the reality that the violence is not fully known (6).

knowledge of the event itself. It is only through historical recuperation—rather than referential authority—that we come to understand an event. As Caruth explains, "Through the notion of trauma, I will argue we can understand that a rethinking of reference is aimed not at eliminating history but resituating it in our understanding, that is, at precisely permitting *history* to arise where *immediate understanding* may not" (11).

For Caruth, trauma "is borne by the act of departure"; "it is the act of leaving that constitutes its central and enigmatic core" (22). Departure, then, constitutes Verdecchia's trauma, but it is what also makes it possible for him to overcome his trauma. Departure holds the key to dealing with trauma because a traumatic event can only gain meaning in another place and time. To deal with a traumatic event one must depart in order to enter historical time. To think of a traumatic event in historical and collective terms means "rethinking of individual trauma as an experience of departure" (Caruth 67). Only at a remove, brought about by departure, are we able to assign historical value to an event.

The shooting in Chile helps Verdecchia understand that in order to orient himself he must *re-enact his departure* from Latin America. Verdecchia can only understand the implications of his first departure by repeating it. This time when he leaves Latin America, he departs not as a toddler but as a clear witness and survivor of a traumatic event. When he witnesses the man's death, he realizes that he needed to witness this in order to understand the violence that drove his family from Argentina. It is this need that makes him feel responsible for the shooting. As he takes photograph after photograph of the dying man, using a variety of lenses, Verdecchia states, "I take photographs and I realize that I have willed this to happen" (39). He has "willed" this murder, so he can finally become a witness and come to grips with the nature of his first departure.

A traumatic event must be transformed into "a historical experience of a survival" because it exceeds "the grasp of the one who survives" (Caruth 67). This transformation is necessary because both the traumatic event and history cannot be articulated within the boundaries of the individual (Caruth 67). To give a traumatic event historical meaning, in other words, one must implicate others, transforming an individual experience of trauma into a collective experience and narrative (Caruth 18). Unfortunately, what Verdecchia witnesses in Latin America, which becomes connected to the history of violence that set his migration in motion, cannot become part of Canadian historical discourse. He belongs to an ethnic group and is not a member of one of the two dominant cultural groups in Canada. The violence in Latin America initiated the first wave of Latin American immigration to Canada, but this thread of Latin American history has not been fully incorporated into a Canadian historical narrative. While Argentina as a nation has worked to come to terms with its violent past, Argentinian immigrants like Verdecchia have not been part of this project to reconcile the past with the present. Living in Canada, Argentina's national historical project cannot help Verdecchia incorporate his past into the present.

Without a space that will allow him to sustain and reproduce his memories, his memories must reside in himself. In Freudian terms, his memories have not been given a psychic meaning, so they enter Verdecchia as something foreign and unintelligible. As a result, his memories are reduced to and located in a sickly body part, transforming his body into something it was never meant to be: an archive. The audience is presented with charts of the human brain and X-rays as Verdecchia attempts to pathologize, locate, quarantine, and eventually expel memory. He tells the doctor to find the source of his nostalgia and surgically remove it. The doctor doesn't find anything, but Verdecchia tells the audience, "I wasn't fooled. I am a direct descendant of two people who once ate an armadillo—armadillo has a half-life of 2,000 years—you can't tell me that isn't in my bloodstream. Evita Peron once kissed my mother and that night she began to feel her cheek rot. You can't tell me that hasn't altered my DNA" (52). The failure to territorialize his memories transforms history and memory into a remainder—an object that has been preserved in Verdecchia's body, undigested. After the physician tells him that there is nothing physically wrong with him, Verdecchia goes to a therapist and confesses, "I feel nostalgia for things I never knew—I feel connected to things that I have no connection with, responsible, involved, implicated in things that happen thousands of miles away" (69). Unfortunately, the therapist focuses on Verdecchia's individual psyche, asking him to give an autobiographical account of his childhood and sex life. This individualist approach fails to cure Verdecchia of the numbness that threatens to immobilize him.

THE STAGE AS THE BORDERLANDS NO-PLACE SPACE OF COLLECTIVE MEMORY

Like Cathy Caruth, Anzaldúa believes that in order to overcome trauma (what she calls the border wound), one must historicize one's memories and connect them to a collective. Where she and Caruth differ, however, is the path one must take to do this. Verdecchia's trauma, as the *brujo* (witch doctor/healer) in the play tells him, is a border wound, and a border wound cannot be cured by nationalist historiography. This is because a border wound, Anzaldúa explains, comes from living on the border between two or more cultures that grate against each other, creating an open, bleeding wound that traumatizes the border subject. A border wound is produced by the imposition of borders, which renders Latinas/os' memories and histories unintelligible, incomplete, or non-existent. To cure themselves of this border wound, Chicana/o cultural producers have focused on creating a non-territorial, no-place space from which to articulate and explore memories and histories. This no-place space is called the borderlands.

Many Chicana/o intellectuals and cultural producers adopted a borderlands approach as a corrective to Chicano nationalism. In the late 1960s and early 1970s, Chicano nationalists used the myth of Aztlán to galvanize the Chicana/o community to political action. According to the myth, around the tenth century CE, the god Huitzilopochtli told the Aztecs to leave Aztlán and to travel south in order to found an empire in present-day Mexico City. It was prophesied that in the period of the Fifth Sun the Aztecs would once again return to their homeland, Aztlán, which is believed to be located in the US Southwest.

Chicana/o nationalists' use of this myth is a perfect example of how collective memory works. Chicana/o collective memory reframed the memory of the myth of Aztlán in order to respond to the Chicana/o community's contemporary political and social circumstances as a beleaguered and oppressed racial minority. At the time, the US was experiencing the largest waves of Mexican immigration it had ever seen. As a result, Anglos cast both Mexicans and Chicanas/os as foreigners and invaders. Chicanas/os responded by reframing the myth of Aztlán in order to change the representation of Mexican immigration from an invasion to a prophesied return to a homeland. This myth of return enabled Chicanos to posit an Aztec/Indigenous origin for the community, thereby establishing a claim to the Southwest that precedes all other claims. Anglos were transformed into foreigners, and Chicanas/os and Mexicans became the rightful heirs to the Southwest. This act of reframing helped bring the Chicana/o community together to fight for political and social change.

Despite the tremendous political significance of Aztlán to Chicana/o politics, however, the myth does not have any inherent political meaning. Its political import depends solely on how the community instantiates its collective memory through its framing practices.[7] Collective memory allows a community to "frame" a certain event, in this case the mythic return to Aztlán, in order to shape how it is read and remembered by the community (Irwin-Zarecka 5). The memory of the myth of Aztlán, to use Crane's words for my purposes, is not a single artifact from the past but "a production that emerges over time and in the present" ("Memory" 49–50). Unlike history, which Pierre Nora defines as a simple reconstruction of the past, memory is constantly evolving in order to create the present (9). Collective memory, in

---

7   In response to the immigration rights rallies in 2006 and 2007, American nativists used the myth to support their political agenda. The myth of Aztlán was reframed in order to support their claims that Mexican immigrants were engaging in a reconquista of the American West. Unlike Chicana/o nationalists, nativists used the myth to cast Mexican immigrants as an invading horde that would transform "proper" Americans into foreigners in their own land. American nativists were able to give the myth of Aztlán a radically different meaning because it is the frame of collective memory—not the content—that gives memories their historical and political significance.

other words, is a dynamic process that responds to political and social circumstances in the present by framing and reframing memories (Irwin-Zarecka 7).

The reframing of the myth of Aztlán helped the community to achieve some major political changes. Nonetheless, the manner in which the memory of this myth was reframed also provides a cautionary tale for the Chicana/o community about the consequences of not adopting a borderlands approach to collective memory. By transforming Chicano history into a history of return, the Chicana/o Movement created an origin story and territorialized its history. In doing so, it could not avoid the pitfalls that often come with a nationalist history of return. It soon adopted the very inside-outside logic of borders that had turned them into outsiders and foreigners. To the community's detriment, Chicana/o nationalists began to exclude feminists, gays, lesbians, and others who would not conform to its masculinist political agenda.

Even before Anzaldúa introduced her borderlands theory, Chicano writers were already criticizing the limits of Chicano nationalism and its focus on territory. For example, two novels, Rudolfo Anaya's *Heart of Aztlán* (1976) and Ron Arias's *The Road to Tamazunchale* (1975), revised the nationalist approach to Aztlán by abandoning a history of origins or land claims. Instead Anaya and Arias used their writing to explore how the use of myth and storytelling could create a no-place space on which to found community relations. Anaya radically transforms Aztlán from a Chicana/o territory to a set of ethical relations that, with the loss of land and property, can only be fostered through myth and storytelling. In his novel, Arias creates Tamazunchale, an imaginary space that can only be reached by going on stage and becoming part of a performance. Through Tamazunchale, he transforms the act of migration into a figural site of departure and arrival. In both novels, characters cannot return to their land or homeland. It is this impossibility of return that creates a need for an imaginary space that will foster the Chicana/o community.

In borderlands theory, it is precisely the absence or inability of return that makes a new relation to history a necessity. By examining the overlaps between Anzaldúa's borderlands theory and collective memory's framing practices, it is clear that they approach the past in a similar fashion. Hames-Garcia's explanation of Anzaldúa's call for an original relation to history can also be used to describe the workings of collective memory: "Anzaldúa calls for something new, something not-yet that will draw from the past but will not be a return to it" (113). Both draw on the past to give memories and events an entirely new contemporary significance. A borderlands collective memory, however, reframes memories in order to enter the realm of imagination and sever the ties between memory and a locus of referentiality or territory; it does not reframe memories in order to claim territory or to create an origin story. A borderlands subject, as Alicia Gaspar de Alba points out, "must be rooted in nonexistence, in the subjunctive netherlands of desire and imagination ('if only I had a homeland'), rather than in the lament for a lost wholeness ('there's no place like home')" (107). A borderlands collective memory constantly reframes memories in order to create a home that will historicize the Latina/o community and render them intelligible. Like democracy, however, this search for a homeland is a never-finished project. The moment collective memory stops its reframing practices, this search for a homeland ends and a territory is established. As a result, a community becomes static, impervious to change, and hence oppressive.

The move from territory to the no-place space of imagination has encouraged Latina/o cultural producers to use their art as a means to historicize their memories and connect them to a collective (i.e. the Latina/o community). In this respect, Latinas/os are like many other marginalized groups, which, according to Lisa Lowe, have a long history of using cultural practices like literature, art, theatre, and music to establish the ground upon which they can launch a critique and counternarrative to official historical discourse. These sites "of cultural forms . . . propose, enact, and embody subjects and practices not contained by the narrative of . . . citizenship" (Lowe 176). For Verdecchia this space of desire and imagination, this site of counternarrative, is the stage. In order to depart from the "reality" of borders, Verdecchia transforms the stage itself into a borderlands space where he can finally place his memories and experiences within the framework of a Latina/o collective memory. Trauma, as I have mentioned above, destabilizes Verdecchia's nostalgic locus of referentiality (Argentina). It is only on a stage in Canada that Verdecchia can give meaning to his traumatic past.

The stage and the performance allow Verdecchia to move away from realism and a dependence on referential authority by providing him a space of imagination. The introduction of the *brujo* signals this departure from realism and an entry into the realm of magic projected on screens, putting on a performance as he proceeds to heal Verdecchia. Unlike the therapist who asks Verdecchia to remember events from his personal life, the *brujo* asks him to remember both the historical and the personal. The *brujo* tells him, "You have a very bad border wound [. . .] and here in Mexico any border wounds or afflictions are easily aggravated" (74). At first Verdecchia is skeptical of the *brujo*, who seems to think the corner of Madison and Bloor is the borderlands (*la frontera*). Not anchored to any place, the *brujo* seems even more lost than Verdecchia. He then tells Verdecchia that he remembers the night Bolívar burned with fever and realized there was no way back to the capital. Verdecchia laughs skeptically and tells him that that must have taken place in 1830. The *brujo* tells him that he remembers the Zoot Suit Riots; he has the scars to prove it. He informs Verdecchia that the only way to cure his border wound is to remember both his past and history. After a failed attempt, Verdecchia begins to remember both:

I remember the French Invasion of Mexico; I remember the Pastry War [. . .] I remember that I had a dream. I was playing the accordion, playing something improvised, which my grandmother recognized after only three notes as a tango from her childhood, playing a tango I had never learned, playing something improvised, not knowing where my fingers were going. [. . .] And I remember that I remembered that dream the first time one afternoon in Paris while staring at an accordion in a stall at the flea market and then found 100 francs on the street. As I passed out El Brujo said, [. . .] "The Border is your Home." I'm not in Canada; I'm not in Argentina. I'm on the Border. I am Home. Mais zooot alors, je comprends maintenant, mais oui, merde! Je suis Argentin-Canadien! I am a post-Porteño, neo-Latino Canadian. I am the Pan-American highway! (75)

Verdecchia is cured of his border wound, his trauma, when he severs his ties to place (Argentina or Canada) and enters the no-place space of a borderlands collective memory. The borderlands allow Verdecchia to give his memories a different meaning, one that does not induce a cultural schizophrenia. As Verdecchia explains to the audience, "I am learning to live on the border. I have called off the Border Patrol, I am hyphenated but I am not falling apart, I am putting together. I am building a house on the border. And you? [. . .] Will you call off the Border Patrol?" (78).

Verdecchia has finally learned how to disconnect memories from territory. In doing so, he subverts the nation's power to impose boundaries on people's histories and memories. Instead of his memories becoming the effect of borders, they are reframed by a borderlands collective memory. A borderlands collective memory allows Latinas/os to introduce their stories and memories into North American culture through their art, music, literature, and drama.

Verdecchia's memories, however, are not simply connected to the Latina/o community; they are connected to a collective that is the audience. In other words, the space of a borderlands collective memory that he has created on stage is open not only to Latinas/os but to others as well. Moreover, the stage on which he chose to perform the play ensures that this no-place space is accessible to a national audience as well. The play premiered at the Tarragon Theatre, which Mayte Gómez notes was founded in 1971 and until very recently has functioned as an institution that helped to maintain the divide between British culture and ethnic groups by focusing on the creation of a national dramatic tradition for English-speaking Canada ("Healing"). However, instead of the Tarragon co-opting Verdecchia's work, she asserts that the inclusion of *Fronteras Americanas* helped to subvert the ideology of multiculturalism by refusing to ghettoize the play and maintain the border between culture and ethnicity. If it had been produced exclusively for a Latina/o audience, she claims, the play's message would have been contained within this single community. The play, Gómez notes, is no longer simply about the Latina/o community or an individual, it is "about the entire country, about all those

Canadians who live on the border." Instead of multiculturalism, it is interculturalism, she continues, "an interaction among living, practicing culture."
The fact that the play was performed on a national stage allows Canada to be
a point from which Verdecchia can reframe his memories and overcome the
trauma of migration. The Tarragon is no longer a bastion of British culture,
but a site for the production of cultural memory that is open to a national
audience and not limited to one ethnic group.

LATINA/O STEREOTYPES AND NORTH AMERICAN COLLECTIVE MEMORY

There are as many different forms of collective memory as there are communities. So far, this paper has focused on a borderlands collective memory. But
the play also devotes a great deal of attention to a North American collective memory. Guillermo Verdecchia's *Fronteras Americanas* scrutinizes how
Latinas/os have been framed within North American collective memory by
addressing two seemingly unconnected borders: the US–Canada and US–
Mexico borders. Centuries of contact between the United States and Latin
America have produced stereotypes about Latinas/os and Latin America that
have been deployed again and again, all the while gaining more strength and
coherence with each repetition. Guillermo Verdecchia shows how stereotypes
are not simply negative representations but memories North Americans pos-
sess of Latinas/os and Latin Americans. Generations of North Americans
have grown up with movies, ads, political speeches, cartoons, dime novels, etc.
that have stereotyped Latinas/os, and they draw upon these stereotypes-as-
memories in order to understand their present interactions with Latinas/os or
Latin America. In other words, stereotyping is a framing practice that instantiates North American collective memories about Latinas/os and Latin America.

How do you create a borderlands collective memory when the dominant
group uses stereotypes to frame Latinas/os and their culture and history?
Verdecchia addresses this issue by creating an alter ego, Facundo, a.k.a.
Wideload McKenna, a Colombian translator/ethnographer who is a few

credits short of his M.A. in Chicano Studies and now lives in Toronto. At first glance, Wideload seems like a grab bag of the worst stereotypes of Latinas/os, and an odd choice for a translator. However, Wideload McKenna establishes a common ground between Latina/o and Anglo Canadians precisely because of the familiarity of the stereotypes and cultural icons—Speedy Gonzalez, Frito Bandito, Sor Juana, greaser, drug dealer, etc.—that he embodies. Wideload draws upon fantasies and images Anglos have about Latinas/os in order to explain Latinas/os in terms that an Anglo audience can understand, only to use these very images and terms to critique North American racism. By the very fact that stereotypes of Latinas/os are products of contact that have wide circulation, they can be wrenched out of their places in popular culture, reframed, and used to open up new areas of meaning and interpretation.

The character of Wideload reminds the audience of how stereotypes are born out of a long history of interaction between North America and Latin America. He also reminds us that due to the long history and prevalence of such stereotypes, Latinas/os cannot ignore them in any attempt at self-definition. When the play translates the word "Chicano" to a Canadian audience, it provides a mixture of stereotypes, ethnic slurs, fact, and location:

> Chicano: a person who drives a loud car that sits low to the ground?
> A kind of Mexican?
> A wetback?
> Generic term for a working class Latino?
> A Mexican born in Saxon America? (26)

There is a refusal to purge stereotypes from any definition of North American Latina/o culture to illustrate how Latinas/os must conceive of themselves within the dynamic of Anglo–Latina/o contact.

Even the character of Verdecchia must embody these stereotypes as he auditions for roles; he tells producers that he specializes in "El Salvadorian refugees, Italian bobsledders, Arab horse-thieves and Uruguayan rugby players who are forced to cannibalize their friends when their plane crashes in the Andes" (64). There is nothing inherently wrong or demeaning about being an El Salvadorian refugee. In and of themselves, for example, Latina/o drug dealers and gang members are not stereotypes. Stereotyping unmoors these people from their socio-political context and transforms them into frames that trap, distort, and make Latinas/os "intelligible" in the racist imaginations of North Americans. What is degrading is being condemned to play the same roles over and over again, whether in a film or in someone's imagination. Stereotyping provides the roles and scenarios available to Latinas/os in the North American mediascape, and can force Latinas/os to embody the very stereotypes that threaten their individuality and dignity. Stereotyping is especially insidious because it constantly threatens to replace and shape North American Latinas/os' understanding of themselves. This is one reason Latinas/os in North America must address two or more cultural frames of reference, so they can combat North American stereotyping-as-framing practice with a practice that instantiates their own collective memory.

Stereotypes provide the characters and the props for scenarios of contact between Anglos and Latinos. In *The Archive and Repertoire*, Diana Taylor defines "scenario" as a paradigmatic set-up that is structured around a schematic plot with an adaptable end. These scenarios exist as a set of possibilities and represent ways of conceiving conflict, crisis, or resolution. One scenario familiar to most North Americans, for example, is the "frontier scenario in the United States, [which] organizes events as diverse as smoking advertisements and the hunt of Osama bin Laden. Rather than a copy, the scenario constitutes a once-againness" (Taylor 32). Scenarios, Taylor contends, form part of a cultural repertoire, which "enacts embodied memory: performance, gestures, orality, movement, dancing, in short all those acts usually thought of as ephemeral nonreproducible knowledge" (20). Unlike the archive, which "consists of items supposedly resistant to change" (19), the repertoire "requires presence: people participate in the production and reproduction of knowledge by 'being there', being part of the performance" (20). The archive and the repertoire, however, work in tandem to create historical and collective memory. These scenarios and stereotypes, in a manner of speaking, are the memories Anglos have of Latinas/os and Latin America.

Wideload allows Verdecchia to draw upon these stereotypes and the repertoire of scenarios of Anglo–Latina/o contact in order to articulate a new borderlands identity and an original relation to history. By having Wideload restage and unpack scenarios of Anglo–Latino contact, *Fronteras Americanas* engages a North American collective memory that has made Latinas/os "visible" and culturally "intelligible" in the US and Canada. Wideload points out how such scenarios of Anglo–Latino contact have become marketing tools and ways of representing Latin America as a site of social disorder and backwardness. Wideload even pitches the idea of using multiple scenarios to create a theme park for Anglos. Wideload explains to the audience:

> I want to cash in on de Latino Boom. [. . .] We are a hot commodity right now. And what I really want to do is get a big chunk of toxic wasteland [. . .] and make like a third-world theme park. You know, you drive up to like big-barbed wire gates with guards carrying machine guns and [. . .] as soon as you're inside somebody steals your purse and a policeman shows up but he's totally incompetent and you have to bribe him to get any action. Den you walk through a slum on the edge of a swamp wif poor people selling tortillas. And [. . .] a drug lord comes along in his hydrofoil and [. . .] [you] watch a multi-media presentation on drug processing. I figure it would be great—you people love dat kinda *shit*. (25)

Wideload strings together a number of scenarios that Hollywood and the popular media have produced about Latin America (Latin American countries as military dictatorships, Latinas/os as thieves, Latin America as corrupt, and Latinas/os as drug dealers). He transfers these scenarios from Latin America to a theme park, an ersatz space near the Trans-Canada highway, making it clear that these scenarios have little to do with Latin America and more to do with satisfying an Anglo-dominant market.

Wideload, as the product of both the archive and the repertoire of Anglo–Latino contact, thus functions as a temporary locus of enunciation that helps Verdecchia lead the audience to the borderlands at the end of the play and to begin to articulate an original relation to history. The play alternates between scenarios of Latin American culture and Verdecchia's attempt to create an original relation to history. There is a clear contrast made between the familiarity and coherence of stereotypes and scenarios and Verdecchia's inability to achieve a similar coherence. While Verdecchia is lost and filled with self-doubt, Wideload is presented as a confident and adept social commentator; he has no identity crisis. As a character, Wideload has acquired his strength and intelligibility from a long history of contact between Latin Americans and North Americans. Wideload's energy, confidence, and cultural knowledge are connected to his focus on contact zones rather than national cultures or histories. In a manner, Wideload represents a locus of enunciation that the character of Verdecchia must work to create for himself. Wideload demonstrates how Anglo-produced stereotypes can indeed be adapted for different ends.

By producing a common ground between Anglos and Latinos, Wideload allows Anglos to see how they have constituted their own identities—as rational, self-disciplined, advanced, law-abiding people—in part through the instantiation of a North American collective memory. This collective memory frames Latinas/os by a continual return to an archive and repertoire of stereotypes and scenarios of Latinos and Latin America. Moreover, Wideload shows how such stereotypes can be redirected to examine and critique North American racism. Instead of fixing Latinos on a social map in a determinate manner, Wideload's engagement with a North American collective memory begins a dialogue between Latinas/os and other North Americans.

The borderlands is not a utopian site free from pain; it is also a space in which the marginalized can address aspects of oneself that have been made ugly and unacceptable by the majority. These aspects have been maligned and stereotyped in order to create other types of boundaries, namely race, class, and gender. Consequently, Latinas/os must deal with the stereotypes and scenarios of Latinos and Latinas that Anglos have created. These stereotypes and scenarios are not only part of Anglos' collective memory, they form a cultural arsenal that can be deployed in a number of different circumstances in order to marginalize or expel Latinas/os. Although these Anglo memories of Latin America and Latinas/os are produced in a contact zone between cultures, they serve to create a boundary between the two groups and to solidify borders. Wideload, however, uses these stereotypes and scenarios as tools that allow him to create a "cultural portrait" of Anglos in order to critique racism. Once these Anglo memories have been reclaimed, the rising action of the play builds toward Verdecchia's epiphany that one can indeed dwell in the borderlands. Verdecchia overcomes his trauma by refusing to allow borders to induce a cultural schizophrenia.

CONCLUSION

In the introduction to "Staging Memory," Verdecchia states, "Bearing witness to the wounds of individual and collective psyches, these plays contend with the staging of trauma and the ways in which trauma narratives might be communicated to a community of witnesses, how trauma might become cultural memory" (8). In Canada, playwrights like Carmen Aguirre, Guillermo Verdecchia, Marilo Nuñez, and Latina/o theatre groups like Alameda Theatre (Toronto), Aluna Theatre (Toronto), and Latino Theatre Group (Vancouver) have drawn on the resources of US Latina/o collective memory to create their own Canadian-specific approach to remembering. Guillermo Verdecchia's *Fronteras Americanas*, influenced by Guillermo Gómez-Peña's performance art and informed by Gloria Anzaldúa's borderlands theory, provides an excellent example of how Canadian Latina/o theatre can perform the instantiation of a collective memory that will render Canadian Latinas/os' memories intelligible both to themselves and to others.[8]

As the play makes clear, claiming a space is an act of negotiation with another culture. The play forces North American Anglos to see themselves already involved in the borderlands. As the first slide in Act Two informs the audience, "Every North American, before this century is over, will find that

---

8   Verdecchia references Anzaldúa's theory of the borderlands and Gómez-Peña's *Border Brujo* in the original publication of *Fronteras Americanas*.

he or she has a personal frontier with Latin America. This is a living frontier, which can be nourished [. . .] by knowledge. [. . .] Or starved by suspicion, ghost stories, arrogance, ignorance, scorn, and violence" (Carlos Fuentes, qtd. in *Fronteras* 54). In an interview about his play, Verdecchia tells the reporter, "I believe that all of us, every Canadian, has to claim their space on the continent. [. . .] We're linked more and more to Mexico, Latin America, and the United States, and those links are going to grow even more over the next decade or two" (Carey). With the ever-closer ties between Latin America and North America, all North Americans may one day also have to call off the border patrol and enter the borderlands to make sense of their own histories and memories.

PERFORMING IMAGINARY HOMELANDS

JIMENA ORTUZAR

> Home is neither here nor there [. . .] rather, itself a hybrid, it is *both* here *and* there—an amalgam, a pastiche, a performance.
> —Angelika Bammer

In an age that increasingly defines itself in terms of global movement, the struggle to make oneself at home in the contemporary world is an endeavour faced by more and more people, whether they consider themselves at home or abroad. Indeed, "not feeling at home" today is one of the most common and shared conditions (Virno 38), not least because we live in a quintessentially migrant era. For many, home entails a place of intimacy and familiarity, safety and stability. While this sense of home often corresponds with a homeland, this is often not the case for migrants or their descendants, who frequently set out in search of their ancestral homelands.[1] Traditionally conceived as the "stable physical centre of [one's] universe—a safe [and still] place to leave and to return to" (Rapport and Dawson 27), the idea of home today no longer corresponds to such conventional conceptualizations. In a world where

---

1   The concepts of homeland and home are frequently used interchangeably in scholarly literature on the basis that home is often located in the homeland. Takeyuki Tsuda defines "homeland" as a place of origin that involves an emotional attachment and "home" as a stable place of residence, familiarity, and security. However, Tsuda's definition of home is challenged by some of his own findings in his analysis of diasporic return to the ethnic homeland, which reveal a disconnect between home and homeland that can lead to an intense identification with the host country rather than with the place of origin. I have thus refrained from placing restrictive boundaries around the meaning of these concepts.

identities are increasingly "formed on the move," the notion of home becomes less fixed and more fluid (Chambers 25). As such, home is no longer just one place: "It is locations [or] that place which enables and promotes varied and everchanging perspectives" and "reveals more fully who we are, who we can become" (hooks 149). Conceived in this way, home is perhaps "no longer a dwelling but the untold story of a life being lived" (Berger 64).

In such conditions of transience and displacement, Salman Rushdie suggests that people "root themselves in ideas rather than in places," and must, "of necessity, make a new imaginative relationship with the world" (124–25). Haunted by a sense of loss, exiles, migrants, and expatriates will inevitably look back in an attempt to reclaim a lost homeland. But faced with the impossibility of recovering what was lost, they instead "create fictions, not actual cities or villages, but invisible ones, imaginary homelands" (Rushdie 10). Perhaps, then, feeling at home again entails a certain degree of alienation or estrangement so as to gain a critical perspective from which to see one's own place more clearly. "The migrant suspects reality," Rushdie reflects, "having experienced several ways of being, he understands their illusory nature. To see things plainly, you have to cross a frontier" (125).

The experience of displacement offers a lens through which to see the world from a new vantage point. However, Ato Quayson and Girish Daswani caution us about privileging diasporic experience by reminding us that "one does not need to be an immigrant to experience the creative restlessness produced by not being at home" ("Diaspora"). Not feeling at home in one's own home (already identified by Theodor Adorno several decades ago)[2] is a distinct feature of the modern condition, one that can be characterized as a predominantly ambivalent mode of being and feeling (Virno 38). Hence alienation, whether as a result of displacement or of feeling displaced in one's own place, has "a performative effect in generating an orientation toward homeliness that incorporates a necessary skepticism toward normalization" (Quayson and Daswani, "Diaspora"). To view one's own home with the detachment of

---

2   See Adorno.

the émigré is to recognize its inherent instability—home as provisional and discursively performed.

What, then, if we were to imagine home as a midway point between these two experiences of being displaced *from* and *in* one's own home? A recent artistic experiment has attempted to imagine such a "thirdspace" conceptually situated somewhere between two real places.[3] Borrowing its title from Rushdie's reflections on the migrant imagination, *Imaginary Homelands* is an experiment that explores the movement of people, ideas, and materials between Canada and Colombia in order to create (or to locate) a liminal place, one that is fictionalized and made tangible through an exhibition of artworks at a gallery space (Chhangur, *Imaginary Homelands*). The three-year project (2009–2012), spearheaded by the Art Gallery of York University (AGYU), involved a series of artist residencies in Toronto during which Colombian artists conceived new works from the perspective of being *in* and being *from* two places simultaneously.[4] The resulting works of this project (on view at the AGYU from 12 September to 2 December 2012) displayed a process of creation that merged fiction with description and fantasy with reality

---

3   Although closely related to Homi K. Bhabha's concept of "third space," I am alluding to Edward Soja's use of the term as an in-between space of radical openness and creativity that also encompasses other notions of betweenness such as margins and border zones, as well as Bhabha's own third space (particularly in the way it allows new subject positions to emerge). See Soja.

4   The artworks are based on real lived experiences and, yet, these experiences are not the outcome of migration in the same way that they are for most people who have moved away from (or returned to) their homelands, whether temporarily or permanently. In other words, the movement of people, ideas, and materials in this process (which is the point of departure for locating this imaginary place) has not been prompted by the political and socio-economic conditions that have historically given rise to various forms of migration and mobility (armed conflicts or global market forces for instance). Nevertheless, the participants of *Imaginary Homelands* still experienced the effects of this kind of displacement. For instance, one of the works was conceived from an artist's difficult experience learning English as a second language during her nine-month stay in Toronto. This particular piece can speak to any immigrant who recalls the sorrows of ESL classes in Toronto public schools (myself included).

to produce a unique vision of home and homeland (Chhangur, *Imaginary Homelands*).

In light of current debates on the ways migrant communities negotiate forms of belonging and self-understanding, it is clear that the value of this cultural and artistic work lies in its potential to yield new insights from the perspective of inhabiting a place that is neither here nor there, or rather, *both here and* there. What becomes evident upon a closer look at the artists' varied works is that our ideas of home are shaped by the material circumstances of our experience in relation to, and in tension with, the various myths and narratives that seek to define those experiences for us (Bammer ix). The participants are, like migrants, crossing a border (both literally and figuratively) that will allow them to do just as Rushdie suggests above: to see things plainly, to gain a fuller sense of the world in all its complexity. This unique perspective allows both places to inform the artists' experiences, inviting new understandings of home, while potentially fostering a more creative and active engagement with the *here* and *there*. In the following pages, I explore how these works and curatorial approach to artistic and social practice can broaden our understanding of the relations between homelands and host nations, particularly in their imaginative potential to blur the symbolic borders crossed between home and abroad.

STAGING TRANSNATIONAL JOURNEYS: FROM COLOMBIA TO CANADA AND BACK AGAIN

Conceived by Toronto-based artist and curator Emelie Chhangur, *Imaginary Homelands* is a thematic framework but also a strategy for exhibition-making (Chhangur, *Imaginary Homelands*). The three-year project involved nine artists from Bogotá, seven of whom completed a series of residencies of various lengths in Toronto and its surrounding areas. Chhangur, whose curatorial practice has a long-standing history of collaboration with Latin American artists, was instrumental in developing the conditions for each of the artists' residencies. Her process-based, collaborative approach to working with artists ensured that each residency was relevant to each artist's own work and interests. For instance, Daniel Santiago, whose work revolves around the notion of "America" in the hemispheric sense, divided his time between Toronto and Northern Ontario, where he learned about First Nations cultures in Canada. For Mateo López, who discovered that houses in the Colombian archipelago of San Andrés were built with wood from Canada, his residency involved visits to places such as the old shipping docks, the Archives of Ontario, and the New Forest Paper Mill, as well as meetings with craftsmen and designers dedicated to upcycling old Canadian wood. In this way, Chhangur facilitated, if not mediated, the circumstances of the artists' multiple border crossings into Canada according to their social, political, and cultural interests, as well as to their aesthetic sensibilities. The result was a series of hybrid creations drawn from a wide range of intersecting itineraries that included encounters, stories, and materials—in short, experiences both individual and shared (Chhangur, *Imaginary Homelands*).

Imaginary Homelands is not the first long-term, large-scale collaborative project for Chhangur. In 2011 she worked with Panamanian artist Humberto Vélez, whose public art performances explore the possibilities of collaborative acts with diverse groups of people, to bring together Indigenous dancers from an Ojibway First Nations community with a group of parkour practitioners from Toronto. Also a three-year project, this intercultural encounter aimed to put different groups and practices in dialogue in order for the participants to learn from one another and thus strengthen each other's voices. The result was the showcasing of a new aesthetic tradition in the making, one in which diverse cultural contexts, popular practices, and multiple points of view collided and converged (Chhangur, *Aesthetics of Collaborations*). While this project was concerned with creating a new approach to intercultural collaboration—one that offers the participants agency in their own representations on stage—it remained anchored in a particular place (in this case, the city of Toronto). In fact, its staging is a place-making strategy that seeks to reinsert excluded groups of people and cultural expression into the public spaces of the city. In contrast, *Imaginary Homelands* is not about the encounter of two groups of people and how their practices can reclaim a place; it is an encounter of two places in the real and imaginary crossings of the participants. As such, it is a project that must be considered under the conceptual categories of diaspora and transnationalism. Indeed, its objective to explore "the oscillation of people, ideas, and materials" between Bogotá and Toronto (Chhangur, *Imaginary Homelands*) is precisely the kind of phenomena that concerns transnational studies. The project's aim is to look at how this oscillation between two places can open up a path toward creating an imaginary midway point.

If home can be conceptualized as this "imaginary point where here and there—where we are and where we come from—are momentarily grounded" (Bammer ix), then the exhibit's conception seems to be guided by the question of what the process of arriving at this point might actually look like as it materializes. Thus, while much literary and artistic work addresses the experience of displacement associated with flows of capital, labour, and people (and Rushdie's work is exemplary in this respect), *Imaginary Homelands* manifests itself as an event. Rather than depicting the experiences of loss and recuperation of migrant or diasporic artists already here—that is, of those already displaced—the project created the conditions of displacement for those that were *not yet here*. It is, thus, the product of a series of transnational relations that were "staged." In order for the artists to engage with a concept of home—one that entails movement and allows for new ways of seeing reality—they had to cross a border. Like many literary and artistic works dealing with diasporic experience, *Imaginary Homelands* blurs the real and the imaginary, but unlike these cultural products, it resists being read as a text; rather, it asks to be experienced as a an event—a performance. Indeed, performance is perhaps "the best potential alternative to the old paradigm of the world as text" because it "refocuses attention on the artist and the process rather than the artwork, exploding the falsely static quality of the product and its self-denying fixation out-of-time" (George 23–24). What then, does this process look like and how are the artists' imaginary homelands performed through their artworks?

ENACTING CARTOGRAPHIES OF HOME AND IDENTITY

If home is the untold story of a life being lived, to experience it beyond the transcendent medium of the text means to experience it as a process, "something materially produced and negotiated through site" (Houston and Nanni 8). Hence, upon the encounter with the artists' imaginary homelands in exhibition, the viewer is presented with a set of relationships between the artists and their places of origin and sojourn. It is not only the artworks that we are asked to consider but also the journeys behind them and the processes that gave rise to them. But even before entering the gallery, we are confronted by a work that has been placed outside the entrance of the AGYU. Its author, Colombian artist Carlos Bonil, was denied a Canadian visa to participate in the residencies of the project. He was thus forced to imagine what it might have been like to experience the journey, and in turn translate this imaginative work into the creation of an imaginary place from the position of having been refused the benefit of a new perspective that such border crossings engender. His piece, titled . . . . *code*, consists of a series of anthems he composed for an imaginary homeland using a number of hybrid homemade instruments. This work and its placement outside the gallery alert us to the fact that despite its imaginative possibilities in thinking about porous boundaries, this project and its participants must function within parameters that are governed by the legal and social institutions of the nation-state. The operations of power that seek to realign nation with state are still very much in effect, particularly in producing stateless populations. Migrancy and deportation are carefully regulated around the globe even as we imagine unrestricted flows of media, technology, and travel moving across existing state borders. Gayatri C. Spivak reminds us "as walls have gone up between the US and Mexico, between Israel and Palestine, and neither India nor China will let the Tibetans cross a border, we are wishfully thinking of a world without borders" (qtd. in Butler viii). In other words, the extent to which we think we have transcended the nation-state is highly debatable, especially when we consider that notions of hypermobility are founded upon patterns of mobility between first-world countries (Butler viii).

That the first work we encounter is centred on the creation of a fictional anthem for an imaginary place suggests that notions of home are still very much tied to the idea of nation, particularly in Benedict Anderson's sense of an "imagined community." Both home and nation are "fictional constructs, mythic narratives, stories the telling of which has the power to create the 'we' who are engaged in telling them" (Bammer ix). Further elaborating this analogy between home and Anderson's sense of nation, Angelika Bammer notes:

> This power to construct not only an identity for ourselves as members of a community ("nation," say or "family"), but also the discursive right to a space (a country, a neighbourhood, a place to live) that is due to us, is—we then claim, in the name of that we-ness we have just constructed—at the heart of what Anderson describes as the "profound emotional legitimacy" of such concepts as "nation" or "home." (ix–x)

Bammer's analogy not only reveals that the concepts of nation and home function within the same mythic field (x), it also points to the significance of place in the production of these ideas. Home is perhaps the most familiar instance of place where people feel a sense of attachment and rootedness—a place most often seen as a field of care (Cresswell 26). For a nation to be considered as a field of care it must act as a place that holds its inhabitants as a community (Cresswell 100). The idea of nation as place, notes Tim Cresswell, entails "all the paraphernalia of national ideology and belonging—flags, anthems, passports, money and more" (100). If the notions of home and homeland help to naturalize the state as nation, it is not surprising then that the creation of an imaginary homeland should include an anthem.

A national anthem is one of the many state symbols adopted by nation-building policies that seek to construct national homogeneity, and hence usually represents the dominant group's language, history, and culture. Such policies, characteristic of Western states, have the effect of rendering minority groups invisible (Kymlicka 62–63). However, that Bonil composed an anthem when he was denied entry into Canada and was (symbolically) excluded from the official space of the gallery is itself a symbolic act of claiming a discursive right to a place—the imaginary homeland from which he is an outsider. What is more, neither the sounds nor the language can be identified as being from any one country in particular. Rather, the anthem is composed of a coded language that is incomprehensible to the listener. As such, it is not the language of Colombians or Canadians, or any particular group, whether dominant or minoritarian. Language thus becomes disarticulated from ideas of nation, homeland, place, culture, and ethnicity that are frequently attached to, and entangled with, notions of home and identity. Reduced to a sequence of sounds and devoid of meaning, language can no longer function to demark a particular place to which to belong, nor can it be used as a source of power over others.[5]

For most migrants, however (and certainly for the seven artists who crossed the border into Canada), the experience of displacement is not only a journey across time and space but also across language. Indeed, language is the site through which several of the participants' works find expression. To enter the gallery is to temporarily arrive at a liminal place where language and meaning collide and converge, most subtly signalled by the EXIT sign above the entrance to the exhibition space that has, in fact, been replaced by a virtually identical luminous red sign with the word EXILE (Fig.1). Conceived by artist Nicolás Consuegra as a result of his own confusion between the two words while learning English as a second language, the sign signals a threshold

---

5   Bonil's . . . . *code* recalls Mexican-based Spanish artist Santiago Sierra's works with national anthems, which consist of several anthems from different countries, one with several nations in South America (belonging to MercoSur) and another with all of the nations in the European Union. The anthems are played simultaneously and continuously or in reverse. Needless to say, the language becomes disarticulated and incomprehensible. Not only does this highlight the way political spaces and populations are being reconfigured within and across borders as a result of neo-liberal strategies of governing, it also touches on the process in which citizenship elements such as rights, nation, and state are being disarticulated from one another. For more on this notion of (dis)articulation, see Ong.

Fig. 1. Nicolás Consuegra, *Untitled (Exile)*, 2007. Modified
back-lit exit sign. 25 x 40 x 8.5 cm. Private Collection, Bogotá.
Photo by Michael Maranda. Photograph courtesy of Art Gallery
of York University.

in which both exit and exile "signify that you are leaving a place, yet entering another" (Consuegra). But whereas exit signs have become ubiquitous
in our everyday life, exile is, as Edward Said puts it, "life led outside habitual
order" ("Reflections" 186). It is a decentred, nomadic, and often marginal
life marked by the instability of time and space—the so-called "chronotope
of exile" that characterizes so much exile literature and is particularly salient
in the writing of Latin Canadian exiles (Torres 183). The sign thus sets the

stage for viewing the artists' works as a liminal condition created by the circumstances of having been uprooted from the familiar places of everyday
life in Bogotá and thrown into a different time and place. But framing the
artists' journeys under the discourse of exile immediately brings into play
a particular temporal dimension at work in the condition of exile. In other
words, *Imaginary Homelands* is not just the creation of a liminal space; it also
involves the liminal temporality of exile in which difference becomes vital to
the artists' experience of displacement.

However, in the experience of exile, difference, warns Luis Torres, is not
a Derridean *différance*:

> [W]here the idea of postponement seems to involve the playful dis-
> placement of the signifier and the willful erasure of meaning. This
> is a time of change where difference is costly to the subject of con-
> sciousness . . . [D]ifference—being other, the process of decentering,
> the tension between temporalities and spaces, the breaking of the
> "natural" relations to signs, is not an unending flow of "jouissance"
> here, but an image of pain. (190)

The temporality found in the writing of exiles, particularly in the case of Latin
American exiles in the Canadian context, is a "textual struggle" to articulate
this pain and "to give it form and direction" (Torres 190). This struggle manifests itself in a maelstrom of conflicting times where the world of the past
floods the present and the images of another space (the homeland left behind)
surface "to break the normality of signs in the new land," thus unsettling the
relationship between the subject and the surrounding world (192). For instance, the main character in Carmen Rodríguez's story "Agujero negro," a
Chilean exile living in Vancouver, experiences her new locality with a strange
familiarity as images of her hometown invade the streets of her present one.
In this momentary confusion she can no longer discern between the two
locales, which leads her to despair. The relationship between the character
and the habitual signs of her present surroundings is thus thrown into crisis
(Torres 193).

It is tempting to read Consuegra's EXILE (exit) sign as a reference to the "dénouement of the crisis of signs" expressed in the exile literature of Latin Canadians (Torres 193),[6] especially given its placement above the entrance to the exhibition space. After all, the act of overwriting the exit sign does indeed "break the normality of signs" (by breaking our habituation to it), hence warning us that we are about to witness artworks that will inevitably reveal the artists' ambivalent relationship with the world around them. But Consuegra's sign also re-performs the incident that led him to conceive the artwork—that is, a momentary confusion in which the act of departure and the condition of displacement become indistinguishable. In doing so, it suggests that such misreadings of the signs in one's new environment are not only generative but also performative. The work thus functions as a denouement of the performativity of the exhibit as a whole, putting the notion of imaginary homelands itself under stress—a tension inscribed between sign and referent that acts on the spectators as they enter and exit the exhibition space of the gallery.

Once inside, we find that the imaginary homelands created by the Colombian artists move away from the pathos that preoccupies the narrative imagination of Latin American exiles. The "exile," suggests Michael Seidel, "is someone who inhabits one place and remembers or projects the reality of another" (ix). In contrast, the artists of *Imaginary Homelands* propose a different relationship between their place of origin and their new temporary home, one that is open to but not haunted by the past and where identity is no longer attached to the fixity of place. This distinction can be easily attributed to the fact that, unlike many Latin American exiles, the artists were not forced into exile as a result of social disruption and political turmoil throughout Latin America (e.g. Argentina's Dirty War, the Pinochet dictatorship, the

---

6   Torres refers to the "dénouement of the crisis of signs" to describe how exile identity is disrupted and unravelled by the surfacing of the past into the world of the present, thus breaking apart its temporal and spatial boundaries. Reality loses its familiarity and the characters no longer recognize themselves in the signs of their immediate surroundings. Images of the homeland, as in the example of "Agujero negro," begin to flood the space of the present. This semiotic crisis, observes Torres, is a pervasive occurrence in the writing of Latin Canadian exiles (192–93).

Mayan genocide in Guatemala, the decades of civil conflict and violence in Colombia), which is not to say that they are unaware of the pain and suffering endured by those forced to leave their homelands. And yet, as Said put so well, "Exile is strangely compelling to think about but terrible to experience" ("Reflections" 173). The artists in this project, however, escape these two extremes by virtue of their voluntary and temporary exile, a state of betweenness that leads not to anxiety but to possibility. The conditions of their displacement are such that they allow the creation of works that creatively explore in the imagination the crossing of boundaries without necessarily having to deal with the traumas that characterize the paradigm of exile.

Whether forced or voluntary, the experience of displacement is one that rarely escapes the tribulations of learning another language. Like Consuegra, Angélika Teuta's work arises from her experience with English as a second language. Her piece, *The Language of Birds*, may have been inspired by the sounds of the many unrecognizable languages she encountered upon her arrival in Toronto, but it is also a response to her own perceived "lack" of language (the official language she endeavoured to learn) during her stay (Chhangur, *Imaginary Homelands*). The imaginary landscape she creates with the use of sound and overhead projection fuses together elements from her home country's rainforests with those of her host country's natural landscape. With the sounds heard in one space and the projected images layered in a single plane, the two worlds merge into a single temporal and spatial illusion in which different languages can coexist harmoniously as a soundscape, as the musical texture of a place (Fig. 2). Teuta's desire to root herself in her new environment without leaving her home points to the sense of simultaneity in migrant experience—what Pnina Werbner describes as the "sharing of space in a continuous social field" across homeland and host country (Werbner). While the illusion of simultaneity can be quickly shattered by the ruptures experienced upon returning to the homeland,[7] it nonetheless remains a powerful experiential force that defines the migrant's sense of self and subjectivity (Werbner).

---

7   Tsuda's study of encounters with the ethnic homeland articulate these ruptures, for instance in the experience of Japanese Brazilian return-migrants to Japan. See Tsuda.

Fig. 2. In the foreground, Angélica Teuta, *The Language of Birds*, 2012, installation with audio, dimensions variable. Commissioned and produced by AGYU. Wooden platform ("wave") designed and fabricated by Brian Davis. Animal drawings by Lena Suksi. Residency supported by AB Projects, Toronto (2012). In the background, Mateo Rivano, *Micro-Mundo / Micro World*, 2012. Mixed media: wood, cardboard, lithographs, and found objects, 9 metres. Commissioned and produced by the AGYU. Wooden armature designed and constructed by Brian Davis. Residencies supported by AGYU (2010) and Fundación Gilberto Alzate Avendaño, Bogotá (2011/'12). Photo by Michael Maranda. Photograph courtesy of Art Gallery of York University.

It is one of the ways, notes Werbner, in which intimate knowledge is sustained in the face of temporal and spatial discontinuities that characterize transnational journeys.

Paradoxically, the exhibition of Teuta's work revealed the mechanisms required in creating the illusion of this fantastical world. Against the image described above (which covered an entire wall of the gallery), miniscule, meticulously crafted and sculpted layers of delicate paper cut-outs could be seen balancing from threads on multiple projectors, along with the miniature fans that kept them in motion. All these elements were in full view of the spectators who had to walk past or around the projectors. The contrast in scale was a remarkable sight, perhaps as marvellous as the images projected on the wall. It is not only the exposure of its design but also the fragility of the materials (and the care needed to maintain them) that reveals just how easily and abruptly the illusion can rupture. The work thus performs this imaginary world by alluding to the reality of how such illusions are sustained. Indeed, as Werbner observes, it is through performance that the illusion of simultaneity sustains migrants in their places of sojourn. But whereas the kind of performance that Werbner is referring to is the cultural practices that are translocated along with the individuals, Teuta's work moves away from specific modes of sociality that link home and host lands by imitating the sounds of birds as a substitute for language and through her use of landscape.

This focus on landscape reveals yet another level on which the experience of displacement might work to both maintain and expose the illusion of continuity. In contrast to place, which is something to be lived and felt, landscape is primarily a visual idea. It has historically been something to be looked at from outside (i.e. landscape painting) (Cresswell 10). However, it is often the case that the image of a homeland—what remains in memory and representation—is indeed the idea of place as landscape. Raymond Williams's novel *Border Country* (1960) beautifully captures this predicament. When the protagonist returns to his place of childhood in the Welsh borders, he realizes that the village of his memory had been nothing more than an image of a vacant site: "[T]he valley as landscape" (Williams qtd. in Creswell 10). He had forgotten the life and work that had taken place in it—in other words, the aspects of lived experience that had made it a place, his home. It is not surprising then that Teuta's imaginary homeland depicts an impossible landscape. *The Language of Birds* certainly emphasizes the act of looking by inviting spectators onto a platform built for viewing the projection.[8] However, its structure, built in the shape of a wave, produces a rather unstable position

---

8   In contrast to (or perhaps complementing) the act of viewing, the subtle elements of the *mise-en-scène*—the impossible sound of birds, the movement of several elements in an otherwise static projection, the wavering paper cut-outs, the sound of the fans—all combine for a much more sensory experience than expected at first sight of this piece.

from which to see (Fig. 3). And without a firm ground on which to stand, we are forced to constantly negotiate our change in perspective.

A particularly unstable perspective is also at work in the presentation of Miler Lagos's *Lat 65.31 N, Long 114.13 W*. These coordinates mark the shores of the Coppermine River in the Canadian Arctic where Lagos documented the northernmost regions of the country by attaching a camera to the bottom of a propeller plane. Seen from above and yet "with our feet firmly planted on the ground," the floating landscape on display disorients the viewer (Chhangur, *Imaginary Homelands*). As a journey of discovery across the Arctic, *Lat 65.31 N, Long 114.13 W* recalls the voyages of nineteenth-century European explorers, particularly the British for whom Northern Canada was a source of imperial ambition. Polar regions fuelled the imagination of the British public during the nineteenth century while their continued exploration was considered a sign of Britain's status in the world, even if its commercial potential was more imagined than real (David 2). But as Said has shown in *Culture and Imperialism*, the dependence upon colonized territories was a central aspect of European imperialism: "Imperialism and the culture associated with it affirm both the primacy of geography and an ideology about control of territory" (93). Today, the Arctic is an essential part of Canadian national identity and yet it remains foreign: the idea of the "True North" that for many of us exists only in the imagination (Chhangur, *Imaginary Homelands*).[9] Nevertheless, the geopolitical significance of the Arctic is indeed real given recent discoveries

---

9   That we know little about our Nordic land and the communities that live in them is illustrated by a journalist's report of the G7 summit Canada hosted in the arctic city of Iqaluit, Nunavut's capital. To the rest of the world leaders, commented a European official, "it looked like the Canadians had just arrived—they didn't know the place any better than we did" (Saunders). Journalist Doug Saunders suggests that, as Canadians, we relate to the Arctic not as a part of our identity, culture, or economy, but rather as a colony—a foreign land we control. The potential of natural resource development, he suggests, "has suddenly turned us into the better sort of colonial masters: We're spending some money, and caring about the people there" (Prime Minister Stephen Harper's recent Northern Strategy to establish both a legal and a public presence in the Arctic region is a case in point) (Saunders).

Fig. 3. Angélica Teuta, *The Language of Birds*, 2012, installation with
audio, dimensions variable. Commissioned and produced by AGYU.
Wooden platform ("wave") designed and fabricated by Brian Davis.
Animal drawings by Lena Suksi. Residency supported by AB Projects,
Toronto (2012). Photo by Michael Maranda. Photograph courtesy of
Art Gallery of York University.

of natural-resource wealth and contending claims about national boundaries and borders—issues that have led Canada to recently launch its Northern
Strategy of military and development measures in an effort to re-establish its
sovereignty and build its public identity as a "northern power" (Saunders).

From the aerial perspective of Lagos's *Lat 65.31 N, Long 114.13 W*, a different topography of the North becomes visible, one where borders have been
erased and mythic representations displaced, even if momentarily. However,

the communities that inhabit this land are also absent from this picture; in other words, all the aspects that might be associated with notions of home and nation have been removed. Lagos's allusion to an imaginary homeland is, like Teuta's work, centred on landscape, a real landscape in this case, but one that becomes increasingly abstract—an undifferentiated area of the planet's surface. As such, it becomes a space that is once again unknown and can be rediscovered anew, both for its aesthetic possibilities and as a site to be invested with new meaning and value. Thus, Lagos's disorienting exploration is one that refuses "an assumed topography, an already 'worlded' world (as Gayatri Spivak might put it)" underlying the vision of a homeland, whether real or imaginary (Clifford, "Notes" 178).

Like Lagos's *Lat 65.31 N, Long 114.13 W*, Daniel Santiago's piece, titled *A treasure, a myth. Dialogues through time*, re-appropriates tropes of exploration and discovery. But whereas Lagos's journey toward an imaginary homeland entails distance and abstraction, Santiago's voyage is an intimate venture across land and water. In an act of redress for the violence of colonialism, particularly its history of pillage that gave rise to legends and myths like El Dorado, Santiago's project involved burying a treasure as a way to "put something back *into* a continent that so much had been taken out of" (Chhangur, *Imaginary Homelands*). The treasure, comprised of personal objects collected over years of travels through the Americas, was buried in Bark Lake, Ontario, where he spent much of his residency. As part of a series of actions the artist describes as "continuing the work of the New World from the perspective of being from there," Santiago's act of repatriation inverts the logic embedded in narratives of imperial conquest (qtd. in Chhangur, *Imaginary Homelands*). The performative journey from Bogotá to Bark Lake was documented and exhibited in the gallery along with photographs of Santiago's personal objects now buried at the bottom of the lake. Its exhibition, however, does not necessarily indicate the end of the journey, as the work remains open to a future when Santiago's collection may be found and recovered.

Both Lagos's and Santiago's creations for the exhibition of *Imaginary Homelands* re-enact their trajectories over land, one from above, the other from below. Against the perceived ubiquity of global travel in our contemporary world and the increasing number of people that are uprooted as a result of market forces and territorial conflicts, Lagos's and Santiago's works ask us to reconsider the land we traverse in our transnational journeys. But whereas Lagos's landscape is depicted as a vast surface by virtue of a bird's-eye view, Santiago's work entails a closer relation to the ground. As such, it pays attention to the particularity of place—an environment that is "uniquely local, which could not be transposed" (Carter 16). And yet, his desire to "return" his collection to the land of this new temporary home is a gesture that links host and homeland as one continent: "America" viewed through a hemispheric lens. In the tradition of Latin American heroes like Simón Bolívar and José Martí, Santiago imagines the whole continent as home. With this gesture, Santiago's performance embodies the transnational character of Latina/o identity in Canada, which has less to do with essence than with the conditions of displacement and, more importantly, with the creative imagery that acts as a narrative about a place—an imagined community that transcends the nation-state.

UTOPIAN LONGING AND BELONGING: LOCATING A SENSE OF HOME

Not so much "Where are you from?" as "Where are you between?"
—James Clifford

The difference between "home" and "abroad" in today's global cities is no longer clearly divided, just like self and other are no longer "spatially distinct," as observes James Clifford in his "Notes on Travel and Theory." No matter how unknown the places of travel were for the explorers of the nineteenth century, the point of departure was always a given—the stable place of home (Clifford, "Notes" 178). For the participants of *Imaginary Homelands*, the concept of home holds no such stability. This may be evident from their imaginative creations on view at the AGYU but, in fact, Chhangur notes that the work of these young artists in Bogotá was very much characterized by the condition

of "not feeling at home" well before they engaged in their transnational journeys to the North (Personal interview). This is not completely unexpected
given that their own homeland is a country marked by violence and crisis as
a result of nearly five decades of civil conflict. But while there is little hope
of putting an end to this undeclared civil war that has had a devastating impact on the civilian population, claiming dozens of thousands of lives and
displacing millions of people internally, these artists display a surprisingly
idealist attitude and an incredibly imaginative output of work—perhaps the
result of the "creative restlessness" of not feeling at home in one's own home.

   When asked why, given the nature of this particular project, she had not
chosen to work with Colombian Canadian artists who were already displaced
and residing in Toronto, Chhangur responded that she was looking to bring
new perspectives rather than those already formed in the shared diasporic
experiences of the Colombian community in Canada (Personal interview). In
other words, this project is about imaginary homelands in the making—in the
very process of creation—rather than about the representation of homeland
myths already operating in diasporic communities. That all the participants
in *Imaginary Homelands* are part of a new generation of young artists in
Colombia suggests a generational change in attitude toward a society where
violence, and the threat of violence, are part of people's everyday experience.
These young artists, observes Chhangur, are moving away from the previous
generations whose work is characterized by a reflexive engagement with the
ongoing crisis and the effects of violence (Personal interview). Having spent
a significant amount of time researching their work in Bogotá, Chhangur
identified in the artists an optimistic outlook and a willingness to imagine
a different scenario than the current condition of conflict allows (Personal
interview). In contrast, many artists of the Colombian diaspora in Toronto
continue to engage with the collective traumas of the homes they left behind.[10] This is not to say that there is no longer a need to tell these stories,

---

10   The recent play *Lizardboy* (2011), published in the companion anthology to this collection, by Colombian Canadian playwright and actor Victor Gómez is a case in point.
Based on his own experience growing up in Colombia during the 1980s, the play depicts

but that striving for newly imagined notions of home and homeland entails moving beyond the limitations that socio-political conditions of migrants' home countries place on the imagination, whether they are experienced at home or are translocated to Canada.

Thus, for Latina/o Canadians, *Imaginary Homelands* opens up a new way of inhabiting the betweenness of life at the border, one in which the imaginative relationship with the world is no longer guided by the loss and recuperation of the homeland. The question that remains is whether the artists' performed displacements in this experiment yield a more open and creative engagement with home and host countries than past and present migrant itineraries allow for. What is evident in many of the resulting works of this project is that the relationship with the place of origin and the place of sojourn is one where the two places are intertwined in new and impossible ways. Perhaps, then, Chhangur's choice of subjects for this project was made on the basis of knowing that the artists' aesthetic inclinations would intuitively gesture toward the utopian—an imaginary condition where the sense of simultaneity would not be an illusion but a fact of experience, where one feels equally "at home" in both places. Indeed, as Marianna Torgovnick asserts, home is one of the few remaining utopian ideals (133). An imagined home where utopia can be experienced and enacted affectively is perhaps best articulated by performance.

For an ideal future to be enacted, argues Jill Dolan (following the theories of Roland Schaer), one must move away from the real and into the realm of the performative ("Performance" 457). The transformative potential of performance for how we imagine ourselves in culture rests in its ability to articulate a vision of a future that can be affectively experienced in the present by means of the intersubjective understanding it provokes. To actively engage with the experience of being in between two places is quite different from envisioning this idea from a singular and sedentary position. For the spectators viewing the culmination of this process—the exhibit of the artists'

---

the struggles of a family coping with the fear of violence and the uncertainties of their living conditions through the eyes of a nine-year-old boy.

imaginary homelands—the trajectories of the artists are embodied in the displayed works by a constant referral to the means by which they were conceived and created—in other words, the journey. The resulting works are hence not only the artists' visions arising from their journeys, they are enactments that are open to the imaginative projections of the spectators.

The significance that this project places on process reveals that, for a diasporic imagination, it is the journeys and not the end results that become "important considerations to an imagination of home and its relation to discontinuity and otherness" (Quayson and Daswani, "Diaspora"). The means is what makes possible not only a double perspective but also, to borrow Said's term, a "contrapuntal awareness" of simultaneous dimensions of being ("Reflections" 186). Perhaps, then, the key to understanding *Imaginary Homelands* is that the project also conceives of place, whether imaginary or real, as a process, as something that is performed—place as event rather than an ontological object that is rooted and bounded. To think of place as an event is to envision place as open and subject to change—to be redefined and reimagined in practice (Cresswell 39). Home can therefore be thought of as an enacted space, in which forms of belonging are established in the multiple ways they are imagined and performed.

Imaginary Homelands is an exercise in fluidity across various real, symbolic, and enunciative borders that challenges the assumptions and stabilities of site and location operating in the concepts of home and homeland. It contests the notion of place as fixed and bounded, not by its approach of multilocality, but by the ambiguity it creates over the limits and boundaries of artwork and place. As such, it engages with the concept of diaspora in a most productive encounter. Whereas diaspora is, as Avtar Brah argues, a critique of fixed origin (197), *Imaginary Homelands* is a critique of fixed performances of location. By creating the conditions for its participants to collectively and individually perform displacement while at the same time experiencing its very real effects, this project allowed for the creation of imaginary homelands that are not located in a particular time and place, least of all in the past. This in-between imaginary place is not found in the space of the gallery, it is embodied in the journeys of its subjects that are articulated in the works displayed. Thus, the utopian gesture of this project rests not in the particular visions of its participants but in the creative productivity that such displacement engenders. What *Imaginary Homelands* reveals is that for migrant and artist alike, imagining a different mode of being and feeling at home means engaging with a critical reflexivity in agency.

WORKS CITED

Adams, Rachel. *Continental Divides: Remapping the Cultures of North America*. Chicago: U of Chicago P, 2009. Print.

---. "Guillermo Verdecchia's Northern Borderlands." Alvarez, *Fronteras* 46–53.

---. "The Northern Borderlands and Canadian Latino Diaspora." *Hemispheric American Studies*. Ed. Caroline F. Levander and Robert S. Levine. New Brunswick, NJ: Rutgers UP, 2008. 313–27. Print.

Adorno, Theodor W. *Minima Moralia: Reflections from Damaged Life*. London: NLB, 1978. Print.

Agosto, Alba. Personal interview by Jeannine M. Pitas. 24 Sept. 2012.

Aguirre, Carmen. *Blue Box*. 2011. TS.

---. *Chile Con Carne. Rave: Young Adult Drama*. Winnipeg: Blizzard, 2000. 57–85. Print.

---. *Qué Pasa with La Raza, Eh? Along Human Lines: Dramas from Refugee Lives*. Winnipeg: Blizzard, 2000. 51–107. Print.

---. *The Refugee Hotel*. Rehearsal draft. 2009. TS.

---. *The Refugee Hotel*. Vancouver: Talonbooks, 2010. Print.

---. *Something Fierce: Memoirs of a Revolutionary Daughter*. Vancouver: Douglas & McIntyre, 2011. Print.

---. *The Trigger*. Vancouver: Talonbooks, 2008. Print.

Ahmed, Sara. *The Cultural Politics of Emotion*. London: Routledge, 2004. Print.

---. *Strange Encounters: Embodied Others in Post-Coloniality*. London: Routledge, 2000. Print.

Alarcón, Norma. "Chicana's Feminist Literature: A Re-Vision Through Malintzín/Or, Malitnzín Putting Flesh Back on the Object." *This Bridge Called My Back: Writings by Radical Women of Color.* Ed. Cherríe Moraga and Gloria Anzaldúa. New York: Kitchen Table, 1983. 182–90. Print.

Alba, Alicia Gaspar de. "There's No Place Like Aztlán: Embodied Aesthetics in Chicana Art." *CR: The New Centennial Review* 4.2 (2004): 103–40. Print.

Alba Emoting North America. "Acting and Emotion: Introducing Alba Emoting." *Alba Emoting North America.* Alba Emoting, n.d. Web. 15 Jan. 2013.

Aluna Theatre. "About Aluna Theatre." *Aluna Theatre Blog.* Aluna Theatre, 24 March 2012. Web. 1 Sept. 2012.

---. "Artistic Mission." *Aluna Theatre.* Aluna Theatre, n.d. Web. 1 Sept. 2012.

---. "History." *Aluna Theatre.* Aluna Theatre, n.d. Web. 1 Sept. 2012.

---. *Nohayquiensepa (No One Knows): A Requiem for the Forcibly Displaced.* Aluna Theatre. Panamerican Routes/Rutas Panamericanas Festival, Theatre Passe Muraille, Toronto. 22–26 May 2012. Performance.

---. *Nohayquiensepa (No One Knows): A Requiem for the Forcibly Displaced.* Program. Toronto: Aluna, August 2009. Print.

---. *Panamerican Routes/Rutas Pamamericanas.* Program. Toronto: Aluna, 15–27 May 2012. Print.

Alvarez, Natalie, ed. *Fronteras Vivientes: Eight Latina/o Canadian Plays.* Toronto: Playwrights Canada, 2013. Print.

---. Introduction. Alvarez, *Fronteras* iii–xxvii.

---. "Realisms of Redress: Alameda Theatre and the Formation of a Latina/o-Canadian Theatre and Politics." *New Canadian Realisms.* Ed. Roberta Barker and Kim Solga. Toronto: Playwrights Canada, 2012. 144–62. Print. New Essays on Canadian Theatre 2.

---. "Transcultural Dramaturgies: Latina Theatre's Third Wave." *Contemporary Women Playwrights.* Ed. Penny Farfan and Lesley Ferris. Basingstoke: Palgrave, 2013. N.p. Print.

Anaya, Rudolfo. *Heart of Aztlán.* Berkeley: Justa, 1976. Print.

Anderson, Benedict. *Imagined Communities: Reflections on the Origin and Spread of Nationalism.* London: Verso, 1991. Print.

Anzaldúa, Gloria. *Borderlands/La Frontera: The New Mestiza.* San Francisco: Aunt Lute, 1987. Print.

Appadurai, Arjun. "Disjuncture and Difference in the Global Cultural Economy." *Theory, Culture & Society* 7.2 (1990): 295–310. Print.

Arendt, Hannah. *On Revolution*. London: Penguin Books, 1977. Print.

Arias, Ron. *The Road to Tamazunchale*. Reno, NV: West Coast Poetry Review, 1975. Print.

Arrizón, Alicia. "Contemporizing Performance: Mexican California and the Padua Hills Theatre," *Mester* 22.2-23.1 (1993–1994): 5–30. Print.

---. *Latina Performance: Traversing the Stage*. Bloomington, IN: Indiana UP, 1999. Print.

---. *Queering Mestizaje: Transculturation and Performance*. Ann Arbor, MI: U of Michigan P, 2006. Print.

Arrizón, Alicia, and Lillian Manzor, eds. *Latinas on Stage*. Berkeley: Third Woman, 2000. Print.

Artaud, Antonin. *Le théâtre et son double suivi de Le théâtre de Séraphin*. Paris: Gallimard, 1964. Print.

Auslander, Philip. " 'Brought to You by Fem-Rage': Stand-up Comedy and the Politics of Gender." *Acting Out: Feminist Performances*. Ed. Lynda Hart and Peggy Phelan. Ann Arbor, MI: U of Michigan P, 1993. 315–36. Print.

Badiou, Alain. *Being and Event*. Trans. Oliver Feltham. New York: Continuum, 2005. Print.

---. *Ethics: An Essay on the Understanding of Evil*. Trans. Peter Hallward. New York: Verso, 2001. Print.

---. *Infinite Thought: Truth and the Return to Philosophy*. Ed. and trans. Justin Clemens and Oliver Feltham. New York: Continuum, 2003. Print.

---. *Logics of Worlds*. Trans. Alberto Toscano. New York: Continuum, 2009. Print.

Bammer, Angelika. "The Question of 'Home.' " Editorial. *New Formations: A Journal of Culture, Theory, and Politics* 17 (1992): vii–xi. Print.

Barker, Roberta, and Kim Solga, eds. *New Canadian Realisms*. Toronto: Playwrights Canada, 2012. Print. New Essays on Canadian Theatre 2.

Barton, Bruce. "Paradox as Process: Intermedial Anxiety and the Betrayals of Intimacy." *Theatre Journal* 61.4 (2009): 575–601. Print.

Bátiz-Benét, Mercedes. Skype interview by Tamara Underiner. 2 Jan. 2013.

Beaunoyer, Jean. "Alberto Kurpel frappe en plein coeur." *La Presse*. 4 June 1987: C8. Print.

Bennett, Jill. *Empathic Vision: Affect, Trauma, and Contemporary Art*. Stanford: Stanford UP, 2005. Print.

Berger, John. *And Our Faces, My Heart, Brief as Photos*. New York: Pantheon Books, 1984. Print.

Bhabha, Homi K. *The Location of Culture*. New York: Routledge, 1994. Print.

Billard, Jean Antonin. Telephone interview by Hugh Hazelton. 23 Aug. 2012.

Blair, Rhonda. *The Actor, Image, and Action: Acting and Cognitive Neuroscience*. New York: Routledge, 2008. Print.

Bloch, Susana. *The Alba of Emotions*. Santiago: Ediciones Ultramarinos PSE, 2006. Print.

Bolívar, Rubí Carreño. "Libercueca: biopoéticas del sexo y la fusión de la cueca urbana chilena." *Revista de Crítica Literaria Latinoamericana* 36.71 (2010): 151–67. Print.

Bonil, Carlos. . . . . *code*. 2012. Art Gallery of York University, Toronto.

Bowden, Charles. *Inferno*. Photographs by Michael P. Berman. Austin: U of Texas P, 2006. Print.

---. *Juárez: The Laboratory of our Future*. New York: Aperture, 1998. Print.

Brah, Avtar. "Diaspora, Border and Transnational Identities." *Cartographies of Diaspora: Contesting Identities*. London: Routledge, 1996. 178–210. Print.

Brecht, Bertholt. *Brecht on Theatre: The Development of an Aesthetic*. Ed. and trans. John Willett. London: Methuen, 1964. Print.

Brooks, Daniel, and Guillermo Verdecchia. *The Noam Chomsky Lectures*. Vancouver: Talonbooks, 1998. Print.

Brooks, David. "The Limits of Empathy." *New York Times*. New York Times Company, 29 Sept. 2011. Web. 12 Feb. 2013.

Brown, Wendy. "Resisting Left Melancholy." *Boundary 2* 26.3 (1999): 19–27. Print.

Butler, Judith. "Performativity, Precarity and Sexual Politics." *AIBR: Revista de Antropología Iberoamericana* 4.3 (2009): i–xiii. Print.

Cabezas, Pedro. Personal interview by Jeannine M. Pitas. 4 Aug. 2012.

Cáceres, Susana. *L'éveil. Théâtre performance et créativité*. Montreal: Humanitas, 1999. Print.

"Canada-Latin America/Caribbean Defence Relations." *National Defence and the Canadian Forces*. Government of Canada, 25 Oct. 2012. Web. 13 Jan. 2013.

Canadian Press. "New Canadian Strategy for Americas Expected." *CBC News.* CBC/Radio Canada, 22 March 2012. Web. 12 Jan. 2013.

Carey, Elaine. "They are no Longer Sleeping with their Bags Packed." *Toronto Star* 20 June 1999: 1. Print.

Carmichael, Harold. "Forget the Hatred." *The Sudbury Star.* Sun Media. 17 Dec. 2011. Web. 29 Sept. 2012.

Carter, Paul. *The Lie of the Land.* London: Faber and Faber, 1996. Print.

Caruth, Cathy. *Unclaimed Experience: Trauma, Narrative, and History.* Baltimore: Johns Hopkins UP, 1996. Print.

Castañeda, Jorge G. *Utopia Unarmed: The Latin American Left After the Cold War.* New York: Vintage, 1994. Print.

Castro, Enrique. Personal interview by Jeannine M. Pitas. 10 Sept. 2012.

Castro Pozo, Tristan. Personal interview by Jeannine M. Pitas. 8 Oct. 2012.

Cawley, Margeurite. "Colombia's 1st Independent Theater Continues To Influence, Create, Innovate." *Columbia Reports.* Columbia News, 15 June 2011. Web. 1 Sept. 2012.

Chambers, Iain. *Migrancy, Culture, Identity.* London: Routledge, 1994. Print.

Chaves, Martha. "Canada Immigration Guide & (Racism)." *YouTube.* Web. 12 Feb. 2013.

---. "De Colores Playwright: Martha Chaves." *YouTube.* Web. 22 Oct. 2012.

---. *Fragile: A Play in Progress.* 2012. TS.

---. "Leather Bar—The Beef With Government of Nicaragua-Vaginista." *YouTube.* Web. 12 Feb. 2013.

---. "Martha Chaves Comedian Commercial-Comedy Out Out Damm Spots." *YouTube.* Web. 12 Feb. 2013.

---. "Martha from Mexico Got Shot." *YouTube.* Web. 12 Feb. 2013.

---. "Sunday Feature: Dying is Easy . . . (From Stand-up To Theatre)." *The Charlebois Post-Montreal.* Charlebois Post, 3 Feb. 2013. Web. 12 Feb. 2013.

---. "The Sunday Feature: First-Person, Martha Chaves: A Day in the Laughs." *The Charlebois Post-Canada.* Charlebois Post, 14 Aug. 2011. Web. 16 Oct. 2012.

---. Telephone interview by Alicia Arrizón. 26 Sept. 2012.

---. Telephone interview by Alicia Arrizón. 22 Oct. 2012.

---. Telephone interview by Alicia Arrizón. 5 Nov. 2012.

Chhangur, Emelie. *Aesthetics of Collaboration*. 2011. Exhibition text. Art Gallery of York University, Toronto.

---. *Imaginary Homelands*. 2012. Exhibition text. Art Gallery of York University, Toronto.

---. Personal interview by Jimena Ortuzar. 12 Dec. 2012.

Childs, Matt D. "An Historical Critique of the Emergence and Evolution of Ernesto Che Guevara's *Foco* Theory." *Journal of Latin American Studies* 27.3 (1995): 593–624. Print.

Cifuentes, María. *Historia Social de La Danza En Chile: Visiones, Escuelas y Discursos 1940–1990*. Santiago: LOM, 2007. Print.

Clifford, James. "Notes on Travel and Theory." *Traveling Theories, Traveling Theorists*. Ed. Cilfford and Vivek Dhareshwar. Santa Cruz, CA: Group for the Critical Study of Colonial Discourse & the Center for Cultural Studies, 1989. 177–88. Print.

---. *Routes: Travel and Translation in the Late Twentieth Century*. Cambridge, MA: Harvard UP, 1997. Print.

Close, David. "The Meaning of Revolution." *Revolution: A History of the Idea*. Ed. David Close and Carl Bridge. Sydney: Croom Helm, 1985. 2–14. Print.

Cohen, Robin. *Global Diasporas: An Introduction*. Seattle: U of Washington P, 1997. Print.

Consuegra, Nicolás. "Exile." *Nicolás Consuegra*. Nicolás Consuegra, 2006. Web. 20 Jan. 2013.

---. *Untitled (Exile)*. 2012. Art Gallery of York University, Toronto.

Corporación Colombiana de Teatro. Corporación Colombiana de Teatro, 2010. Web. 1 Sept. 2012.

Council of Canadians. "Update: Remembering Water Justice Activist Kimy Pernia Domico." *Council of Canadians*. Council of Canadians, 30 May 2011. Web. 27 Sept. 2012.

Crane, Susan A. "Memory, Distortion, and History in the Museum." *History and Theory* 36.4 (1997): 44–63. Print.

---. "Writing the Individual Back into Collective Memory." *The American Historical Review* 102.5 (1997): 1372–85. Print.

Cresswell, Tim. *Place: A Short Introduction*. New York: Blackwell, 2004. Print.

David, Robert G. *The Arctic in the British Imagination, 1818–1914*. Manchester: Manchester UP, 2000. Print.

Debray, Régis. *Revolution in the Revolution? Armed Struggle and Political Struggle in Latin America*. Trans. Bobbye Ortiz. New York: MR P, 1967. Print.

DeLyser, Dydia. *Ramona Memories: Tourism and the Shaping of Southern California*. Minneapolis, MN: U of Minnesota P, 2004. Print.

Deutschmann, David, ed. *The Che Guevara Reader*. Melbourne: Ocean P, 2003. Print.

Díaz, Junot. *The Brief Wondrous Life of Oscar Wao*. New York: Riverhead Books, 2007. Print.

---. "*Mil Máscaras*: An Interview with Pulitzer-Winner Junot Díaz" by Matt Okie. *Identity Theory*. Identity Theory, 2 Sept. 2008. Web. 21 Sept. 2012.

Díaz López, Isis. "Alberto Kurapel: Utilicé la carencia como un medio expresivo." *Facultad de Arts*. Universidad de Chile, 6 Oct. 2010. Web. 26 Feb. 2013.

Dolan, Jill. "Feminist Performance Criticism and the Popular: Reviewing Wendy Wasserstein." *Theatre Journal* 60.3 (2008): 433–58. Print.

---. *The Feminist Spectator as Critic*. Ann Arbor, MI: U of Michigan P, 1991. Print.

---. "Performance, Utopia, and the 'Utopian Performative.' " *Theatre Journal* 53.3 (2001): 455–79. Print.

Dostoevsky, Fyodor. *The Brothers Karamazov*. Trans. Constance Garnett. New York: Signet, 1999. Print.

Eliot, T.S. "The Love Song of J. Alfred Prufrock." *Prufrock and Other Observations*. London: Egoist, 1917. N. pag. *Bartleby*. Web. 28 Feb. 2013.

Esquilo [Aeschylus]. *Prometeo, encadenado. Tragedias completas*. Trans. Fernando Segundo Brieva. Madrid: EDAF, 1989. 23–68. Print.

Fajardo, Jorge. "La subversion de la plenitude dans le *Prométhée enchaîné* d'Alberto Kurapel." Prologue. Kurapel, *Prométhée* 27–36.

Faúndez Carreño, Tania. "Alberto Kurapel. Una 'neo' vanguardia." Diss. Universidad de Chile, 2008. *Tesis Electrónicas de la Universidad de Chile*. Web. 26 Feb. 2013.

---. "La repetición en el teatro-performance de Alberto Kurapel." *Cuadernos de Pensamiento Latinoamericano* 18 (2011): 91–103. Web. 8 Feb. 2013.

Fellner, Astrid. "*Fronteras Americanas* and the Latino Canadian Diaspora." *A Fluid Sense of Self: The Politics of Transnational Identity*." Ed. Silvia Schultermandl and Sebnem Toplu. Berlin: Lit Verlag, 2010. 231–45. Print.

Fischer, Virginia. *Tres hombres de teatro.* Santiago: Nascimento, 1985. Print.

Fisher, Mark. *Capitalist Realism: Is There No Alternative?* Ropley, UK: Zero Books, 2009. Print.

Flores, Juan. "The Latino Imaginary: Meanings of Community and Identity." *The Latin American Cultural Studies Reader.* Ed. Ana Del Sarto, Alicia Ríos, and Abril Trig. Durham, NC: Duke UP, 2004. 606–21. Print.

Foster, Susan Leigh. *Choreographing Empathy: Kinesthesia in Performance.* New York: Routledge, 2011. Print.

Freud, Sigmund. *Beyond the Pleasure Principle.* Trans. C.J.M. Hubback. New York: International Psycho-Analytical P, 1922. Print.

Gallese, Vittorio. "Empathy, Embodied Simulation and the Brain: Commentary on Aragno and Zepf/Hartmann." *Journal of the American Psychoanalytic Association* 56 (2008): 769–81. Print.

Gallese, Vittorio, et al. "Action Recognition in the Premotor Cortex." *Brain* 119 (1996): 593–609. Print.

George, David E.R. "Performance Epistemology." *Performance Research* 1.1 (1996): 16–25. Print.

Gogol, Nikolai. "The Nose." *The Mantle and Other Stories.* Trans. Claud Field. New York: Frederick Stokes, 1915. *Project Gutenberg.* Web. 28 Feb. 2013.

Gómez, Mayte. "Healing the Border Wound: *Fronteras Americanas* and the Future of Canadian Multiculturalism." *Theatre Research in Canada/Recherches Théâtrales au Canada* 16.1-2 (1995): n. pag. *Érudit.* Web. 25 March 2013.

---. "Infinite Signs. Alberto Kurapel and the Semiotics of Exile." *Canadian Literature* 142-143 (1994): 38–43. Web. 7 Feb. 2013.

Groneman, Claudia, and Cornelia Sieber. "Nuevas cartografías en las performances de latinoamericanos en Norteamérica: Guillermo Gómez-Peña, *Border Brujo* (1993), y Alberto Kurapel, *Off, off, off ou Sur le toit de Pablo Neruda* (1986)." *Acercamientos al teatro actual (1970–1995): historia—teoría—práctica.* Ed. Fernando de Toro and Alfonso de Toro. Madrid: Iberoamericano, 1998: 277–89. Print.

Guevara, Ernesto. "Guerrilla Warfare: A Method." Deutschmann 70–84.

---. "Letter to Fidel Castro." Deutschmann 386–87.

---. "Socialism and Man in Cuba." Deutschmann 212–28.

Guevara, Lina de. "Civic Participation Through Theatre." *Ruptures, Continuities and Re-Learning. The political participation of Latin Americans in Canada*. Ed. Jorge Ginieniewicz and Daniel Schugurensky. Toronto: Transformative Learning Centre, Ontario Institute for Studies in Education, 2007. N. pag. *Lina de Guevara*. Web. 8 Feb. 2013.

---. *Journey to Mapu*. Alvarez, *Fronteras* 353–400.

---. Message to Tamara Underiner. 23 Jan. 2013. Email.

---. "PUENTE Theatre: In the Beginning there Was the Interview!" *alt.theatre* 9.2 (2011): 40. *Lina de Guevara*. Web. 15 Jan. 2013.

---. "Sisters/Strangers: A Community Play about Immigrant Women." *Canadian Theatre Review* 90 (1997): 28–31. Print.

---. Skype interview by Tamara Underiner. 8 Nov. 2012.

---. "Staging the Immigrant Experience: It Takes One to Know One." *alt.theatre* 1.4 (2000): n. pag. *Lina de Guevara*. Web. 15 Jan. 2013.

---. "Telling Stories: PUENTE Theatre and the Immigrant Experience." *Untold Stories of British Columbia*. Ed. Paul Wood. Victoria: Humanities Centre, U of Victoria, 2003. N. pag. *Lina de Guevara*. Web. 15 Jan. 2013.

---. "Welcoming Speech—Sharing the Legacy Symposium." *Lina de Guevara*. Lina de Guevara, 17 Nov. 2011. Web. 15 Jan. 2013.

Guevara, Lina de, et al. *Crossing Borders/Aventuras de Chepe (a Musical Play)*. 1990. TS. Collection of Tamara Underiner.

Habell-Pallán, Michelle. " 'Don't Call Us Hispanic:' Popular Latino Theater in Vancouver." *Latina/o Popular Culture*. Ed. Michelle Habell-Pallán and Mary Romero. New York: New York UP, 2002. 174–89. Print.

---. "Epilogue: 'Call Us Americans, 'Cause We Are All from the Américas': Latinos at Home in Canada." *Loca Motion: The Travels of Chicana and Latina Popular Culture*. New York: New York UP, 2005. 205–20. Print.

---. Rev. of *¿Qué Pasa Con La Raza, Eh?*, by Carmen Aguirre. Latino Theatre Group, Firehall Arts Centre and Headlines Theatre, Vancouver. *Theatre Journal* 52.1 (2000): 112–14. Print.

Hames-Garcia, Michael. "How to Tell a Mestizo from an Enchirito®: Colonialism and National Culture in the Borderlands." *Diacritics* 30.4 (2000): 102–22. Print.

Hardt, Michael, and Antonio Negri. *Empire*. Cambridge, MA: Harvard UP, 2001. Print.

Hazelton, Hugh. "Latin American Writing In Canada: Formation of a Literature." Introduction. *Latinocanadá: A Critical Study of Ten Latin American Writers of Canada.* Montreal: McGill-Queen's, 2007. 3–27. Print.

---. "Quebec Hispánico: Themes of Exile and Integration in the Writing of Latin Americans Living in Quebec." *Canadian Literature* 142-143 (1994): 120–35. Print.

Henríquez, Jorge. Personal interview by Jeannine M. Pitas. 24 Sept. 2012.

Hitchens, Christopher. "Why Women Aren't Funny." *Vanity Fair.* Condé Nast, Jan. 2007. Web. 3 Nov. 2012.

hooks, bell. *Yearning: Race, Gender, and Cultural Politics.* Boston: South End P, 1990. Print.

Houston, Andrew, and Laura Nanni. "Heterotopian Creation: Beyond the Utopia of Theatres and Galleries." *Canadian Theatre Review* 126 (2006): 5–9. Print.

"i AM LET On: La Furia." *relazion@rte.* relazion@rte, n.d. Web. 7 Sept. 2012.

ICA Victoria. "With Open Arms." *YouTube.* Web. 15 Jan. 2013.

Irwin-Zarecka, Iwona. *Frames of Remembrance: The Dynamics of Collective Memory.* New Brunswick, NJ: Transaction, 1994. Print.

Jackson, Helen Hunt. *Ramona.* Boston: Roberts Brothers, 1884. Print.

Jacome, Diego. Personal interview by Jeannine M. Pitas. 24 Sept. 2012.

"Jerry Lewis: Not Funny." *People Magazine.* Time Inc., 29 Oct. 1998. Web. 3 Nov. 2012.

Joy, Penny, and Robin J. Hood, prod. and dir. *Changing Rhythms.* Media Network Society, 1990. *YouTube.* Web. 24 Oct. 2012.

---, prod. and dir. *Creating Bridges.* Media Network Society, 1988. *YouTube.* Web. 15 Jan. 2013.

Keith, Toby. "Stays in Mexico." *Greatest Hits 2.* Dreamworks, 2004. CD.

Kirby, Kathleen M. *Indifferent Boundaries: Spatial Concepts of Human Subjectivity.* New York: Guilford, 1996. Print.

Klein, Kerwin Lee. "On the Emergence of *Memory* in Historical Discourse." *Representations* 69 (2000): 127–50. Print.

Knowles, Ric. "Performing Intercultural Canada." Introduction. *Theatre Research in Canada/Recherches théâtrales au Canada* 30.1-2 (2009): v–xxi.

---. *Theatre & Interculturalism*. Basingstoke: Palgrave, 2010. Print.

Knowles, Ric, and Ingrid Mündel. Introduction. *"Ethnic," Multicultural, and Intercultural Theatre*. Ed. Knowles and Mündel. Toronto: Playwrights Canada, 2010. vii–xvii. Print. Critical Perspectives on Canadian Theatre in English 14.

Koltai, Judith. "Welcome to Embodied Practice®." *Embodied Pratice—Judith Koltai*. Embodied Practice, n.d. Web. 15 Jan. 2013.

Kowalchuck, Lisa. "Nicaraguans." *Encyclopedia of Canada's Peoples*. Ed. Paul Robert Magocsi. Toronto: U of Toronto P, 1999. 1008–12. Print.

Kristeva, Julia. *Powers of Horror: An Essay on Abjection*. Trans. Leon S. Roudiez. New York: Columbia UP, 1982. Print.

Kuftinec, Sonja. *Staging America: Cornerstone and Community-Based Theater*. Carbondale, IL: Southern Illinois UP, 2003. Print.

Kurapel, Alberto. *3 Performances teatrales de Alberto Kurapel*. Montreal: Humanitas, 1987. Print.

---. *10 Obras inéditas: teatro-performance*. Montreal: Humanitas, 1999. Print.

---. *El actor-performer*. Santiago, Chile: Cuarto Propio, 2010. Print.

---. "Alberto Kurapel // Actor, Dramaturgo, Poeta, Cantautor." *El catalejo*. El catalejo, n.d. Web. 27 Feb. 2013.

---. *Berri-UQÀM*. Montreal: Écrits des Forges, 1992. Print.

---. *La bruta interférence*. Trans. Jean Antonin Billard. *Canadian Theatre Review* 79 (1994): 134–49. Print.

---. *La bruta interférence*. Trans. Jean Antonin Billard. Montreal: Humanitas, 1995. Print.

---. *Carta de ajuste ou Nous n'avons plus besoin de calendrier*. Montreal: Humanitas, 1991. Print.

---. *Colmenas en la sombra ou L'espoir de l'arrière-garde*. Trans. Jean Antonin Billard. Montreal: Humanitas, 1994. Print.

---. *Estética de la insatisfacción en el teatro-performance*. Santiago, Chile: Cuarto Propio, 2004. Print.

---. *Margot Loyola. La escena infinita del folklore*. Santiago, Chile: Fondart, 1997. Print.

---. "Montreal/Santiago: The First Installment of a Trilogy (Alberto Kurapel Collaborates with Chilean Performers on *America desvelada ou Mon nom sera toujours auprès de vous*)." *Canadian Theatre Review* 75 (1993): 72–76. Print.

---. Personal interview by Hugh Hazelton. 21 June 1996.

---. *Prométhée enchaîné selon Alberto Kurapel le Guanaco gaucho/Prometeo encadenado según Alberto Kurapel le Guanaco gaucho*. Montreal: Humanitas, 1989. Print.

---. *Prometheus Bound According to Alberto Kurapel, the Guanaco Gaucho*. Trans. Hugh Hazelton. Alvarez, *Fronteras* 11–44.

---. "Re: otra pregunta sobre Prometeo." Message to Hugh Hazelton. 3 Sept. 2012.

---. *Station artificielle*. Montreal: Humanitas, 1993. Print.

Kymlicka, Will. "The Forms of Liberal Multiculturalism." *Multicultural Odysseys: Navigating the New International Politics of Diversity*. Oxford: Oxford UP, 2007. 61–87. Print.

Laborde, Rosa. *Leo*. Toronto: Playwrights Canada, 2006. Print.

LaCapra, Dominick. *Writing History, Writing Trauma*. Baltimore: Johns Hopkins UP, 2001. Print.

Lagos, Miler. *Lat 65.31 N, Long 114.13 W*. 2012. Art Gallery of York University, Toronto.

Le Blanc, Huguette. *Alberto Kurapel. Chant et poésie d'exil*. Montreal: Éditions Coopératives de la Mêlée, 1983. Print.

Limon, John. *Stand-up Comedy in Theory, or, Abjection in America*. Durham, NC: Duke UP, 2000. Print.

López, Ana M. "Of Rhythms and Borders." *Everynight Life: Culture and Dance in Latin/o America*. Ed. Celeste Fraser Delgado and José Esteban Muñoz. Durham, NC: Duke University Press, 1997. 310–44. Print.

Lowe, Lisa. *Immigrant Acts: On Asian American Cultural Politics*. Durham, NC: Duke UP, 1996. Print.

Lowell, Amy. *Tendencies in Modern American Poetry*. New York: MacMillan, 1917. Print.

MacLeod, Joan. *Amigo's Blue Guitar*. Toronto: Summerhill P, 1990. Print.

"Mandate." *PUENTE Theatre*. PUENTE Theatre Society, n.d. Web. 15 Feb. 2013.

Mann, Laurin. "'Stanislavski' in Toronto." *Theatre Research in Canada/Recherches Théâtrales au Canada* 20.2 (1999): 207–26. Print.

Markard, Anna. *The Green Table: The Labanotation Score, Text, Photographs, and Music*. New York: Routledge, 2003. Print.

Martínez, Sergio. "Teatro chileno en Canadá: 'Nos han cambiado hasta la geografía.' " *Análisis* 178 (1987): 47–48. Print.

McConachie, Bruce. *Engaging Audiences: A Cognitive Approach to Spectating in the Theatre.* New York: Palgrave, 2008. Print.

McHugh, Kathleen. "Giving 'Minor' Pasts a Future: Narrating History in Transnational Cinematic Autobiography." *Minor Transnationalism.* Ed. Françoise Lionnet and Shu-mei Shih. Durham, NC: Duke UP, 2005. 155–178. Print.

McWilliams, Carey. *North from Mexico: The Spanish Speaking People of the United States.* Philadelphia: J.B. Lippincott, 1949. Print.

Mejia, Louis. "KOGI: Lost Tribe of Pre-Colombian America." *Labyrinthina.* Kathy Doore, n.d. Web. 1 Sept. 2012.

Merritt, Shaun. "Toronto: Meeting Place or Fish Corral?" *Torontoist.* St. Joseph Media, 8 Feb. 2007. Web. 30 Sept. 2012.

Mesa, Maria Elena. Personal interview by Jeannine M. Pitas. 22 Sept. 2012.

Mignolo, Walter. *The Idea of Latin America.* Oxford: Blackwell, 2005. Print.

---. *Local Histories/Global Designs: Coloniality, Subaltern Knowledges, and Border Thinking.* Princeton, NJ: Princeton UP, 2000. Print.

M.O.A.R. Adapt. by Oscar Laurencio Ortiz Quiroz and Enrique Castro. Double Double Performing Arts. York Hall, Glendon College, Toronto. 24 Oct. 2012. Rehearsal.

Mojica, Monique, and Ric Knowles, eds. *Staging Coyote's Dream: An Anthology of First Nations Drama in English.* 2 vols. Toronto: Playwrights Canada, 2003–2009. Print.

Moll, Sorouja. "Tango and the Archive: *Fronteras Americanas.*" *Nineteenth Century Girl.* Wordpress. 19 Jan. 2011. Web. 19 March 2013.

Moss, Jane. "Immigrant Theatre: Traumatic Departures and Unsettling Arrivals." *Textualizing the Immigrant Experience in Contemporary Quebec.* Ed. Susan Ireland and Patrice J. Proulx. Westport, CT: Praeger, 2004. 65–82. Print.

Murphy, Gretchen. *Hemispheric Imaginings: The Monroe Doctrine and Narratives of U.S. Empire.* Durham, NC: Duke UP, 2005. Print.

Murphy, Kim. "Drug War on Another Border: Canada." *Los Angeles Times.* Tribune Company, 30 June 2009. Web. 11 Jan. 2013.

"News Release—Canada Imposes a Visa On Mexico." *Citizenship and Immigration Canada.* Government of Canada, 13 July 2009. Web. 13 Jan. 2013.

"Nicaraguan Immigration." *Encyclopedia of Immigration*. Encyclopedia of Immigration, 23 Feb. 2011. Web. 12 Feb. 2013.

Nieto-Phillips, John M. *The Language of Blood: The Making of Spanish-American Identity in New Mexico, 1880s–1930s*. Albuquerque, NM: U of New Mexico P, 2004. Print.

Nora, Pierre. "Between Memory and History: Les Lieux de Mémoire." *Representations* 26 (1989): 7–24. Print.

Nothof, Anne. "The Construction and Deconstructions of Border Zones in *Fronteras Americanas* by Guillermo Verdecchia and *Amigo's Blue Guitar* by Joan MacLeod." *Theatre Research in Canada/Recherches Théâtrales au Canada* 20.1 (1999): 3–15. Print.

Ong, Aihwa. *Neoliberalism As Exception: Mutations in Citizenship and Sovereignty*. Durham, NC: Duke UP, 2006. Print.

The Original Latin Divas of Comedy. Dir. Scott L. Montoya. Perf. Marilyn Martinez, Sara Contreras, Monique Marvez, and Sandra Valls. Kosmic Films Entertainment, 2007. DVD.

Ortiz, Oscar. Personal interview by Jeannine M. Pitas. 22 Sept. 2012.

Palmer, Alisa. *A Play About the Mothers of Plaza de Mayo*. 1992. TS.

Peña Ovalle, Priscilla. *Dance and the Hollywood Latina: Race, Sex, and Stardom*. New Brunswick, NJ: Rutgers UP, 2010. Print.

Pitas, Jeannine M. "Performing Communities: Latino Theatre in Toronto." *alt. theatre* 8.4 (2011): 8–13. Print.

Pizano, Beatriz. *La Comunión*. TS.

---. *For Sale*. 2006. TS.

Pizano, Beatriz, and Trevor Schwellnus. Personal interview by Jessica Riley and Ric Knowles. 29 Aug. 2012.

Pontaut, Alain. "Un Prométhée antifasciste." *Le Devoir* 21 March 1988: C2-1. Print.

Pozo, José del. *Les Chiliens au Québec: Immigrants et réfugiés, de 1955 à nos jours*. Montreal: Boréal, 2009. Print.

Quayson, Ato, and Girish Daswani, eds. *A Companion to Diaspora and Transnationalism*. New York: Blackwell, 2013. Print.

---. "Diaspora and Transnationalism: Scapes, Scales and Scopes." Quayson and Daswani n. pag.

Rackow, Frank. "Knockin' on Neruda's Door." *Cinema Canada* 154 (1988): 7. Print.

Radulescu, Domnica. *Women's Comedic Art As Social Revolution: Five Performers and the Lessons of Their Subversive Humor.* Jefferson, NC: McFarland, 2011. Print.

Ramirez, Pablo. "Collective Memory and the Borderlands in Guillermo Verdecchia's *Fronteras Americanas." Latin American Identities After 1980.* Ed. Gordana Yovanovich and Amy Huras. Waterloo: Wilfrid Laurier UP, 2010. 273–86. Print.

Rapport, Nigel, and Andrew Dawson. *Migrants of Identity: Perceptions of Home in a World of Movement.* Oxford: Berg, 1998. Print.

Rayter, Scott. "Thinking Queerly about Canada." Introduction. *Queerly Canadian: An Introductory Reader in Sexuality Studies.* Ed. Maureen FitzGerald and Rayter. Toronto: Canadian Scholars', 2012. xv–xxvi. Print.

Reid, Robert. "*Fronteras Americanas* Fascinating." *The Record* [Kitchener, ON] 21 Oct. 1999: D20. Print.

Ricoeur, Paul. *Memory, History, Forgetting.* Trans. Kathleen Blamey and David Pellauer. Chicago: U of Chicago P, 2006. Print.

---. *Time and Narrative.* Trans. Kathleen Blamey and David Pellauer. Vol. 3. Chicago: U of Chicago P, 1990. Print.

Ricourt, Milagros, and Ruby Danta. *Hispanas de Queens: Latino Panethnicity in a New York City Neighborhood.* Ithaca, NY: Cornell UP, 2003. Print.

Rivera-Servera, Ramón H. "Musical Trans(actions): Intersections in Reggaetón." *Revista Transcultural de Música* 13 (2009): n. pag. Web. 27 Feb. 2013.

---. *Performing Queer Latinidad: Dance, Sexuality, Politics.* Ann Arbor, MI: U of Michigan P, 2012. Print.

Rojas, Luis. Personal interview by Jeannine M. Pitas. 24 Sept. 2012.

Román, David. *Performance in America: Contemporary U.S. Culture and the Performing Arts.* Durham, NC: Duke UP, 2005. Print.

"Roster Acts 2012—Martha Chaves." *Funny Business, Inc.* Funny Business, n.d. Web. 16 Oct. 2012.

Rushdie, Salman. *Imaginary Homelands: Essays and Criticism, 1981–1991.* London: Granta Books, 1991. Print.

Said, Edward W. *Culture and Imperialism.* New York: Knopf, 1993. Print.

---. "Reflections on Exile." Said, *Reflections* 173–86.

---. *Reflections on Exile and Other Essays.* Cambridge, MA: Harvard UP, 2000. Print.

Saldívar, José David. *Border Matters: Remapping American Cultural Studies*. Berkeley: U of California P, 1997. Print.

Salverson, Julie. Introduction. *Community Engaged Theatre and Performance*. Ed. Salverson. Toronto: Playwrights Canada, 2011. vii–xiv. Print. Critical Perspectives on Canadian Theatre in English 19.

Sandoval-Sánchez, Alberto. *José, Can You See?: Latinos On and Off Broadway*. Madison, WI: U of Wisconsin P, 1999. Print.

Santiago, Daniel. *A treasure, a myth. Dialogues through time*. 2012. Art Gallery of York University, Toronto.

Santos, Boaventura de Sousa. "Beyond Abyssal Thinking: From Global Lines to Ecologies of Knowledges." *Eurozine*. Eurozine, 29 June 2007. Web. 28 Feb. 2013.

Saunders, Doug. "We See our Arctic as a Colony." *The Globe and Mail*. The Globe and Mail Inc., 12 Feb. 2010. Web. 20 Dec. 2012.

Schwellnus, Trevor. "Interview Series—Nohayquiensepa." Interview by Geneviève Trilling. *SummerWorks Theatre Festival*. SummerWorks Theatre Festival, 18 July 2009. Web. 2 Sept. 2012.

---. "Nohayquiensepa (No One Knows), Toronto March 26 2011." *Vimeo*. Web. 28 Sept. 2012.

---. "Why a Festival of Theatre for Human Rights?" *Aluna Theatre Blog*. Aluna Theatre, 20 May 2012. Web. 15 Feb. 2013.

"Seasonal Agricultural Workers Program Mexico—Canada." *Consulado General de México en Toronto*. Estados Unidos Mexicanos, 11 March 2011. Web. 13 Jan. 2013.

Seidel, Michael. *Exile and the Narrative Imagination*. New Haven, CT: Yale UP, 1986. Print.

Sepúlveda Corradini, Gabriel. *Víctor Jara: hombre de teatro*. Santiago: Sudamericana, 2001. Print.

"Sexual Anxiety, Personality Predictors of Infidelity, Study Says." *University of Guelph*. U of Guelph, 27 July 2011. Web. 28 Feb. 2013.

Shaffeeullah, Nikki. "The Conversation: How We Talk About Cultural Diversity in Theatre." *alt.theatre* 9.4 (2012): 10–16. Print.

Sher, Emil. "One in a World of Exiles: Quebec's Alberto Kurapel." *Canadian Theatre Review* 56 (1988): 31–34. Print.

Siemerling, Winfried, and Sarah Phillips Casteel. "Canada and Its Americas." Introduction. *Canada And Its Americas: Transnational Navigations*. Ed. Siemerling and Casteel. Montreal: McGill-Queens UP, 2010. 3–28. Print.

Smith, Tracey Erin. "About Us." *SoulOTheatre*. SoulOTheatre, 2012. Web. 12 Feb. 2013.

Soja, Edward. *Thirdspace: Journeys to Los Angeles and Other Real-and-Imagined Places*. New York: Blackwell, 1996. Print.

Solari, Maria. "Ballet Nacional de la Universidad de Chile." *Revista Musical Chilena* 75 (1961): 32–38. Print.

Spurrier, Christian. "No Bar To Love: Christian Spurrier On the Tragedy of Gramsci's Prison Years as Revealed in Letters To His Wife and Sons." *The Guardian*. Guardian Media Group, 11 Feb. 2006. Web. 12 May 2012.

Stanley, Alessandra. "Who Says Women Aren't Funny?" *Vanity Fair*. Condé Nast, April 2008. Web. 3 Nov. 2012.

Stastna, Kazi. "Canada's Migrant Farm Worker System—What Works And What's Lacking." *CBC News*. CBC/Radio Canada, 8 Feb. 2012. Web. 12 Jan. 2013.

Tan, Marcus Cheng Chye. *Acoustic Interculturalism: Listening to Performance*. Basingstoke: Palgrave, 2012. Print.

Taylor, Charles. "Modernity and Difference." *Without Guarantees: In Honour of Stuart Hall*. Ed. Paul Gilroy, Lawrence Grossberg, and Angela McRobbie. New York: Verso, 2000. 364–74. Print.

Taylor, Diana. *The Archive and the Repertoire: Performing Cultural Memory in the Americas*. Durham, NC: Duke UP, 2003. Print.

Teuta, Angélika. *The Language of Birds*. 2012. Art Gallery of York University, Toronto.

"Tina Fey, Chevy Chase, Dana Carvey: *A Saturday Night Live* Class Reunion." 12 April 2011. *The Oprah Winfrey Show*. Web. 15 Feb. 2013.

Torgovnick, Marianna. "Slasher Stories." *New Formations: A Journal of Culture, Theory, and Politics* 17 (1992): 133–45. Print.

Toro, Alfonso de. "Figuras de la hibridez: Carlos Fuentes, Guillermo Gómez Peña, Gloria Anzaldúa y Alberto Kurapel." *Aves de paso: Autores latinoamericanos entre exilio y transculturación (1970–2002)*. Ed. Birgit Mertz-Baumgartner and Erna Pfeiffer. Frankfurt: Vervuert; Madrid: Iberoamericano, 2005: 83–101. Print.

---. " 'Transversalidad'—'Hibridez'—'Transmedialidad' en las *performances* de Alberto Kurapel: una teatralidad menor." *Estrategias postmodernas y postcoloniales en el teatro latinoamericano actual. Hibridez—Medialidad—Cuerpo*. Ed. Toro. Frankfurt: Vervuert; Madrid: Iberoamericano, 2004: 237–58. Print.

Toro, Fernando de. "Identidad, alteridad y tercer espacio: el teatro de Alberto Kurapel." *Intersecciones II, ensayos sobre cultura y literatura en la condición posmoderna y post-colonial.* Ed. Toro. Buenos Aires: Galerna, 2002. 70–88. Print.

Torres, Luis. "Writings of the Latin-Canadian Exile." *Revista Canadiense de Estudios Hispánicos* 26.1-2 (2001–2002): 179-198. Print.

Torrini, Emilíana. "Beggar's Prayer Lyrics." *Metro Lyrics.* MetroLyrics, n.d. Web. 15 Feb. 2013.

Trezise, Bryoni. "Spectatorship that Hurts: Socìetas Raffaello Sanzio as Meta-affective Theatre of Memory." *Theatre Research International* 37.3 (2012): 205–20. Print.

Trotsky, Leon. *The Russian Revolution: The Overthrow of Tzarism and the Triumph of the Soviets.* Ed. F.W. Dupee. Garden City, NY: Doubleday, 1959. Print.

Tsuda, Takeyuki. "When the Diaspora Returns Home: Ambivalent Encounters with the Ethnic Homeland." Quayson and Daswani n. pag.

Velasco, Juan. "Automitografias: The Border Paradigm and Chicana/o Autobiography." *Biography* 27.2 (2004): 313–38. Print.

Vélez-Ibáñez, Carlos G., and Anna Sampaio. "Processes, New Prospects, and Approaches." Introduction. *Transnational Latina/o Communities: Politics, Processes, and Cultures.* Ed. Vélez-Ibáñez and Sampaio. Lanham, MD: Rowan & Littlefield, 2002. 1–37. Print.

Verdecchia, Guillermo. *Another Country. Another Country – bloom.* Vancouver: Talonbooks, 2007. 13–92. Print.

---. "Contending with Rupture: Memory-Work in Latina-Canadian Playwriting." *Signatures of the Past: Cultural Memory in Contemporary Anglophone North American Drama.* Ed. Marc Maufort and Caroline De Wagter. Brussels: Peter Lang, 2008. 115–28. Print.

---. *Fronteras Americanas (American Borders).* Toronto: Coach House, 1993. Print.

---. *Fronteras Americanas: American Borders.* 2nd ed. Vancouver: Talonbooks, 2012. Print.

---. "*Leo* at the Tarragon: Naturalizing the Coup." *Theatre Research in Canada/Recherches Théâtrales au Canada* 30.1-2 (2009): 111–28. Print.

---. "Mapping the Canada-America(s) Border: New Latin(a)-Canadian Playwriting." *Zeitschrift für Kanada-Studien* 26.2 (2006): 147–58. Print.

---. "Staging Memory: Constructing Canadian Latinidad." M.A. thesis. U of Guelph, 2006. Print.

---. "Tango's Cross-Cultural Dance." *Canadian Theatre Review* 139 (2009): 17–24. Print.

---. *The Terrible But Incomplete Journals of John D. Canadian Theatre Review* 92 (1997): 50–67. Print.

---. *The Terrible But Incomplete Journals of John D.* Rumble Productions, 1998. CD.

---. " 'We Win': Memory, Forgetting, and the Audience in *¿Que Pasa con La Raza, eh?*" *Essays in Theatre/Études théâtrales* 21.1-2 (2002–2003): 141–51. Print.

Villegas, Juan. *Historia multicultural del teatro y las teatralidades en América Latina.* Buenos Aires: Galerna, 2005. Print.

Virno, Paolo. *A Grammar of the Multitude: For an Analysis of Contemporary Forms of Life.* Los Angeles: Semiotext(e), 2004. Print.

Walker, John. "3 performances teatrales de Alberto Kurapel." *Canadian Theatre Review* 56 (1988): 83–84. Print.

Werbner, Pnina. "Migration and Transnational Studies: Between Simultaneity and Rupture." Quayson and Daswani n. pag.

Wesso, Antonio. Personal interview by Jeannine M. Pitas. 28 Oct. 2012.

Williams, Raymond. *Keywords: A Vocabulary of Culture and Society.* New York: Oxford UP, 1985. Print.

Wilson, Ann. "Border Crossing: The Technologies of Identity in *Fronteras Americanas.*" *Australasian Drama Studies* 29 (1996): 7–15. Print.

Wintrop, Norman. "Marx, Lenin, and Modern Revolutions." *Revolution: A History of the Idea.* Ed. David Close and Carl Bridge. Sydney: Croom Helm, 1985. 89–119. Print.

World Rainforest Movement. "Colombia: The Embera Katio's Struggle for Life." *WRM.* World Rainforest Movement, 29 Dec. 1999. Web. 27 Sept. 2012.

Xiomara. "Colombian Cumbia Dance Performance with Xiomara." *YouTube.* Web. 27 Sept. 2012.

Zorc-Maver, Darja, and Igor Maver. "Guillermo Verdecchia and the *frontera* in Contemporary Canadian Diasporic Writing." *Acta Literaria* 43 (2011): 119–26. Print.

NOTES ON CONTRIBUTORS

Natalie Alvarez is an associate professor at Brock University's Department of Dramatic Arts where she teaches in the Theatre Praxis concentration. Her work on contemporary performance, performance theory, and Latina/o theatre has appeared in a number of periodicals such as *Theatre Journal, Journal of Dramatic Theory and Criticism*, and *Janus Head*, as well as in national and international essay collections. Her current SSHRC-funded book project, *Enactments of Difference*, examines simulations, interculturalism, and performance in military training and dark tourism. She also serves as co-editor of the *Canadian Theatre Review's* Views and Reviews.

Alicia Arrizón is currently a professor in the Department of Women's Studies at the University of California, Riverside (UCR), where she has also recently served as Departmental Chair (2006–2012). The core of her scholarship has been contemporary cultural and performance studies, with a strong commitment to the study of race and ethnicity and their interchange with gender and sexuality. She is the author of *Latina Performance* (Indiana UP, 1999), *Queering Mestizaje: Transculturation and Performance* (U of Michigan P, 2006), and co-editor of *Latinas On Stage* (Third Woman Press, 2000). Some of her articles have appeared in *Women and Performance: A Journal of Feminist Theory, The Drama Review, Theatre Journal*, and *Theatre Research International*.

Hugh Hazelton is a writer and translator who specializes in the comparison of Canadian and Quebec literatures with those of Latin America, as well as in the work of Latin American writers of Canada. He has written several books of poetry and translates from Spanish, French, and Portuguese into English; his translation of *Vétiver* (Signature, 2005), a book of poems by Joël Des Rosiers, won the Governor General's Literary Award for French-English translation in 2006. His third collection of poems, *Antimatter*, was republished with a CD by Broken Jaw Press in 2010; a Spanish edition, *Antimateria* (Split Quotation/La Cita Trunca), came out in 2009. He is co-director of the Banff International Literary Translation Centre and a professor emeritus of Spanish translation and Latin American civilization at Concordia University in Montreal.

Ric Knowles is Professor of Theatre Studies at the University of Guelph, co-editor of *Theatre Journal*, and general editor of the New Essays on Canadian Theatre series. His most recent book is *Theatre and Interculturalism* (Palgrave, 2010).

Martha Nandorfy's work focuses on social and environmental justice issues in the borderlands and the Americas generally. She is Associate Professor of English in the School of English and Theatre Studies at the University of Guelph and author of *The Poetics of Apocalypse: García Lorca's Poet in New York* (Bucknell University Press, 2003). She is co-author with Daniel Fischlin of a trilogy on the intersections between rights and storytelling entitled *Eduardo Galeano: Through the Looking Glass* (Black Rose Books, 2001), *The Concise Guide to Global Human Rights* (2007), and *The Community of Rights/The Rights of Community* (2012). She has published extensively on storytelling and communitarian politics in such diverse contexts as the Zapatista Movement in Chiapas and the queer utopianism of filmmaker Pedro Almodóvar. Her current research focuses on literary journalism and Indigenous storytelling as alternative sources of information and inspiration.

Jimena Ortuzar is a Ph.D. candidate at the Centre for Drama, Theatre and Performance Studies and the Centre for Diaspora and Transnational Studies at the University of Toronto. She received her M.A. from Tisch School of the Arts/NYU where she earned the Leigh George Odom Memorial Award for Distinguished Masters Students. Her research focuses on performing alternative modes of citizenship and belonging under conditions of displacement. Her artistic practice includes performance art, film and video art, as well as various theatre collaborations in Toronto and New York City. Her professional experience includes labour relations and human rights for the Canadian Union of Public Employees.

Jeannine M. Pitas is a Ph.D. candidate at the University of Toronto's Centre for Comparative Literature, where she is completing a dissertation on twentieth century Southern Cone poets Delmira Agustini, Alejandra Pizarnik, and Marosa di Giorgio. She has written various articles on diasporic Latin American cultures in Toronto, and she is the English-language translator of Uruguayan poet Marosa di Giorgio's *The History of Violets* (Ugly Duckling Presse, 2010).

Pablo Ramirez received his Ph.D. in American Cultures from the University of Michigan. He is presently an associate professor in the School of English and Theatre Studies at the University of Guelph. His current project is a book tentatively titled *Consent of the Conquered: Californio Romances and Contractual Freedom in Nineteenth-Century America.*

Jessica Riley is a Ph.D. candidate at the School of English and Theatre Studies, University of Guelph. Her research interests include contemporary Canadian developmental dramaturgy and early modern English drama.

Ramón H. Rivera-Servera is Associate Professor and Director of Graduate Studies in the Department of Performance Studies at Northwestern University. His research focuses on contemporary performance in North America and the Caribbean with special emphasis on the ways categories of race, gender, and sexuality are negotiated in the process of migration. His work documents US Latina/o, Mexican, and Caribbean performance practices ranging from theatre and concert dance to social dance, fashion, and speech. He is author of *Performing Queer Latinidad: Dance, Sexuality, Politics* (University of Michigan Press, 2012), a study of the role performance played in the development of Latina/o queer publics in the United States from the mid-1990s to the early 2000s.

Tamara Underiner is Associate Professor and Director of Graduate Studies at Arizona State University's School of Theatre and Film, where she also directs the doctoral concentration in Theatre and Performance of the Americas. She is the author of *Contemporary Theatre in Mayan Mexico: Death-Defying Acts* (U of Texas P, 2004) and has published on Indigenous and Latina/o theatre and critical pedagogy in *Theatre Journal*, *Signs*, *Baylor Journal of Theatre and Performance*, *TDR*, and critical anthologies from the University of Arizona and Routledge Presses.

Guillermo Verdecchia is a writer of drama and fiction as well as a direc-tor and actor. He is the recipient of a Governor General's Award for Drama for his play *Fronteras Americanas* and a four-time winner of the Floyd S. Chalmers Canadian Play Award. His work, which includes the Governor General's Award–shortlisted *Noam Chomsky Lectures* (with Daniel Brooks), the *Seattle Times*'s Footlight Award–winning *Adventures of Ali & Ali* (with Marcus Youssef and Camyar Chai), *A Line in the Sand* (with Marcus Youssef), *bloom*, and *Another Country* has been anthologized, translated into Spanish and Italian, produced in Europe and the US, and is studied in Latin America, Europe, and North America. As a director and actor he has worked at theatres across Canada, from the Stratford Shakespeare Festival, where he directed Sunil Kuruvilla's *Rice Boy*, to Vancouver's East Cultural Centre. Currently an associate artist with Toronto's Soulpepper Theatre, where he heads new play development, Guillermo is also a Ph.D. Candidate at the Centre for Drama, Theatre, and Performance Studies at the University of Toronto. He has published a number of articles and contributed book chapters on as-pects of intercultural theatre practice in Canada. He has an M.A. from the University of Guelph, where he received a Governor General's Gold Medal for Academic Achievement.

INDEX